Chris O'Rourke is Lecturer in Film & TV History at the University of Lincoln, UK. He has published widely on aspects of British cinema history, in particular the silent film period, including contributions to the DVD release of *Shooting Stars* (BFI, 2016). He received his PhD from the University of Cambridge in 2012, and held a postdoctoral Research Associateship at University College London.

'O'Rourke has significantly broadened our understanding of the contours of British film culture in the 1920s and 1930s, showing how filmmakers, agents, publicists, publishers, novelists and journalists simultaneously encouraged, castigated and cynically exploited a nascent mass yearning for screen stardom.'

– Jon Burrows, University of Warwick

'With flair and imagination, this book traces the debates about the professionalisation of acting, the everyday experiences of both those who aspired to and those who did make their living as film actors, and the fan cultures that surrounded the industry. It is an object lesson in the rich possibilities of archival research: beautifully written, authoritative and absorbing.'

– Lawrence Napper, King's College London

Cinema and Society series
General Editor: Jeffrey Richards

Acting for the Silent Screen: Film Actors and Aspiration between the Wars
Chris O'Rourke

The Age of the Dream Palace: Cinema and Society in 1930s Britain
Jeffrey Richards

Banned in the USA: British Films in the United States and their Censorship, 1933-1960
Anthony Slide

Best of British: Cinema and Society from 1930 to the Present
Anthony Aldgate & Jeffrey Richards

Beyond a Joke: Parody in English Film and Television Comedy
Neil Archer

Brigadoon, Braveheart and the Scots: Distortions of Scotland in Hollywood Cinema
Colin McArthur

Britain Can Take It: British Cinema in the Second World War
Tony Aldgate & Jeffrey Richards

The British at War: Cinema, State and Propaganda, 1939-1945
James Chapman

British Children's Cinema: From the Thief of Bagdad to Wallace and Gromit
Noel Brown

British Cinema and the Cold War: The State, Propaganda and Consensus
Tony Shaw

British Film Design: A History
Laurie N. Ede

Children, Cinema and Censorship: From Dracula to the Dead End Kids
Sarah J. Smith

China and the Chinese in Popular Film: From Fu Manchu to Charlie Chan
Jeffrey Richards

Christmas at the Movies: Images of Christmas in American, British and European Cinema
Edited by Mark Connelly

The Classic French Cinema 1930-1960
Colin Crisp

The Crowded Prairie: American National Identity in the Hollywood Western
Michael Coyne

The Death Penalty in American Cinema: Criminality and Retribution in Hollywood Film
Yvonne Kozlovsky-Golan

Distorted Images: British National Identity and Film in the 1920s
Kenton Bamford

The Euro-Western: Reframing Gender, Race and the 'Other' in Film
Lee Broughton

An Everyday Magic: Cinema and Cultural Memory
Annette Kuhn

Family Films in Global Cinema: The World Beyond Disney
Edited by Noel Brown and Bruce Babington

Femininity in the Frame: Women and 1950s British Popular Cinema
Melanie Bell

Film and Community in Britain and France: From La Règle du jeu to Room at the Top
Margaret Butler

Film Propaganda: Soviet Russia and Nazi Germany
Richard Taylor

The Finest Years: British Cinema of the 1940s
Charles Drazin

Frank Capra's Eastern Horizons: American Identity and the Cinema of International Relations
Elizabeth Rawitsch

From Moscow to Madrid: European Cities, Postmodern Cinema
Ewa Mazierska & Laura Rascaroli

The Hollywood Family Film: A History, from Shirley Temple to Harry Potter
Noel Brown

Hollywood and the Americanization of Britain: From the 1920s to the Present
Mark Glancy

Hollywood Genres and Postwar America: Masculinity, Family and Nation in Popular Movies and Film Noir
Mike Chopra-Gant

Hollywood Riots: Violent Crowds and Progressive Politics in American Film
Doug Dibbern

Hollywood's History Films
David Eldridge

Hollywood's New Radicalism: War, Globalisation and the Movies from Reagan to George W. Bush
Ben Dickenson

Licence to Thrill: A Cultural History of the James Bond Films
James Chapman

The New Scottish Cinema
Jonathan Murray

Past and Present: National Identity and the British Historical Film
James Chapman

Powell and Pressburger: A Cinema of Magic Spaces
Andrew Moor

Projecting Tomorrow: Science Fiction and Popular Cinema
James Chapman & Nicholas J. Cull

Propaganda and the German Cinema, 1933-1945
David Welch

Shooting the Civil War: Cinema, History and American National Identity
Jenny Barrett

Spaghetti Westerns: Cowboys and Europeans from Karl May to Sergio Leone
Christopher Frayling

Spectacular Narratives: Hollywood in the Age of the Blockbuster
Geoff King

Typical Men: The Representation of Masculinity in Popular British Cinema
Andrew Spicer

The Unknown 1930s: An Alternative History of the British Cinema, 1929-1939
Edited by Jeffrey Richards

Withnail and Us: Cult Films and Film Cults in British Cinema
Justin Smith

ACTING FOR THE SILENT SCREEN

Film Actors and Aspiration between the Wars

Chris O'Rourke

BLOOMSBURY ACADEMIC
LONDON • NEW YORK • OXFORD • NEW DELHI • SYDNEY

BLOOMSBURY ACADEMIC
Bloomsbury Publishing Plc
50 Bedford Square, London, WC1B 3DP, UK
1385 Broadway, New York, NY 10018, USA
29 Earlsfort Terrace, Dublin 2, Ireland

BLOOMSBURY, BLOOMSBURY ACADEMIC and the Diana logo
are trademarks of Bloomsbury Publishing Plc

First published by I. B. Tauris
This paperback edition published in 2021

Copyright © Chris O'Rourke, 2017

Chris O'Rourke has asserted their right under the Copyright,
Designs and Patents Act, 1988, to be identified as Author of this work.

For legal purposes the Acknowledgements on p. xi constitute
an extension of this copyright page.

All rights reserved. No part of this publication may be reproduced or
transmitted in any form or by any means, electronic or mechanical,
including photocopying, recording, or any information storage or retrieval
system, without prior permission in writing from the publishers.

Bloomsbury Publishing Plc does not have any control over, or responsibility for,
any third-party websites referred to or in this book. All internet addresses given
in this book were correct at the time of going to press. The author and publisher
regret any inconvenience caused if addresses have changed or sites have
ceased to exist, but can accept no responsibility for any such changes.

A catalogue record for this book is available from the British Library.

A catalog record for this book is available from the Library of Congress.

ISBN: HB: 978 1 78453 279 6
PB: 978 1 3502 4285 2
ePDF: 978 1 78673 059 6
eBook: 978 1 78672 059 7

Series: Cinema and Society

To find out more about our authors and books visit
www.bloomsbury.com and sign up for our newsletters.

Contents

List of illustrations		ix
Acknowledgements		xi
General editor's introduction		xiii
	Introduction: Winifred Hopcroft's story	1
1	In and out of the studio: The silent film actor in Britain	14
2	Learn to act for the cinema in your own home: Instructional guides to film acting	43
3	The common round: Finding film work in interwar London	69
4	Stand forth, Mary Pickford the second! Searching for British stars	99
	Epilogue: From silence to sound	133
	Notes	142
	Select filmography	182
	Select bibliography	183
	Index	195

List of illustrations

I.1.	Winifred Hopcroft. 'The film lure', *Daily Mirror*, 16 July 1920, p. 1.	2
I.2.	W.K. Haselden, 'The craze for "getting on the films"', *Daily Mirror*, 20 January 1922, p. 5. © Mirrorpix.	4
1.1.	A letter to 'crowd players' from the Samuelson Film Manufacturing Company. Courtesy of the Teddy Baird Collection, British Film Institute Special Collections.	26
1.2.	Inside the Famous Players-Lasky British studios in Islington. L.C. MacBean, *Kinematograph Studio Technique* (London: Pitman, 1922), frontispiece. Courtesy of Cambridge University Library.	30
1.3.	Clive Brook and Brian Aherne. Postcards, *c.* 1930s. Author's collection.	35
1.4.	Mabel Poulton and Chili Bouchier. Postcards, *c.* 1920s and 1930s. Author's collection.	39
2.1.	Front cover of Fred Dangerfield and Norman Howard, *How to Become a Film Artiste: The Art of Photo-Play Acting* (London: Odhams, 1921). Courtesy of Cambridge University Library.	51
2.2.	Geraldine Farrar demonstrates her emotional range. 'The expressions of Geraldine Farrar', *Picture Show*, 16 April 1921, p. 9. © Time Inc (UK) Ltd.	61
2.3.	'How to register expressions'. Violet Hopson, 'Hints for the kinema actress', in *Cinema Acting as a Profession: A Splendid Course in 10 Lessons* (London: Standard Art Book, n.d. [*c.* 1919]), Lesson 9. Courtesy of the Bill Douglas Cinema Museum, University of Exeter.	64
3.1.	The main office of the Victoria Cinema College. *Victoria Cinema College and Studios: A Guide to Cinema Acting* (London: Victoria Cinema College, *c.* 1917). Courtesy of the Bill Douglas Cinema Museum, University of Exeter.	77

List of illustrations

3.2. The studio at the Victoria Cinema College. *Victoria Cinema College and Studios: A Guide to Cinema Acting* (London: Victoria Cinema College, c. 1917). Courtesy of the Bill Douglas Cinema Museum, University of Exeter. 78

3.3. Marion Quigley, also known as Jessie Wilding. 'Swindler unmasked', *News of the World*, 13 January 1924, p. 6. © News Corp UK & Ireland Ltd. 91

3.4. A would-be film star, as imagined by *Picturegoer*. Victor Hilton, 'That film school', *Picturegoer*, May 1928, p. 50. Courtesy of the British Film Institute Reuben Library. 98

4.1. Sybil Rhoda, the winner of *Picture Show*'s 'sporting chance' contest. 'A *Picture Show* reader gets her screen chance', *Picture Show*, 10 October 1925, front cover. © Time Inc (UK) Ltd. 104

4.2. Finalists in the 1919 *Sunday Express* Cinema Star Competition. 'On the first rung of the ladder of fame', *Sunday Express*, 29 June 1919, p. 2. © Sunday Express/N&S Syndication. 108

4.3. Advertisement for the 1928 Amami Film Star Quest. 'To some lucky Amami girl', *Weekly Dispatch*, 11 March 1928, p. 9. Courtesy of Cambridge University Library. 123

4.4. Margaret Leahy, the '*Daily Sketch* Girl'. Postcard, c. 1922. Author's collection. 125

4.5. Margaret Leahy with Buster Keaton on the set of *The Three Ages* (Buster Keaton and Edward F. Cline, 1923). Images from the Margaret Leahy Collection, courtesy of the British Universities Film & Video Council. 131

Acknowledgements

This book has been made possible with the help of many individuals and institutions. I gratefully acknowledge the assistance of the Arts and Humanities Research Council, who funded the doctoral research on which parts of this book are based. I owe many thanks to my PhD supervisor at the University of Cambridge, Jean Chothia, who guided the work through its initial stages, and to my advisors, David Trotter and Pam Hirsch, for their generous support throughout the process. Thanks also to Judith Buchanan, whose meticulous comments on my doctoral dissertation helped me to see new areas of research to explore. At UCL, I wish to thank my colleagues at the Centre for Humanities Interdisciplinary Research Projects and the Centre for Multidisciplinary and Intercultural Inquiry. I am especially grateful to Lee Grieveson for his mentorship and advice. Thanks to the series editor and editorial staff at I.B.Tauris – Jeffrey Richards, Philippa Brewster and Anna Coatman – and especially to Maddy Hamey-Thomas and David Campbell for seeing the book through to completion.

Research for this book has been greatly aided by the staff at the British Library, Cambridge University Library, Senate House Library, Guildhall Library, the Women's Library at LSE, the National Archives, the Parliamentary Archives, London Metropolitan Archives and by Kathleen Dixon and Steve Tollervey at the BFI National Archive. I would particularly like to thank Phil Wickham at the Bill Douglas Cinema Museum, University of Exeter, Jonny Davies and Nathalie Morris at BFI Special Collections, Anastasia Kerameos at the BFI Reuben Library and Linda Kaye at the British Universities Film & Video Council for their help locating materials and for allowing me to reproduce images from their collections. Thanks to the organisers of the British Silent Film Festival and British Silent Film Festival Symposium for giving me the opportunity to present aspects of my work-in-progress. Parts of this book appeared as '"On the first rung of the ladder of fame": Would-be cinema stars in silent-era Britain', *Film History*, 26/4 (2014), 84–105. Thanks to Indiana University Press for permission to reproduce this text.

A number of people have commented on drafts of this work at various stages, gone out of their way to share their knowledge with me, or otherwise helped with their friendship and encouragement. Thanks to Valerie Appleby for her services as copy-editor. Thanks also to John Arnold, Mara Arts, Ruth Austin, Jocelyn Betts, Chris Brown, Jon Burrows, Piotr Cieplak, Bryony Dixon, Polly Goodwin, Matt Houlbrook, Sam James, Roland-François Lack, Sara Levavy, Luke McKernan, Lawrence Napper, Gary Piele, Laraine Porter, Amy Sargeant, Andrew Shail, Trish Sheil, Rosie Šnajdr and Peter Walsh, among others.

Most of all, thanks to my partner, Rory Devine, for his love and support. I dedicate the book to my parents, Hilary and Conal, and to the memory of my grandmothers, Olive and Audrey, who passed away while this book was being written. Gran, this is for you.

General editor's introduction

Cinemagoing was the principal leisure activity in Britain between the 1920s and the 1950s. Social surveys revealed that the most assiduous cinema patrons were young, urban and more often female than male. It was from this demographic that were frequently to be found sufferers from a new malady 'the cinema craze', the overpowering desire to become a film star. The 'craze' was fed by the proliferation of film magazines, full of accounts of the lives of the stars, studio gossip, advice columns and competitions. They succeeded in imbuing film acting with a potent aura of glamour, which some impressionable youngsters found irresistible. In this book, Chris O'Rourke explores 'the cinema craze' in all its aspects in the period from the end of World War I to the advent of the talkies. He traces the emergence of film acting as a profession and describes working conditions in the early British studios, drawing on the memories of such notable British screen stars as Clive Brook, Brian Aherne, Mabel Poulton and Chili Bouchier. He examines the new genre of instructional manuals such as *How to Become a Film Artiste* (1921) and *Film Acting as a Career* (1929) which gave advice on how to seek employment in the industry, the art of applying screen makeup and the way to portray emotion and character by gesture and facial expression. He explores the role of employment agencies specialising in film work and the more suspect area of cinema schools, many of them fraudulent concerns seeking only to fleece their innocent young clients. Then there is the 'star search' phenomenon – at least eight of them between 1918 and 1929. Most were organised by film magazines and national newspapers, mainly to improve their circulation. None of them produced an enduring British film star. O'Rourke trawls widely not just in films, newspapers and magazines but in novels, instructional manuals, trade papers, court reports, memoirs and scrapbooks to produce a comprehensive analysis of 'the cinema craze' and to explore what it tells us about the role of cinema in changing attitudes, values and aspirations in British society in the 1920s. In so doing, he adds an entirely new dimension to our understanding of the relationship between films and their audience.

Jeffrey Richards

Introduction: Winifred Hopcroft's story

On Saturday, 10 July 1920, a young woman from the village of Rothley near Leicester went missing from her family home. Aged only 15, Winifred Agnes Hopcroft was described as 'a prepossessing young girl'. She had been working as a typist until, for reasons unknown, she received a fortnight's notice from her employers.[1] Winifred, known as Winnie, was tall for her age, with a fresh complexion (according to the description released by Scotland Yard), blue eyes, dark curly hair and a round face, which combined to make her look older than her years.[2] In a photograph printed on the front page of the *Daily Mirror*, she stares directly at the camera, her chin resting on her hand in a casual, self-assured pose (Figure I.1).[3] Winnie's ambition was to be a film star. She had been told by her friends that she was 'a second Mary Pickford', and on the day that she disappeared she explained to an acquaintance at Rothley railway station that she was going to London to pursue a screen career. A few days later, Winnie's father received a letter from her imploring him not to worry, adding that she would be well looked after and that she would be careful about the company she kept.[4]

Winnie's letter was traced to a hotel in Kensington, and the next day Mr Hopcroft travelled to London to find his daughter. Having alerted the police, he was able, with the help of detectives, to follow her trail from the hotel to the offices of Sidney Jay, a well-known film and theatre agent

Figure I.1. Winifred Hopcroft. 'The film lure', *Daily Mirror*, 16 July 1920, p. 1.

in London's West End.[5] Winnie had written to Jay three months earlier, asking him if he would help her find an engagement in the studios were she to come to London. 'She said that she was very clever,' one newspaper reported, 'and was considered to have a striking film face.'[6] Jay sent the photograph back to Winnie with the reply that, without professional experience, her chances of getting film work were extremely remote. It was the same reply he gave to her in person when she showed up at his door that July.[7] Winnie left Jay's office and went on her way through central London, possibly to try her luck at other film agencies nearby. After this, the trail goes cold. No more film industry witnesses came forward with information, and Winifred Hopcroft's name disappeared from the newspapers. For the press, this was an unfortunate case of a young woman who had been 'magnetised by the glamour of film fame' – another 'cinema-struck' girl who had come to London to find stardom, then gone astray.[8]

Introduction: Winifred Hopcroft's story

Winnie's story was by no means an isolated example. In the 1910s and 1920s, the British press regularly reported on women, and sometimes men, who were similarly 'cinema-struck'. A police detective investigating the case of a housemaid accused of stealing money from her mistress in 1915 told the court about incriminating letters and pictures he had found in the maid's lodgings 'showing that she was obsessed with the idea that she could become a cinema actress'.[9] A kitchen maid in 1920 apparently stole a small fortune's worth of furs, dresses and underwear from her employer, the stage actress Marie Lohr, to impress film producers and feed her fantasies of stardom.[10] In 1918, the local press in Hull related the case of the 13-year-old son of a butcher who had pawned a gold necklace from his home and used the money to get lodgings in London. 'I wanted a job as a cinema actor, and got one,' he explained in a half-apologetic, half-triumphant letter to his father.[11] A few years later, a 'film-struck page-boy', who had deserted his post with the Marquis of Huntly, was giving the national press a similar account of himself. 'I have always loved "the pictures",' he said, 'and a long while ago I determined that I would be a film actor. Please help me if you can – I can't bear to think of being a page-boy again.'[12]

It was not just typists, housemaids and pageboys who were keen to find employment in Britain's early film studios. Members of the upper classes, such as Lady Angela Forbes's girl Flavia and other 'daughters of Belgravia', were said to have succumbed to the modern condition of 'cinemaitis' in 1919, when they signed up for lessons in film acting.[13] Lady Diana Cooper, formerly Diana Manners, daughter of the Duke of Rutland, made headlines the same year when she 'consented' to star in a series of British films.[14] The involvement of the aristocracy in filmmaking was taken as a sign of cinema's increasing social and cultural legitimacy in Britain. As Cooper's biographer Philip Ziegler speculates, before World War I, 'the fact that a duke's daughter made money by acting for the cinema would have outraged society'. At the start of the 1920s, he says, only a scattering of upper-class 'diehards' and middle-class snobs found it shocking.[15] But Lady Diana's entry into film work was also understood as a marker of the universalising tendencies of the cinema, whose popularity cut across, and perhaps chipped away at, the class system. The newspaper cartoonist W.K. Haselden satirised the screen

Figure I.2. W.K. Haselden, 'The craze for "getting on the films"', *Daily Mirror*, 20 January 1922, p. 5. © Mirrorpix.

ambitions of Lady Diana and her peers in 1922, joking that 'the craze for "getting on the films"' threatened 'to affect the whole of society', upper and lower class alike, with the result that there would soon be nobody left to watch the pictures (Figure I.2).[16]

The 'craze' for film acting

Haselden was not alone in thinking about the enthusiasm for the cinema – and for film acting, in particular – as a 'craze'. As Shelley Stamp notes of the response to early film fandom in America, cinemagoers – especially female ones – were often caricatured as immature, irrational and even mad in their desire to see themselves on the screen.[17] Similar 'diagnoses' of crazed movie fans were made in Germany around the same time, and were also directed chiefly at women.[18] In Britain, the craze for film acting was one of many fads identified by commentators in the early twentieth century, forming part of a popular culture in which the turnover of ideas and fashions was seen to be accelerating at a rapid pace, fuelled by the apparently insatiable need to be up-to-date with the latest trends.[19] Like other crazes in the interwar period – for jazz music, new dance steps, crossword puzzles, psychoanalysis – the craze for 'getting on the films' had a life-cycle, albeit a longer one than some.[20] Already circulating by the mid-1910s, reports of 'film-' or 'screen-struck' youngsters were still appearing at the end of the 1920s, when the period of silent films gave way to the era of 'talkies'.[21]

The height of the craze for film acting, if the evidence of surviving newspapers, novels and films is to be believed, came in the years immediately following World War I, when stories of film actors and would-be actors proliferated. Cinema attendance in Britain had rocketed during the war, reaching around 21 million visits per week in 1917.[22] Cinemagoing had become a national pastime, particularly among young people who had grown up with moving pictures. The interest in becoming a film actor was partly an expression of a wider fascination with the cinema. In June 1920, a month before Winnie Hopcroft came to London, the extent of the public interest in films and their stars was amply demonstrated when the screen actress Mary Pickford, the 'world's sweetheart', and her husband Douglas Fairbanks travelled from Hollywood to Britain. They were mobbed by large crowds in London, and prompted outpourings of popular admiration that some sources depicted as mass hysteria.[23] Similar scenes would accompany Charlie Chaplin's 'homecoming' visit the following year.[24] But public attention was not only directed at Hollywood films and personalities. Already at the start of 1920 there were half a dozen 'how-to' guides to film acting on the British market, including a ten-part guide containing contributions from homegrown stars.[25] For much of the year, at least two well-publicised film 'star search' contests played out across national newspapers and newsreels, claiming to attract entries in the tens of thousands.[26] That autumn, a new British film, *The Romance of a Movie Star* (Richard Garrick, 1920), based on one of numerous serialised novels about the lives of fictional film actors, went on general release in cinemas, purporting to show film fans 'the conditions under which their favourite stars work'. The only danger, said a reviewer, was that 'the exhibition of the film will inevitably result in a tremendous rush of aspirants for screen honours'.[27] Images of the glamorous off-screen lives of film stars or the behind-the-scenes world of the studio, it was assumed, all exerted an inescapable force on British audiences, propelling them headlong towards the studio doors.

This book follows the experiences of film actors and aspiring film actors in silent-era Britain, focusing on the period from the end of World War I to the transition to sound cinema at the end of the 1920s. It argues that, while people like Winnie Hopcroft were undoubtedly on the periphery of the British film industry, attending to their stories is of central importance for understanding the nature of film culture, and of popular culture more broadly, between the wars. One of the contentions I explore in this book is that the craze for 'getting on the films' identified so often by contemporary commentators was not just narcissism or naivety on the part of a 'cinema-struck' populace, but a reflection of genuine enthusiasm for the career opportunities offered by film acting, especially for those people already busy climbing, or attempting to climb, the social ladder. Many people in Britain between the wars were interested in the possibilities of film acting as a job. Some, including Winnie Hopcroft, took active steps to pursue their interest, and a few were able to make a living by appearing in front of the cameras.

At the same time, it is clear that the craze for film acting was also invented, or at least perpetuated, by journalists, fiction writers, publicists and those who put themselves forward as experts on the art of performing for the 'silent stage'. Crazes, note Robert Graves and Alan Hodge in their history of the interwar years, were ultimately a product of newspaper headlines and editorials, whatever their basis in fact.[28] So, this book also looks critically at the depictions of would-be actors in the popular press, at the products and services that emerged to cater to their ambitions and at the responses that the 'rush of aspirants for screen honours', whether real or imagined, left in its wake.

Film acting and the British silent cinema

I should say early on that this is not a book dedicated to analysing film performances. Equally, while I draw on the evidence provided by the careers of individual film actors, it is not my intention to examine their surviving films and public personae in depth. Both of these approaches have been applied elsewhere to acting in the silent cinema, resulting in detailed studies of performance styles in early films by D.W. Griffith and performances by Lillian Gish and Charlie Chaplin, and in numerous works on the social and cultural meanings encoded in selected 'star images'.[29] Much of the scholarship on silent film acting has concerned Hollywood stars. But there has also been valuable research into the contribution made to British silent cinema by theatre actors and the promotion and reception of British silent film performers, including Alma Taylor and Ivor Novello.[30]

Instead of embarking on a textual analysis of silent screen performance, this book focuses on the history of film acting as a job. Chapter 1 traces the emergence of film acting as a distinct profession in Britain in the early part of the twentieth century. It charts the changing social status of film actors and explores the working conditions and institutional structures encountered by actors in the British film industry. In this respect, the book follows the approach of theatre historians including Michael Sanderson and Tracy Davis, who have attempted to place the work undertaken by stage actors in the context of larger economic and social developments.[31] It also responds to recent historical scholarship on silent film production in America that has shed light variously on labour disputes and attempts to unionise among film actors, regulation of working conditions and the experiences of people who found themselves on the margins of the Hollywood studio system, working as bit players or extras.[32]

Film production in Britain during the period of silent films was invariably on a smaller scale than it was in America, and the opportunities for film actors in British studios were much more limited. Jobseekers were frequently reminded of this fact. 'So far as Britain is concerned,' Herbert Morgan told readers of his guide to *Careers for Boys and Girls* in 1926, 'the film industry is yet to be established.' Eighty per cent of the films shown in British cinemas were American, he said – a figure backed up by subsequent estimates.[33] Those already working in the British production sector could be equally pessimistic. 'It is ridiculous for girls to leave regular employment in an effort to earn a living on the films,' warned the producer Cecil Hepworth. 'There is not even enough employment for tried and trained screen artists.'[34] Nevertheless, despite the very real obstacles faced by British films on the domestic and international markets, Britain remained a film-producing nation throughout the 1910s and 1920s. Revisionist scholarship on the British cinema of the silent period has revealed not only the variety of the work being undertaken in British studios, but also the extent of popular interest in local films and stars among British audiences.[35] Examining the British silent cinema from the point of view of its actors provides another perspective on the possibilities and peculiarities of British filmmaking during these years.

Participation and self-improvement

Although this is not a book about screen performance styles, it does look at what was thought to constitute good screen acting technique in the silent period. Chapter 2 looks at a number of early 'how-to' guides to film acting published in Britain, placing them in the context of a 'participatory' film culture. As Anne Morey observes of the Hollywood film industry in the 1910s and 1920s, film producers and their publicists were keen to create 'a culture of moviegoing that was, at least ostensibly, participatory rather than passive', seeking through various means 'to establish a continuum, rather than an unbridgeable separation, between the audience and industry'.[36] As other historians of American cinema have shown, this continuum had the effect of encouraging film audiences to invest emotionally, creatively and, above all, financially in the products of the Hollywood studio system.[37] Chapter 2 shows that a similar dynamic emerged between films and audiences in Britain. As well as being taught to appreciate the differences between stage and screen acting, readers of instructional guides were invited to imagine themselves as part of the filmmaking process and to take existing film performers as models of professional and, to some extent, personal conduct.

Introduction: Winifred Hopcroft's story

The advice given to would-be actors in early guides to film acting can also be understood with reference to developments that reached beyond film culture. In addition to the crazes sweeping the post-World War I public, the interwar years saw more fundamental changes to British society. Some of these stemmed from shifts in the job market, including the decline in Britain's industrial power and the shock of mass unemployment. Historians have also pointed to expansion in other areas of the economy, such as electrical, chemical and consumer goods manufacturing, and to the significant rise in service jobs, especially in the clerical and retail sectors.[38] The increase in these 'white collar' (or 'white blouse') occupations proved to be especially important to women. Shop and office work offered alternatives to traditional 'women's jobs' in factories or domestic service.[39] Combined with memories of the economic opportunities afforded to women – if only temporarily – during the war, the rise in 'white collar' employment seems to have done much to raise women's career expectations. A new generation of 'ambitious young women', Ray Strachey wrote, looking back on the years after the Armistice from the vantage point of the 1930s, sought to build on the freedoms won during wartime by exploring new fields of employment, while equally ambitious parents 'began to think seriously about their daughters' careers'.[40] In general, there was greater fluidity in the British labour market between the wars, with more men embarking on occupations that differed from those of their fathers.[41] But young working-class women, more than their brothers, were especially likely to experience upward social mobility, searching out jobs that would give them more money, more leisure time and a better social standing.[42]

Women in Britain may have been especially primed for the promises of fame, glamour and success that were made – often with numerous caveats – by the writers of instructional guides to film acting. But the idea of getting ahead through self-improvement was widespread. While Britain was still undeniably a class-conscious society between the wars, there were signs that people's attitudes and cultural values were beginning to change.[43] The culture of the suburban, upwardly mobile and moderately affluent lower-middle-class, or 'new middle class', that took shape in the early part of the twentieth century was 'more mobile', says Ross McKibbin, and 'less attached to older class cultures'.[44] With greater disposable income than those lower down the social scale and fewer ties to traditional institutions than the 'traditional' middle classes, people in this group turned instead to sports, clubs, hobbies, voluntary and religious groups and, especially, commercial culture to find their place in society.[45] They also enrolled in university extension courses and evening classes in substantial numbers. 'Absorbed in the business of learning how to live,' Peter Bailey remarks, 'those in the lower middle class were eager subjects for instruction.'[46]

For these and other groups in Britain between the wars, film stars became useful role models, or 'popular idols', as *The Times* said of Mary Pickford.[47] This was not least because they were seen to be largely removed from traditional British class hierarchies, representing a version of success that was potentially accessible to everyone, no matter their background. As D.L. LeMahieu suggests, it was easier for most people to imagine themselves becoming a film star than an aristocrat, even if the chances of this happening in real life were still slim.[48] Film actors, more than other public figures, were also attuned to what historians have described as a new emphasis, visible in contemporary self-help books and advertising, on the importance of projecting a distinctive personality, or 'inner self', through appearance, gesture and behaviour.[49] The popular interest in film acting as a profession thus coincided with the notion, encouraged by proponents of consumer culture, that individuals needed to cultivate the skills of the actor in everyday life in order to be successful in the modern world.[50]

The idea that film stars served as templates for everyday appearance and behaviour is perhaps more familiar in accounts of Britain in the 1930s. It is captured in J.B. Priestley's description, in his *English Journey* (1934), of a new nation dominated by cinemas and dance halls, in which factory girls look like film actresses.[51] It has been examined more closely in discussions of 1930s youth culture and, particularly, in Annette Kuhn's study of the habits and memories of 1930s cinema audiences.[52] There are no equivalent social survey or oral history records of British cinema audiences in the 1920s. But historians have increasingly turned to the evidence provided by popular film magazines, along with other aspects of fan culture, to understand how audiences were routinely addressed outside of the picture theatre and to piece together what fans made of their encounters with the cinema and its stars during the silent period.[53] The material explored in this book adds to our picture of cinema's reception in Britain during the late 1910s and 1920s, and of cinema's role in the transformation of attitudes and cultural values that was taking place in British society at this time.

Exploiting ambition

It wasn't only the writers of instructional guides who encouraged the British public to nurture and pursue their dreams of film stardom. Chapters 3 and 4 focus on two ways in which the aspirations of would-be film actors were shaped and, to a large extent, exploited in the interwar years. Chapter 4 looks at the network of film employment agencies and training establishments that emerged in London in the silent period. It outlines the different ways in which people went about seeking work as film actors and examines the response that greeted their attempts in the pages of trade journals and the popular press. In particular, the chapter follows the controversy caused by the proliferation of 'cinema schools' in the years after World War I. Throughout the 1920s, cinema schools, which offered lessons in film acting, were characterised as – at best – parasitic and misleading, and – at worst – fraudulent and cruel in the promises they made to their students.

As Chapter 3 shows, the local and national authorities were eager to regulate cinema schools, while members of the British film industry made frequent attempts to shut them down. At the same time, they continued to be one of the first ports of call for people who were serious about film acting as a career. Similar to film employment agencies, they were places where popular fantasies of stardom met with the harsher realities of the interwar job market and the limitations of the British film production sector. Drawing on the trail of court cases left behind by one especially notorious cinema school proprietor, Chapter 3 searches for evidence of the men and women whose ambition or curiosity about film acting took them into the territory of London's 'filmland'.

As the coverage of Winnie Hopcroft's disappearance in 1920 suggests, the British press tended to report on those it identified as 'cinema-struck' with a mixture of concern and disapproval. But, beneath the moral panic, the interwar media was also increasingly invested in the cinema, along with other aspects of commercial culture, in its ongoing attempt to keep step with popular tastes, to attract readers and to sell advertising space.[54] Chapter 4 looks in detail at a number of 'star search' competitions in Britain, almost all of which were sponsored or supported by national newspapers. These elaborate beauty and talent contests, designed to identify and launch new British film stars and aimed almost exclusively at young women, were major events in the 1920s. Similar schemes were launched in America during the silent period, and at least one star – the 'It Girl' Clara Bow – owed her success partly to a fan magazine competition.[55] In Britain, though, such contests often carried a nationalist message and were typically presented as ways to combat or compete with the appeal of Hollywood. Producers, keen to stimulate interest in British film production, offered winners supporting roles in feature films or long-term contracts with their studio stock companies. Investigating the development of early star search competitions, including the involvement of newsreel, 'cinemagazine' and advertising firms, reveals the number of groups that saw their own opportunities to get ahead in the 1920s by latching onto the cinema craze.

As with modern media talent contests, British star search competitions were invariably more profitable for their organisers than for the people who entered them.[56] Chapter 4 ends by reconstructing the brief career of Margaret Leahy, the winner of one of the most high-profile film competitions of the 1920s, who, in a controversial departure from the patriotic thrust of most British contests, was sent to America to appear in a Hollywood film. In a similar way to the stars she encountered in Hollywood, Margaret Leahy was promoted not just as a film actor, but as an example of the new type of transatlantic celebrity that was becoming more common between the wars.[57] As far as the film trade press was concerned, however, hers was a cautionary tale, and her fame and success as a film performer were ultimately fleeting.

Similar to Winnie Hopcroft, Margaret Leahy and other aspiring stars have left a few scant but intriguing traces behind of their ambitions, their motives and their experiences. More successful British film actors have left behind bigger caches of information in published and unpublished autobiographies, personal papers and publicity materials. Throughout this book, I bring together evidence from a wide variety of sources – films, newspapers, novels, instructional guides, fan magazines, trade papers, court reports, memoirs, scrapbooks – in order to provide a more rounded understanding of some underexplored areas of British film and social history between the wars. By drawing on the experiences of people who were

Introduction: Winifred Hopcroft's story

able to make the transition from film fan to film star, and of those who were not, my hope is also to give space for members of what was, effectively, the first generation in Britain to imagine themselves on the screen to tell their stories in their own words.

1

In and out of the studio: The silent film actor in Britain

A cartoon submitted to a fan magazine in 1918 by a young female reader imagined what was involved in the life of a film actor. Responding to a recently launched contest to find an 'English Mary Pickford', the reader put herself in the place of the winner. She drew herself, as a film star, swimming and 'basking in the sunshine', lying in bed and signing portraits for fans and talking pleasantly with her friends about money, clothes, flowers and music. Puncturing the fantasy, the final image depicted the young reader with an apron and bucket, ready for domestic chores, with the caption: 'And then I wake up.'[1]

The division between film acting and the working world that is implicit in this fan magazine cartoon is a common one. As Paul McDonald notes, while some 'serious' screen actors are credited with doing a complex job in front of the camera, more often the image of the film star is of someone who enjoys 'all play and no work'.[2] This wasn't always the case. In the early cinema, before World War I, accounts of film acting stressed how physically demanding and even dangerous the work of the film performer could be, with actors regularly 'called upon to risk life and limb' in the effort to secure 'exciting and sensational' scenes.[3] The association of film acting with danger continued to play a part in the publicity images of certain stars, especially those working in action genres.[4] But, from the mid-1910s, the discourse surrounding film actors tended to downplay the labour involved in film acting, preferring instead to present an image of the actor's work as more or less an extension of his or her leisure time. Hollywood stars posed for publicity photographs in the midst of their luxurious homes, next to their swimming pools, playing sports or driving their motorcars.[5] Just as the cinema was popularly understood as a place removed from everyday concerns, the people who populated the screen were seen to inhabit a space of daydreams, where the demands of housework or the practicalities of paid employment no longer applied.

But, for people actively seeking work in the film industry, the cinema also represented a viable field of employment. Although potentially more exciting than most occupations, film acting, for them, was one potential job among others. Many would-be stars may well have been naive to the actual behind-the-scenes life of the film actor. Nonetheless, there was a great deal of information available to aspiring actors about the skills required for film work and the material conditions of the studios, even if the details were sometimes distorted or exaggerated. Before turning, in the next chapter, to examine the information contained in screen acting manuals and other instructional literature, this chapter outlines the characteristics of film acting as a profession. It starts by examining how acting for a living fitted into social and cultural understandings of work in Britain at the beginning of the twentieth century. It then looks at the development of film acting as a profession in the early cinema, and at the working conditions that film actors encountered in British studios. To explore the social context of film acting in interwar Britain further, the chapter ends by following the professional lives of a number of actors who began their screen careers in the 1920s.

Acting for a living

Although film acting was a novel occupation in the interwar period, interest in acting as a profession was by no means a new phenomenon. Since the beginnings of the commercial theatre in the sixteenth century, would-be actors had gravitated to the London and provincial stages.[6] But, for much of the intervening time, the work of the actor remained marginal. As Tracy Davis writes of nineteenth-century performers, actors were 'everywhere and nowhere' in British society, 'only nominally classifiable as a group, and diverse as possible in their rank in the social pecking order'.[7] Actors' wages differed vastly, and they worked in places that ranged widely in cultural status – from the major commercial theatres to the cheapest 'penny gaffs'.[8] The diversity of actors' experiences of work was reflected in the uncertainty surrounding their classification in early census reports. Depending on the year and the idiosyncrasies of the census enumerator, actors were grouped variously with fine artists, men of letters, skilled artisans or other entertainers, such as equestrians, acrobats and prizefighters.[9]

Theatre historians have argued that Victorian and Edwardian Britain witnessed a gradual rise in the social status of the actor. At the start of the nineteenth century, moralists and religious groups regarded the theatre as a corrupting influence, and most people viewed actors with suspicion. Critics of the stage accused actors of being dissolute, immodest and prone to vice.[10] Actresses, in particular, faced social stigma as women who were seen to make a living from deception and dissembling, and on account of the longstanding association of the theatre with sexual promiscuity and prostitution.[11] The nature of theatrical entertainment meant that actors tended to work unconventional hours, with irregular patterns of employment. They also had to travel widely in the course of their work, which made it difficult for them to put down roots in any one community. The traditional routes into employment in the theatre further contributed to the sense that actors were a class apart. Many actors had grown up in theatrical families, and marriage between actors was common.[12]

The status of actors in Britain began to alter towards the end of the nineteenth century. Under the restrictive patent-theatre system that pertained up to the 1840s, only a small number of royally sanctioned theatres were permitted to stage spoken, or 'legitimate', drama. When this was finally abandoned, more people were able to establish theatres and acting companies, and thus expand the opportunities for employment. Michael Baker argues that, in the wake of these changes, the insular nature of the acting community was challenged by new entrants from non-theatrical families, including many from middle-class backgrounds. His evidence suggests that actors making their stage debuts after 1860 were more likely than before to be the children of lawyers, army officers, journalists, civil servants and even clergymen, or to have trained as officers and lawyers, themselves.[13] According to one contemporary observer, by the 1880s, the wings of West End theatres had been invaded by 'drawing-room dilettantes' from middle-class and aristocratic backgrounds, who competed for even the smallest 'walk-on' parts.[14] The shift in the social origin of actors coincided with changes in dramatic taste among certain sectors of the British theatregoing public, and particularly with a growing audience for 'polite' dramas of middle-class life.[15]

In addition to the new entrants into the theatre, the working conditions for actors were also changing. The decline of repertory companies and the emergence of a system based on long runs of the same play – typically beginning in big cities and touring during the summer months – narrowed the employment opportunities for players in the provinces. But it gave other actors, especially those based in London, greater job security and a break from the schedule of daily rehearsals.[16] In line with many other occupations in the late nineteenth and early twentieth centuries, acting became increasingly professionalised.[17] As one aspect of this, there was a renewed interest in initiating standardised training for actors.[18] In the Edwardian period, this led to the creation of two influential institutions, the Academy of Dramatic Art (later RADA) and the Central School of Speech and Drama, both in London.[19] There were also attempts to establish professional organisations. The first of these, the Actors' Association, was founded in 1891 with the aims of improving conditions for performers backstage and mediating in disputes between actors and their employers.[20] Other professional bodies and trade unions followed in subsequent decades.

For many, the knighthood awarded to the actor Henry Irving in 1895 was a confirmation of the new social respectability that the acting profession had attained by the end of the Victorian era.[21] Celebrated actors, such as Irving and Charles Wyndham, were admitted to aristocratic and professional circles as guests in private homes or in London gentlemen's clubs and fashionable restaurants.[22] Theatre stars could earn as much as £150 or £170 a week by 1914, and actor-managers, who ran or owned their own theatres, amassed considerable fortunes.[23] Acting for a living at the start of the twentieth century clearly had different social and cultural connotations than it had a century or so earlier. However, the notion that acting had become, effectively, a middle-class occupation by the 1900s has been challenged on a number of fronts. While actors in the upper echelons of the legitimate theatre in the big cities enjoyed new levels of social recognition and wealth, the same was not true for the majority of actors, or for performers working in non-legitimate genres, such as melodrama, burlesque, ballet, pantomime or music hall.[24] The experience of actors in the principal theatres in London's West End was also very different from that of their counterparts elsewhere in the country. At the turn of the twentieth century, acting remained an itinerant occupation for many. Middle-class entrants to the profession often found it difficult to adjust to life on the provincial theatre circuit, where accommodation in lodging houses could be unpleasant or hard to secure, and where conditions backstage were frequently spartan.[25] Alma Ellerslie, an actress in the Victorian provincial theatre, embarked on her career 'dream[ing] of a life of poetry and romance'. But, in her diary, she recorded her disappointment at the realities of life on the road: 'Unutterably wretched last night […]. A tiny room, and a tiny window that could not be seen through or opened. Too tired to eat anything; went to bed unhappy, dreary and desolate.'[26]

Moreover, while social attitudes towards the acting profession, in general, were changing, actresses continued to be viewed as morally suspect. Some star players, such as Mrs Patrick Campbell or Ellen Terry (who was granted a damehood in 1925), were able to move in respectable circles, despite living unconventional lives by the standards of the day.[27] But, in general, women employed in the theatre continued to encounter assumptions about their behaviour off the stage, and many had to contend with sexual misconduct from their employers.[28] In England and Wales, the number of actors – male and female (including music hall performers) – quadrupled around the turn of the twentieth century from 4,565 in 1891 to 18,247 in 1911.[29] Vying against fellow actors for roles was an everyday reality for all workers in the theatre, but the smaller proportion of star parts for women meant that competition for work among actresses was especially intense. In this environment, actresses with a middle-class upbringing, who had been educated in 'accomplishments' such as singing, dancing and foreign languages, and who had the means to support themselves between engagements, were more likely to succeed.[30]

During the interwar years, working conditions for stage actors in Britain continued to change. There were more opportunities for formal training and there was greater interest in trade unionism, with the establishment of the British Actors' Equity Association in 1929.[31] This was partly in response to new structures of management within the theatre, as the leading actor-managers of the Edwardian period, who had recruited and run their own companies, were replaced by more business-minded entrepreneurs who relied more on agents and producers to cast and direct their plays.[32] There were also changes in dramatic taste. According to some critics, audiences began to favour more restrained and relaxed styles of acting in place of the sweeping gestures and sonorous voices of earlier generations of theatrical stars.[33] Outside of the theatre, there were new employment opportunities for actors in broadcast radio (from 1922), as well as in cinema.[34] However, the social origin of stage actors seems to have remained consistent with the situation before World War I, with actors coming mainly from commercial or professional backgrounds, or from longstanding theatrical families.[35] Michael Sanderson writes that, in the 1920s, acting, at least in the theatre, 'was still a profession that children from a working-class background found very difficult to enter, even if it occurred to them to try'.[36]

Despite the obstacles, many people of all classes did try to find work on the stage. If legitimate drama was seen as inaccessible to people from working-class backgrounds, other areas of the theatre seemed more welcoming. The job of the chorus girl in musical comedy or revue was a popular goal for many young women in the early part of the twentieth century. The chorus at London's Gaiety Theatre, in particular, had achieved something of a 'collective star status' by the Edwardian period, which fed into early constructions of film celebrity.[37] The continuing success of musical comedy and revue meant that the popular appeal of the chorus girl as a figure of aspiration remained strong after World War I.[38] But, by that point, as the following section shows, film acting had emerged as another possible – and in some ways more accessible – source of employment for those determined to find work in the entertainment industries.

Actors in the early cinema

In the history of cinema, the increasing importance of actors constitutes one of the major transformations undertaken in the medium's first 20 years.

This transformation was, in turn, closely connected to other changes in the way that films were made and viewed, and in the type of films made. In the early cinema, before around 1905, actors were not a central part of the majority of films.[39] For the first decade after the advent of projected moving pictures in the 1890s, most films produced were non-fiction. Screens were dominated by scenes of everyday life, news films, travel and nature films, or recordings of novelties and extraordinary feats. Some films involved performers from music hall and vaudeville, ballet or legitimate theatre, who reprised a famous role or live act for the camera. In 1898, the matinee idol Lewis Waller was filmed in an episode from his stage production of *The Three Musketeers* by the British Mutoscope and Biograph Company.[40] A year later, the same company recorded the actor-manager Herbert Beerbohm Tree in a series of scenes from his forthcoming revival of *King John* at His Majesty's Theatre, with the full stage cast and scenery.[41] But, although early filmmakers sometimes made use of theatrical material and performers in this way, they did not depend on either for the majority of their output.

Where actors were needed, in the case of early fiction genres, they tended to be drawn from the production crew or from family and friends. As Charles Musser writes of early filmmaking in America, until around 1904, 'production personnel, non-professionals, and stage actors took turns performing for the camera'.[42] The same seems to have been true of early filmmaking in Britain. The producer Cecil Hepworth cast his cutting-room assistant Mabel Clark in the lead role of his 1903 version of *Alice in Wonderland*.[43] For *Rescued by Rover* (Lewin Fitzhamon, 1905), both Hepworth and his wife acted for the camera, as did their 8-month-old daughter and (in the title role) the family's pet dog. In the same film, Hepworth and his company made use – for the first time – of professional actors from the stage, paying Mr and Mrs Sebastian Smith each 10s 6d for their services, which included the cost of their train fares from London.[44] However, casting stage actors had not yet become standard practice. As the film's director, Lewin Fitzhamon, recalled, Hepworth, like other early filmmakers, generally preferred to use local non-professional actors where he could, in order to save time and money.[45]

The professional status of film acting altered as fiction films began to overtake non-fiction films in popularity. Internationally, the rising demand for story films, fuelled by the growth of dedicated picture theatres, encouraged some producers to recruit fulltime stock companies. By 1905, the French company Pathé Frères had amassed a large production staff, including companies of regular actors and directors, capable of turning out up to six films per week.[46] Film companies in America also formed stock companies around 1907–8.[47] In contrast to the situation in France, these companies were generally under the collaborative control of cameramen and producers. However, by 1909, some early filmmakers, such as D.W. Griffith, were given the freedom to hire and direct their own regular cast and crew.[48] In Britain, there was limited development of the stock company system in film production. Hepworth began to assemble a company of actors around 1910. For the sum of 4s a day, Chrissie White commuted from her home in London around this time to the Hepworth studio in nearby Surrey, where she took part in the company's series of *Tilly the Tomboy* comedies and other films.[49] White joined fellow performers, including Gladys Sylvani, Alma Taylor, Hay Plumb, Jack Hulcup and Claire Pridelle, in what became a core group of regular Hepworth players. Around the same time, the Clarendon Film Company started to employ its own salaried performers. As a young woman of 17, Dorothy Bellew recalled signing a three-year contract with Clarendon in 1910 or 1911.[50] The British and Colonial Kinematograph Company (known as B&C) also began to build up a small stock company for its fiction film output in these years.[51]

Other British firms had more informal relations with both professional and non-professional actors. The filmmaker Dave Aylott recalled the typical casting procedure when he joined the film company Cricks and Martin in 1909: 'We had a file of artists who were available for films and from these we would choose the characters for the particular plots we were working on.' Professional theatre actors were given preferential treatment. Of the performers on file, Aylott wrote, 'very few were actors or music hall artists, but those who were we looked after and kept regularly at work.'[52] The practice of casting actors on a per film basis remained common. Will Barker, head of Barker Motion Photography, described the audition process for his film adaptation of *Hamlet* in 1910:

> All being ready to take, and having arranged with a man – who knew the part – to play Hamlet, we turn up the 'Rogue's Gallery,'

that is a newspaper-cutting book in which we have pasted the photos of all the artists who applied to us for work. Any who wanted more than 10s per day was NOT written to. Well, we got the artists into the studio at 8.30 a.m. in the morning. I stand on a chair and look the lot over. 'Here,' I say, 'you're nice and tall, you can play The Ghost.' 'Can any lady swim?' A hand goes up. 'You will play Ophelia, Miss,' and that's how Polonius, the Queen, and all the other characters were chosen.[53]

Barker claimed to have cast and shot the entire film in a single day. Other filmmakers made use of the theatrical press to recruit actors for one-off roles. By 1912, Lewin Fitzhamon had begun to advertise in the theatrical trade paper *The Era* for supporting parts, such as children or 'a Public School' or 'Varsity man' type, for individual productions.[54]

The casual and largely anonymous nature of much early film work meant that film acting wasn't yet widely recognised as a distinct profession. A career guide from the early 1910s encouraged readers to consider the work of the film actor (or the 'bioscope model') as a supplemental employment for theatre actors in the summer, with 'much of the work being done when things are dull on the stage for the rank and file workers in that profession'.[55] Some evidence of how early film performers thought about their work in front of the camera can be gleaned from the way in which they described their occupation in official documents. The household schedules for the 1911 census, which are the earliest to survive in the householders' own words, rather than in the standardised transcripts of census enumerators, give a sense of the variety of ways in which film acting was described by the people involved.[56] The Hepworth stock company actress Gladys Sylvani (then sharing a flat in Bloomsbury with her servant) described herself in 1911 as an 'actress and cinematograph artist', suggesting that she thought about her film acting as a separate, if not necessarily less important, occupation to her work on the stage.[57] Sylvani's fellow Hepworth employees Hay Plumb, Jack Hulcup and Clare Pridelle (all lodging together in a fisherman's cottage near the Hepworth studio) gave their occupations as 'actor' and 'actress', making no explicit mention of film.[58] The B&C actress Dorothy Foster also described herself simply as an 'actress'.[59] Apparently alone among early film performers, only Bertie Harold Brett, a bit player and writer for B&C living in East London, gave his occupation solely as 'cinematograph artiste'.[60]

Picture personalities and crowd players

In the 1910s, film actors began to get more public credit for their work. As fiction films became the dominant cinematic product internationally, and as competition between producers became fiercer, companies began to promote particular actors as selling points. Eventually, they began to provide distributors and cinema owners with promotional materials, such as posters, postcards and photographs of their leading players. The attempts of American film companies to establish a star system have been seen as pivotal in this respect. Certainly by 1910, almost every major producer had started to publicise members of their stock companies by name as 'picture personalities'.[61] Already in France, though, the comic actor Max Linder was given special advertising as a film celebrity from 1909, possibly suggesting to American producers a way to capitalise on and fuel the growing public interest in their regular performers.[62] The market value of casting and marketing named performers was further demonstrated by efforts to entice well-known theatre stars, including Sarah Bernhardt and Gabrielle Réjane, to become more involved in film production.[63] In Britain, as Jon Burrows shows, film companies were particularly keen to recruit stars from the West End stage. Beginning with Godfrey Tearle's 1908 *Romeo and Juliet* for the Gaumont Company and continuing with Will Barker's high-profile collaboration with Beerbohm Tree on the film of *Henry VIII* (1911), British producers repeatedly tried to harness the drawing power of famous and well-respected theatre actors to boost the reputation of the domestic cinema industry.[64]

By the start of World War I in 1914, an early star system had emerged in Europe and America. Performers such as Asta Nielsen and Mary Pickford had become central to the organisation of their national film industries, and were increasingly known internationally for both their films and their off-screen personalities.[65] *The Film Life of Mary Pickford*, a pamphlet published around 1915 by the British film renter J.D. Walker, provides a compendium of the strategies used by film companies to promote film actors to the public and to use the popularity of high-profile film actors to generate interest in new releases.[66] Liberally illustrated with photographs of Pickford in her recent roles in *Tessibel of the Storm Country* and *Hearts Adrift* (both Edwin S. Porter, 1914), the pamphlet also included a poem dedicated to

Pickford ('The World's Sweetheart'), praise for her performances taken from trade press reviews and a biography of her young life and career, including anecdotes about her childhood, her husband and her many fans. Carefully constructed for local audiences, Pickford's *Film Life* was quick to distinguish her not only as a worldwide celebrity, but also as a 'British' star, by virtue of her Canadian parentage.[67]

In Britain, several production companies made concerted efforts to publicise their regular film actors before World War I along comparable lines. The Hepworth Manufacturing Company embarked on a marketing campaign for its stock players around 1912, and the leading lady Gladys Syvlani was especially heavily promoted. 'Her portrait is everywhere', one journalist wrote.[68] Articles about her were published in popular magazines, and her image appeared on London underground platforms and in commemorative photograph albums.[69] Similar treatment was given to the beauty contest winner Ivy Close when she joined the company later that year, and to the young actress Alma Taylor.[70] Hepworth's strategies seem to have paid off. In a 1915 fan poll, Taylor was voted as the favourite British film performer, finishing ahead of Charlie Chaplin, with her co-star Stewart Rome in third place.[71] Other companies also contributed to the promotion of celebrity film actors in Britain. Elisabeth Risdon, the second-most popular film actress in the 1915 fan magazine poll, was one of several actors promoted by B&C, along with Dorothy Foster and Percy Moran, who was most often referred to by the name of his on-screen persona, Lieutenant Daring.[72] Clarendon also publicised their contract players Dorothy Bellew and P.G. Northcote, who was better known for his portrayal of another fictional naval hero, Lieutenant Rose.[73] The promotion of film celebrities in Britain, both homegrown and imported, continued to gain pace during the war years, accelerated by the launch of more specialist film magazines.[74]

The market value that was increasingly being attached to star film performers is reflected in the proportion of film costs set aside for actors. At the end of the 1920s, it is estimated that British producers spent 20 per cent of their budgets on actors, compared with 10 per cent on the director and around 7 per cent on the script.[75] This could translate into relatively high earnings for the biggest names. Although Cecil Hepworth refused, on principle, to pay his star Alma Taylor more than £60 a week, feature film actors in other British companies could expect around £70–100 by the mid-1920s.⁷⁶ Aurèle Sydney, star of the popular *Ultus* film series (George Pearson, 1915–17), was reportedly promised 'a salary of approaching three figures a week' when he signed an exclusive three-year contract with Gaumont in 1919.⁷⁷ If this news is accurate, it would have put him in roughly the same wage bracket as the leading West End theatre actors of the day.⁷⁸ A year later, Betty Balfour, one of the most consistently popular British film stars of the 1920s, was said to have signed with the producers Welsh-Pearson for an undisclosed 'record salary'.⁷⁹ However, similar to reports of theatre actors' wages, reports of film actors' wages could be misleading. A surviving contract from the early sound period suggests that such high payments related only to those weeks when the actor was filming, whereas a much smaller retainer was paid for the rest of the year.⁸⁰ Expenses incurred in the course of their work could also deplete the income of film actors. A sample contract drawn up by Atlantic Union Films, the producers of *Owd Bob* (Henry Edwards, 1924), stipulated that actors were required to pay their own way to the studio and any other filming locations within a 25-mile radius, and to supply their own costumes.⁸¹ This last stipulation reflected standard theatre practice, and could mean that a significant part of an actor's wages would be spent on clothes.⁸² A guide to film acting from the early 1920s recommended that performers invest, at a minimum, in morning suits and evening suits for men and evening gowns for women, noting that 'companies do not provide wardrobe, even for leading players, except in the case of costume plays', when special outfits were hired from theatrical costumiers.⁸³ Some producers even expected actors to supply their own historic outfits. A letter from the Samuelson Film Manufacturing Company in 1918 requested actors to turn up on location dressed 'in the oldest fashioned way you can' for a drama set in the 1890s (Figure 1.1).⁸⁴

Throughout the silent period in Britain, salaried film actors, such as Aurèle Sydney and Betty Balfour, were in the minority. In 1913, the film trade magazine *The Bioscope* wrote that, while many performers might act occasionally in films or split their professional life between stage and screen, no more than 50 actors in the country could subsist entirely on film work.⁸⁵ Five years later, *The Era* estimated that there were only 40 actors working fulltime for British film companies, representing a tiny fraction of the more than 15,000 people who would describe themselves as actors of some kind in the national census two years later.⁸⁶ This number

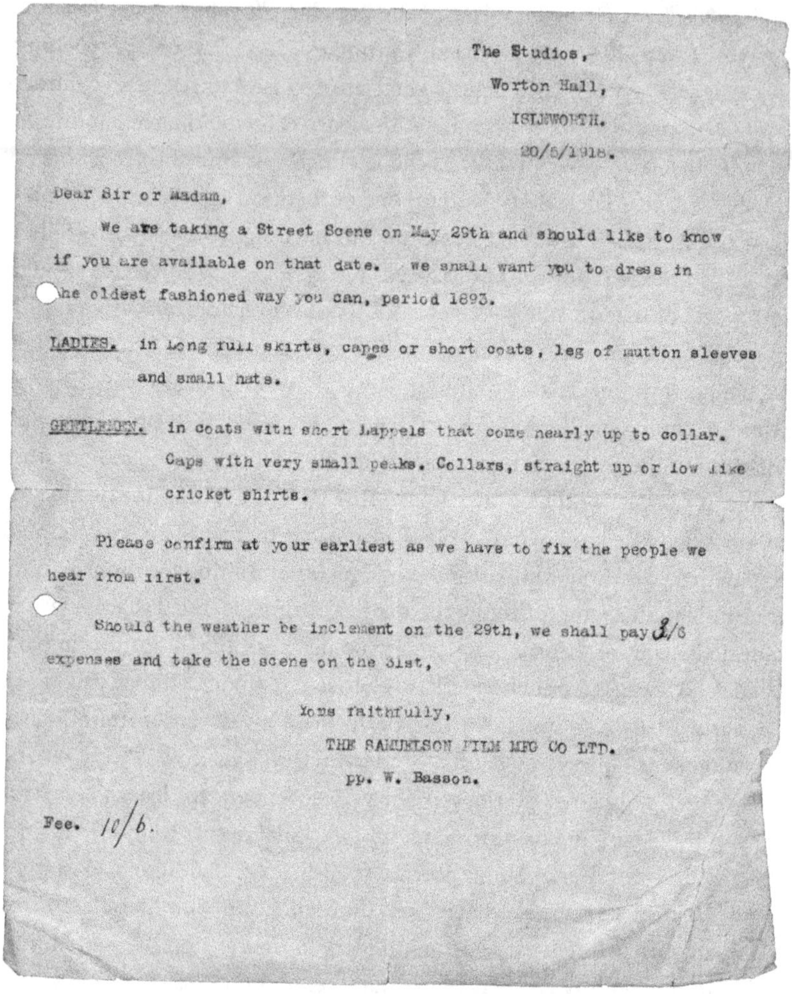

The Studios,
Worton Hall,
ISLEWORTH.
20/5/1918.

Dear Sir or Madam,

We are taking a Street Scene on May 29th and should like to know if you are available on that date. We shall want you to dress in the oldest fashioned way you can, period 1893.

LADIES. in long full skirts, capes or short coats, leg of mutton sleeves and small hats.

GENTLEMEN. in coats with short lappels that come nearly up to collar. Caps with very small peaks. Collars, straight up or low like cricket shirts.

Please confirm at your earliest as we have to fix the people we hear from first.

Should the weather be inclement on the 29th, we shall pay 3/6 expenses and take the scene on the 31st,

Yours faithfully,
THE SAMUELSON FILM MFG CO LTD.
pp. W. Basson.

Fee. 10/6.

Figure 1.1. A letter to 'crowd players' from the Samuelson Film Manufacturing Company. Courtesy of the Teddy Baird Collection, British Film Institute Special Collections.

undoubtedly fluctuated during the 1920s, along with levels of production in British studios. However, in most cases, actors continued to be hired on a per film basis. An international study of working conditions in the film industry published in 1931 estimated that 99 per cent of film actors in America and Europe were being paid per film or even by the day.[87] In Britain, visiting performers from the theatre or from America were sometimes paid large sums for one-off engagements. The theatre star John Martin-Harvey was paid £1,000 by Astra Films for acting in *The Breed of the Treshams* (Kenelm Foss, 1920), while, later in the decade, G.B. Samuelson offered the Hollywood actress Betty Blythe £2,000 to appear in *She* (Leander de Cordova, 1925).[88] But the majority of the film industry's casual workforce was composed not of celebrities moonlighting in British pictures, but of more lowly extras.

Also known in Britain as 'supers' (theatrical shorthand for supernumeraries), or 'crowd' players, extras were essential but habitually marginalised parts of fiction film production.[89] The life of a film extra was notoriously unpredictable. Iris Carpenter, who reported for the fan magazine *Picturegoer* on her single 'day of superdom' on the set of *Remembrance* (Bert Wynne, 1927), said that the majority of crowd players were 'ekeing out a miserable existence on a pound a day minus agent's fees, lunches and fares', and were 'getting only one day's work perhaps in every three weeks'.[90] At the start of the 1930s, a representative from the British film industry was slightly more optimistic, claiming that 'crowd artistes consider themselves lucky to be given employment on two days a week', but adding that many extras 'live very precariously and, indeed, dangerously near to what may be called the "hunger line"'.[91] For this reason, the studio 'crowd' could become a powerful symbol of the wider surplus of labour in Britain's interwar cities, especially during the frequent periods of high unemployment. When the eponymous heroine of Arthur Applin's novel *The Beautiful Miss Barry* (1925) arrives at the studio for her first day of work, she is shocked to see a queue of people from all walks of life waiting outside in the rain for a chance of work: 'Very old men and women bent with age, youth, children. A few smartly dressed, others looked like the artisan class out of work, and many flotsam and jetsam of the city, unemployable.'[92]

As a full-time job, extra work was unreliable. Nevertheless, as supplemental employment, it could be remunerative. Guides to film acting in the 1920s recorded that film extras could expect to be paid between 10s and a guinea (£1 1s) a day, going up to as much as £1 10s by the end of the decade.[93] These figures are largely born out by the evidence provided by the young actor Edward ('Teddy') Baird, who kept a record of his studio engagements and earnings as an extra in British films over a four-year period.⁹⁴ In 1917, aged 15, Baird took home only £2 from five engagements. However, as his experience as an extra grew, so did his wages. Over the course of 1918, he received around £22 for a total of 31 days of filming, making £26 for 28 days' work the following year. By 1920, Baird was regularly being paid a guinea or more per engagement, recording payments totalling over £85 for 81 filming days. By the time his diary entries stopped in July 1921, he had made a further £39. Baird's annual income as an extra during these years was not lavish. But, as a casual labourer – performing, as he did, as a nightclub patron for *Castles in Spain* (Horace Lisle Lucoque, 1920) or acting as a Venetian partygoer in *Carnival* (Harley Knoles, 1921) – he may have found more enjoyment than he otherwise might have in some of the more traditional 'blind alley' jobs open to male school-leavers, such as errand boy, messenger and shop boy.⁹⁵ As Baird's subsequent experiences show, work as an extra could also provide entry into more profitable and rewarding film careers for those willing or able to persist. After continuing to work as a crowd player for several more years, from 1928 Baird found work behind the camera as a cutting-room assistant for British Instructional Films (BIF), before going on to form a close working relationship as a producer with the BIF director Anthony Asquith.⁹⁶ The cinematographer Jack Cardiff also served an unofficial apprenticeship as an extra in the 1920s before making the transition to cameraman.⁹⁷

By the interwar period, it was more generally accepted that film acting was a distinct occupation from acting on the stage. While commentators often worried that the British film industry was underdeveloped compared to other national cinema industries elsewhere in Europe and in America, the immediate post-World War I years brought new levels of financial investment to the British production sector.⁹⁸ This translated into an increasing optimism about the future for British film workers and for actors, in particular. A vocational guide from 1919 wrote that, although would-be actors should not expect 'to obtain the fabulous sums earned by film stars, [...] it is often possible to make a very good income'.⁹⁹ Actors who did find employment in British studios in the 1920s encountered working conditions that were very different to those experienced by the previous generation of film performers.

Working conditions

Working conditions in British studios varied enormously during the silent period, as did the studios, themselves. The earliest studio facilities, such as those constructed by Hepworth for his company in Walton-on-Thames, were basic wooden structures designed simply to provide a backdrop for outdoor filming. 'All we wanted,' Hepworth later wrote, 'was a bit of floor for "actors" to walk on and some scenery flats [...] to give the appearance of a room, kitchen or drawing or what-not.'[100] But producers soon expanded to larger premises, and, by the end of World War I, there was around 87,000 feet of studio space available in Britain.[101] This was mostly in indoor studios in or around London that had been converted from halls, warehouses or stately homes, and that were reliant on daylight provided by glass roofs. During the 1920s, British producers invested in a further 200,000 feet of studio floor space, enlarging existing facilities and constructing new studios at Islington, Cricklewood, Welwyn and Elstree, equipped with multiple stages and artificial lighting, which reduced the reliance on good weather conditions.[102]

For inexperienced actors, the film studio could be a disorienting place. Descriptions of studio life from the silent period tended to emphasise the busy and chaotic atmosphere that greeted the uninitiated. The writer Thomas Burke, who toured the Islington studios built by the British subsidiary of the American company Famous Players-Lasky in the early 1920s (Figure 1.2), remarked on the jumble of scenery he encountered: 'On all sides were little islands of "sets," and we were led through halls, through a drawing-room, through a dining-room, through the forecourt of a country mansion, and stumbled over cables.'[103] Filming indoors required extensive lighting, and many actors commented on the resulting tangle of wires as well as the blinding glare of the lights. In her novelistic portrait of British filmmaking in the 1920s, the actress Joan Morgan wrote of a studio 'littered with cables [...], tripping you up, hissing at you and blowing fuses', and of the long blue tubes of the mercury-vapour lamps, which 'photographed themselves on your retina and returned to keep you awake as soon as you closed your eyes'.[104] Elsewhere, she recalled suffering periodically from the form of conjunctivitis known as 'Klieg eye' (named after the Klieg arc lamps), as a result of her prolonged exposure to studio lights.[105] For newcomers, the

Acting for the Silent Screen

Figure 1.2. Inside the Famous Players-Lasky British studios in Islington. L.C. MacBean, *Kinematograph Studio Technique* (London: Pitman, 1922), frontispiece. Courtesy of Cambridge University Library.

sound caused by the work of studio carpenters and electricians and by cameras being cranked could also be overwhelming. Jack Cardiff said of his experience of extra work at the St Margaret's studios in Twickenham and at Wharton Hall in Isleworth that 'the noise on the set as we worked could be deafening in those "silent" days'.[106]

Once familiar with its workings, though, actors could find the studio a collegial and friendly environment. As in the theatre, in the film industry, actors passed on advice and knowledge to less experienced colleagues. During his first film, the young actor John Stuart was given a lesson in applying screen make-up by the veteran performer Stewart Rome.[107] Film studios could also be egalitarian places. Thomas Burke found it remarkable that the whole of the Famous Players-Lasky cast and crew lunched together at the Islington studio, with 'no line of demarcation' between them. 'The cinema is a democratic institution,' he reflected, 'and it was pleasant to see the democratic spirit alive at headquarters.'[108] Similar to the stage, the studio was notable for being a mixed-gender workplace at a time when the division between men and women's labour was usually strictly observed.[109] The possibility of an easy male-female camaraderie leading to romance was demonstrated by several high-profile marriages between film stars, including, in Britain, the relationship between Chrissie White and Henry Edwards, whose engagement in 1922 made headlines in the popular press.[110]

The studio's egalitarian image did not always ring true, however. At Stoll's Cricklewood premises, the studio layout was explicitly hierarchical, with a separate refreshment room for stars and heads of department, another for 'small part artistes and supers' and a bigger canteen for the rest of the staff.[111] Those who worked as extras found themselves differentiated from salaried actors in other ways, too. Stanley Bruce wrote about his three months' experience of 'doing "crowd" work in the studios round London' in 1919, remarking on the 'unbusinesslike attitude' of producers and studio managers, who kept extras waiting long hours in uncomfortable conditions and treated them like props.[112] Recalling his days as an extra in the late 1920s, Basil Karslake likewise noted how some productions could be especially trying for bit players. Directing a scene set in a Russian Orthodox church for *Tesha* (1928), Victor Saville apparently refused his extras toilet or refreshment breaks, even when none of them was in shot. Conversely, on some films, producers used the presiding 'democratic' atmosphere to their advantage. 'As there were no demarcations, save for electrics,' Karslake wrote of his time working at Elstree on *Piccadilly* (E.A. Dupont, 1928), 'we all mucked in in moving furniture and anything else that required doing – nobody minded.'[113]

For all actors, from stars to extras, preparing for a scene in front of the camera could take considerable time. Most film actors in the 1920s vividly recalled the make-up necessary to make skin tones appear natural on the early orthochromatic film stock. Typically, the area around a film performer's eyes was shaded dark red, brown or blue, eyebrows were outlined in black and lips were coloured crimson.[114] The standard yellow greasepaint applied to white skin for most of the silent period, Leichner no. 5, was eventually side-lined by the introduction of more sensitive panchromatic film stock and advances in studio lighting.[115] But it was ubiquitous enough to be known, even in 1930, as 'moving picture yellow'.[116] The yellow faces of film actors added to the surreal impression made on many studio visitors. Burke commented that, away from the light of the arc lamps, film actors 'showed ghastly yellow', while 'those within the glare looked seasick'.[117]

Because films were usually shot out of narrative sequence, film actors were reliant on the script or the explanations of directors (or producers, as they were known for much of the period) to know their place in the story. The director and studio manager L.C. MacBean said that it was usual for leading actors to receive only a synopsis of the film's plot, rather than the complete scenario, or screenplay.[118] Once on the set, the working relationship between film actors and directors varied immensely depending on the studio and the production. MacBean thought that 'a good producer will carefully explain each scene to his artistes, running through a part himself, where necessary, to emphasize his requirements and give confidence to the players'.[119] In the days before synchronised sound, many film actors recalled directors providing guidance on their performance while the cameras were turning. In one of his more substantial roles as a child actor, Jack Cardiff remembered being told what to do in a scene between him and the actress Violet Hopson by a director (possibly Walter West) 'shouting instructions through a long megaphone': 'Look over to Miss Hopson … You LOVE her … SMILE a little … Take his hand, Violet … Jackie, look up at her and SMILE … More, son – that's good….'[120] There were other aids for film actors, too. In some cases, studios employed a group of musicians to provide accompaniment for important scenes. The producer Michael Balcon recalled that Betty Compson, the American star of his early film *Woman to Woman* (Graham Cutts, 1922), was able to cry real tears, but only with the help of a three-piece orchestra playing the sentimental song 'Mighty Like a Rose'.[121] Other actors recalled being able to request their favourite 'mood music' to suit the emotional demands of the scene.[122]

Waiting, as film actors often complained, was a common experience of life in the studio.[123] This was due to not only the schedules of production, but also seasonal problems such as fog, which could affect even indoor studios in and around London during the winter months.[124] Some studios, including those used by Hepworth and the Broadwest Film Company, had green rooms 'where the artistes dressed for their parts can rest, read and smoke until they are wanted for a scene'.[125] Studios built in the 1920s, including the Stoll facilities at Cricklewood, were also equipped with multiple dressing rooms for supporting actors and stars.[126] But for scenes filmed on location, conditions for actors were sometimes uncomfortable. Of her time filming *The Sorrows of Satan* (Alexander Butler, 1917), Gladys

Cooper wrote: 'I have seldom been so miserable. It was snowy weather, and for half-a-day I crouched over a horrible little fire, waiting to be called to do my bit in evening clothes.'[127] Her fellow actress Fay Compton also remembered braving gale force winds while being asked to imagine 'the stillness of a sultry evening', when filming a love scene on the English coast for *Diana of the Crossways* (Denison Clift, 1922).[128] Stories of accidents or encounters with baffled locals while filming on location were common in the silent period, invariably serving as a marker of cinematic realism.[129] For would-be actors, though, trips to the countryside or journeys to foreign locations were presented as benefits of the job, with the outdoor life of 'fresh air' and 'lovely scenery' enjoyed by film actors set in contrast to the static setting and stuffier atmosphere of the theatre.[130]

Whereas in 1910 Will Barker claimed to be casting and shooting his films in a single day, by the 1920s the length of films and production schedules had grown considerably.[131] In 1919, some companies were making low-budget films in as short a time as 18 days, but, according to Michael Balcon, the average working schedule for a British feature film was between four and five weeks.[132] Most actors would not be working for all of this time, and, while Basil Karslake managed to secure 22 days on the set of *Piccadilly*, crowd players would typically be needed only for a day or two.[133] The longest film engagement Teddy Baird recorded in his diary was six days for the political biopic *The Life Story of David Lloyd George* (Maurice Elvey, 1918).[134] At the end of their time on the film set, extras collected their pay from a cashier's window and returned to the dressing room to remove their greasepaint, hoping to be called again the following day.[135]

To gain a better understanding of the actors who populated British film studios in the 1920s, and the experiences and expectations they brought with them, the remainder of the chapter focuses on the working lives of four British film actors whose screen careers began after World War I. Although by no means exhaustive, their stories highlight the diversity of actors working in British films during the silent period and the range of social and professional backgrounds that film actors came from at that time. The evidence that these performers left behind in films, memoirs, scrapbooks and publicity material sheds further light on the place of actors in British film production. Their stories demonstrate, among other things, the continuing overlaps between the professional worlds of stage and screen, and how the film studio both replicated and challenged the hierarchies of gender and class that characterised British society in the interwar years.

Stage and screen: Clive Brook and Brian Aherne

Geoff Brown notes that, in contrast to the situation in America, where Hollywood and Broadway are some 2,000 miles apart, the main British film studios and the centre of the commercial theatre in Britain are separated by only a short train journey.[136] The conclusion that Brown draws from this fact – that early British filmmakers invariably settled for basking 'in the reflected glory' of the nation's theatrical tradition – has been rightly challenged.[137] But his observation that the physical proximity of the leading West End theatres to the major centres of film production has made it easier for actors to combine work across stage and screen is hard to dispute. The early careers of two British film actors, Clive Brook and Brian Aherne, demonstrate the different ways in which performers attempted to negotiate a career across these two spaces in the 1920s (Figure 1.3).

Clive Brook, born in London in 1887, came to professional acting relatively late in life, aged 32. He grew up in a series of middle-class homes in North London and Dulwich, attending a private school and later a commercial college, where he learned the skills needed for a career in business. 'The thought of "going on the stage", he later wrote, 'never occurred to me,' although, as a child, he had staged plays with his brother and been tutored in music and dancing.[138] While working for an assurance company in the City, Brook became involved in amateur dramatics and invested in elocution lessons. During World War I, he served as an officer in France and performed in plays and recitals staged to entertain the troops. After the war, Brook decided to pursue acting as a career, and gained introductions to stage producers through contacts he had made in the army. He toured the provinces in a series of plays and variety sketches, meeting his future wife and returning to London for performances at West End theatres and music halls.[139]

Brook's entry into film work came several years into his theatrical career, when a number of agents approached him to appear in films. Pretending to have pre-World War I experience in film acting, he was cast in the Broadwest detective drama *Trent's Last Case* (Richard Garrick, 1920). He recalled being disoriented by the process of filmmaking and confused

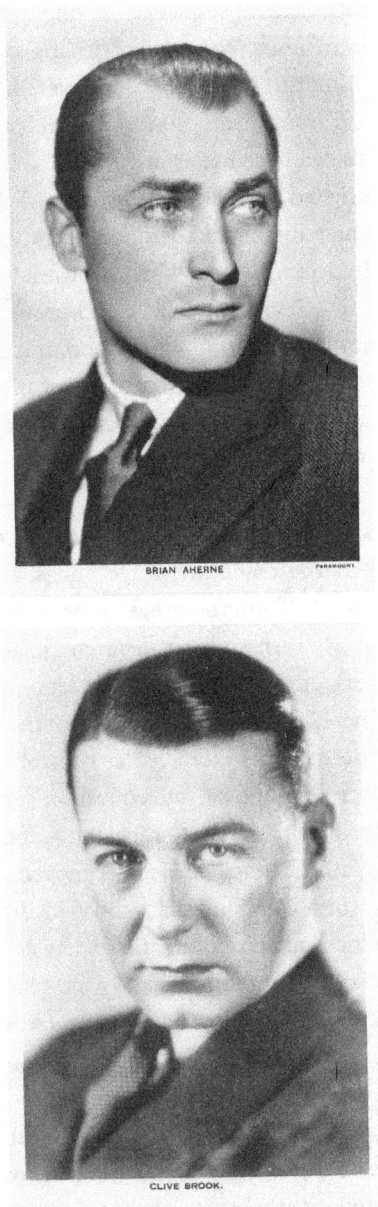

Figure 1.3. Clive Brook and Brian Aherne. Postcards, *c.* 1930s. Author's collection.

by the need to perform simple sequences multiple times. 'My first day's work,' he wrote in his memoirs, 'consisted of driving a car a few yards, stopping, getting out and shutting the door.'[140] However, in Brook's account, his professional transition from theatre to film was relatively swift. He acted in several more films for Broadwest, often with overlapping production schedules, and soon signed a three-film contract with the company for £25 a week.[141] Although he remembered being frequently disheartened by the limited production budgets of British films, his work took him to locations and studios in Scotland, France and Italy, and brought him into contact with performers and directors from Hollywood, including the American star Betty Blythe. The international circulation of his films attracted the attention of American producers, and, in 1924, after finishing a film in the Pathé studios in Paris, he left British films to the join the Thomas Ince company in America.[142]

Whereas Brook's theatre and film careers intersected only briefly, his fellow actor Brian Aherne combined stage and studio work for much of the 1920s. Born in 1902, Aherne grew up near Birmingham and was educated privately at Malvern College. As a child, his mother, who was a keen amateur actress, enrolled him in dance lessons at the Italia Conti School in London. There, he gained his first taste of the West End stage in a Christmas play produced by the actor Charles Hawtrey. But, as with Brook, Aherne's family background and private education set him up for a more firmly middle-class profession, and, after leaving school, he began to train as an architect at his father's practice. He later moved to Liverpool, where he worked as a clerk in a company that managed British assets in West Africa, and joined a local amateur dramatic society as a hobby. He moved to London in 1923. According to his memoirs, he gravitated towards professional stage work only when a 'proper job' in the City or in shipping failed to materialise, using his mother's limited contacts in the theatrical world to secure himself a meeting with an agent.[143]

Once he had been acting in plays for about a year and was receiving favourable reviews in the press, Aherne was asked by Joseph Grossman, the studio manager for Stoll Picture Productions in Cricklewood, to appear in a film, *The Squire of Long Hadley* (Sinclair Hill, 1925).[144] During the production, Aherne worked two jobs simultaneously, getting a bus to Cricklewood at 6am to start early, then leaving at 5pm to get back to the Playhouse Theatre in the West End, where he was performing in a long run of the play *White Cargo*. Similar to other actors, Aherne recalled detesting the 'Leichner greasepaint and heavy lipstick' he had to wear in the studio.[145] He suffered from 'Klieg eye' and found the process of acting in front of the camera frustrating. 'At Stolls,' he wrote, 'they were usually building other sets all around, and the hammering, shouting, and crashing noises that went on were highly distracting.'[146] However, the £40 a week he received from Stoll was a considerable sum compared to the £12 a week he earned from his role at the Playhouse, and he continued to combine film and theatre work over the next year, sometimes travelling long distances on Saturday nights to film on location on Sundays, when the theatres were closed.[147]

Over the years that followed, Aherne acted in several more films, including *A Woman Redeemed* (Sinclair Hill, 1927) and *Shooting Stars* (A.V. Bramble and Anthony Asquith, 1928), in which he played a film actor who becomes the country's leading director. By the end of the decade, he was one of several actors that *The Bioscope* thought should be more systematically publicised as a British film star.[148] But, despite his growing reputation in films, the majority of Aherne's professional life in this period was spent on the stage, either in long theatrical runs in the West End or on international stage tours. Whereas Brook effectively abandoned the theatre for the film studio, for Aherne, acting in films was only part of his job, and one that invariably had to fit around his theatrical engagements. The example of Aherne's early career is a reminder that, while the skills required of film actors may have increasingly been seen as distinct from those required for stage acting, the professional worlds of film and theatre were closely intertwined in the 1920s. It was only when Aherne went to Hollywood in the 1930s, following the example of Brook, Ronald Colman and other British actors, that he became more-or-less a fulltime film actor, largely because – in contrast to British producers – his new employers were less willing to accommodate competing theatrical commitments.[149]

A 'nice' job for girls: Mabel Poulton and Chili Bouchier

In his study of the British acting profession, Michael Sanderson suggests that male actors during the silent period were more mobile than actresses when it came to crossing the boundaries between stage and screen.[150] To counter Sanderson's assertion, there were, in fact, a number of female performers working in Britain, including Florence Turner, Fay Compton and Gladys Cooper, who successfully combined engagements in music halls or legitimate theatres with their work in film studios.[151] But women, and especially working-class women, still faced challenges when embarking on a film career. The early lives of two silent film actresses, Mabel Poulton and Chili Bouchier, demonstrate why film acting, even more than stage acting, could be particularly appealing to young women in the 1920s, while at the same time revealing how actors' experiences of the British film industry were informed by broader social attitudes to class and gender (Figure 1.4).

Mabel Poulton was born in 1901 and grew up in London's East End. Her father worked as a 'clicker', cutting patterns for boots and shoes, while her mother ran a market stall selling costume jewellery.[152] In common with many of her contemporaries, such as those in Jerry White's study of nearby Islington, Poulton found the options for girls in her working-class neighbourhood limited, revolving mainly around factory work, paid (and unpaid) domestic work and motherhood, and she thought of a stage career as a means of escape.[153] However, once Poulton left school, she was required to contribute to the family income, and so she took the more reliable route – followed by an increasing number of young women during the first decades of the twentieth century – and embarked on clerical work.[154] After working in a series of offices in central London, she secured a job at the Alhambra Theatre in the West End, working in the press office as a typist. With her mother's help, she paid for acting lessons and was advised that, because of her 'slight Cockney accent', she would be more employable in films, in which her class-inflected speaking voice would not be an issue.[155] Poulton had at least one engagement as a crowd player in the course of her acting tuition, but her first significant studio engagement came about through her proximity to the entertainment world at the Alhambra. In 1920, when the theatre was hosting an extended run of the film *Broken Blossoms* (D.W. Griffith, 1919), Poulton's manager noticed her resemblance to the film's star, Lillian Gish, and asked her to perform in a live prologue and epilogue staged at every screening. Seeing Poulton's performance, the producer George Pearson offered her a contract worth £20 a week to act for the production company Welsh-Pearson in the comedy *Nothing Else*

Figure 1.4. Mabel Poulton and Chili Bouchier. Postcards, *c.* 1920s and 1930s. Author's collection.

Matters (Hugh E. Wright, 1920), alongside the music hall performer Betty Balfour, who was also making her screen debut.[156]

By the end of the 1920s, Poulton was a well-respected film performer, especially famous for her leading role as Tessa in *The Constant Nymph* (Adrian Brunel, 1928). Similar to Clive Brook, her acting work allowed her to travel widely, and she acted alongside performers from around Europe and America. But Poulton's autobiographical writings also record more ambivalent memories of filmmaking, including the potential for sexism within the male-dominated film industry, expressed most notably in a distressing encounter with the director Thomas Bentley, who tried to sexually assault her during a trip to film on location.[157] Despite the early publicity charting Poulton's rise from typist to film star, her writings also reveal long periods of unemployment, which she supplemented by returning to clerical work (including a job in the Welsh-Pearson office) and through engagements as a dancer in pantomime and cabaret.[158] Poulton's experiences suggest the uncertainty – and in some cases the vulnerability – that actors reliant on British film production in the 1920s could expect to face.

Several years younger than Mabel Poulton, the actress Chili Bouchier had a similarly circuitous route into the film industry. Born Dorothy Boucher in London in 1909, her nickname 'Chili' was given to her as a teenager (in honour of the popular song 'I Love My Chili Bom-Bom'), and she added the 'i' to her surname at the start of her acting career to lend her screen persona an air of foreign glamour.[159] Her strategy worked, and in some cases she was even advertised as an 'Anglo-French' film star.[160] Growing up in a lower-middle-class household in Fulham, and later in one of the new estates outside London in Roehampton, Bouchier had ambitions to become a dancer, although her enthusiasm for the cinema eventually won out. 'I spent all my pocket money on the pictures,' she recalled. 'I was enthralled by the glamour of it all and each time I went, my determination to be one day up there on the silver screen grew in leaps and bounds.'[161] Like Poulton, her first jobs after leaving school were in offices, but she found that she preferred retail work, securing employment as a shop assistant and later as a 'mannequin' (or model) in West End department stores, including one of the ladies' clothing departments at Harrods. Working in such an 'elegant' and 'perfumed' setting, Bouchier was able (retrospectively, at least) to see the job as 'a step closer' to the glamour of the screen.[162] She also took acting lessons and, through this, made the acquaintance of an agent who found her work in advertising films, short sound films and, eventually, feature films, beginning with a supporting role opposite Brian Aherne's leading man in *Shooting Stars*.[163] Starring roles followed, and by the start of the 1930s she was a contract player with the production firm British and Dominions, making as much as £100 a week.[164]

Bouchier's transition from 'mannequin to film star' made for good journalistic copy and prompted numerous remarks about the importance for film actresses to be able to wear clothes gracefully on the screen.[165] But it also highlights how, for both Poulton and Bouchier, the meaning attached to film work was strongly shaped by their early experiences of the labour market. As social historians have noted, it was increasingly common in the interwar period for young women to make decisions about their working lives based not only on the skills and wages involved in a job, but also on more culturally determined factors, such as the perceived 'niceness', or social respectability and prestige, that accompanied a particular line of work.[166] As a young girl, Poulton had envisaged an acting career both as a means of self-expression and as a way to afford 'lovely clothes' and 'a nice house' for herself, her mother and her siblings.[167] Bouchier later remembered herself as a modern 'daughter of the Twenties', for whom film acting was associated with glamour, but also with new levels of social and financial independence that her family life did not allow.[168] In the paternalistic environment of Harrods, Bouchier's behaviour was also closely monitored, and she was eventually dismissed when it was discovered that she was in a sexual relationship with a male co-worker.[169] In this context, the image of easy camaraderie associated with the film studio held an extra appeal. Bouchier later wrote: 'I found the freedom I longed for in the studios because there was no discipline as such – only the discipline one imposed on oneself, such as being on time at the studio and ready when called onto the set.'[170] Her debut feature film performance as the 'bathing beauty' Winnie in *Shooting Stars*, who gossips and jokes with the studio stock company and crew, undoubtedly contributed further to this socially liberal image.

As these brief career outlines demonstrate, there was a wide variety of routes into the British film industry for actors in the 1920s. Whereas two decades earlier, film acting had been understood as the work of amateurs or as a stopgap between theatrical engagements, by the interwar period it was recognised as a distinct and potentially lucrative form of employment. The glamour attached to film stardom in the popular imagination, fuelled by the intensive publicity campaigns begun in the 1910s, often obscured the day-to-day realities of professional film acting. But the recollections of people who were part of, or who observed, British production companies in the silent period reveal the complex hierarchies and working practices that characterised studio life. In Britain, the boundaries between the stage and the screen continued to be porous, with some actors able (or forced) to combine work across different branches of the entertainment industry. In the days prior to synchronised sound, national boundaries were also flexible, and many British film actors found work abroad or acted alongside performers from other countries.

This chapter has pointed to some of the ways in which the working conditions for film actors, along with the social meanings attached to film acting, changed during the silent period. But what did actors actually do when they got in front of the camera? The next chapter explores the skills and techniques involved in acting for the silent screen, as related by the authors of early film acting manuals and other instructional literature. It shows that instructional guides worked hard to validate film acting as an art form, even as they encouraged the public to see screen technique as something that could be practised by anyone with enough time, discipline and enthusiasm for the cinema.

2

Learn to act for the cinema in your own home: Instructional guides to film acting

In John Galsworthy's satirical play *A Family Man* (1921), two rebellious daughters are determined to escape their overbearing father by earning a living for themselves. At the start of the play, Athene, the eldest daughter, has already caused a scandal by moving in with a man outside of marriage and taking up painting. Meanwhile, her younger sister, Maud, is intent on joining 'the movie people' as an actress. Having been given a chance to act in a film in the role of 'guilty typist', she rehearses alone in her father's study. In a short, self-conscious scene, Maud sits with her hands stretched over a typewriter, explaining to herself: 'I must get that expression.' The stage directions call for her to strike a furtive pose, hold it, then dash across the room to scrutinise her face in the mirror. When a manservant enters, Maud quizzes him about her performance: 'What should you say I was?' 'Guilty, Miss,' he replies, before adding approvingly: 'You *have* got a film face.'[1]

The idea that film acting could be rehearsed at home, discreetly or furtively, was a common one in the 1920s. Maud, in Galsworthy's play, had her Hollywood counterparts in Mabel Normand's Sue Graham in *The Extra Girl* (F. Richard Jones, 1923), who subjects her childhood sweetheart to 'endless rehearsals' in her parents' front room when her father is out of the house, and in Colleen Moore's maid-of-all-work and aspiring film actress in *Ella Cinders* (Alfred E. Green, 1926), who practises screen acting alone in her attic in the dead of night. Such scenes reflect the moral suspicion that was seen to linger around the cinema and around acting, especially as an occupation for women. They also suggest that there was still something illicit and potentially subversive in the idea of women aspiring to a career at all.

The instructional guides to screen acting that first appeared in the 1910s made a virtue of the living room rehearsal. 'Learn to act for the cinema in your own home' was the advertising strapline of a ten-part course in film acting published in 1919. 'The great advantage of these lessons,' one advertisement explained, 'is that they can be studied in your spare time' without the need for 'inconvenient and worrying trips to some studio or other perhaps miles away from where you are living.'[2] Handbooks such as this were sold as the first resort for would-be film actors in the interwar years. They promised to provide training exercises that could be fitted around the working day, and offered advice on how to take the difficult step from the home, factory, shop or office in the direction of the film studio.

These manuals serve as useful historical departure points for thinking about the skills required of silent film actors, the conditions in early film studios and the development of screen acting technique. For a period of film history from which only a small proportion of films survive (somewhere in the region of 15 per cent), guides to acting provide important clues about the ways in which screen performance styles developed over time and in different national contexts, and several historians have drawn from them in this way.[3] However, instructional guides remain problematic as accurate depictions of historical film acting practice, not least because they were written by a wide variety of authors, whose connections to filmmaking are often unknown. As David Mayer says of nineteenth-century stage acting manuals, they also tend to present the work of the actor out of context, stripped of the accompanying narratives, scenography and music that made their movements and gestures meaningful to audiences at the time.[4]

Instructional guides to acting are no substitute for lost films. But they can shed light on popular understandings of the work that film actors did. They also suggest how would-be actors were encouraged to integrate their ambitions for stardom into their everyday lives. As Amy Sargeant notes, while instructional guides are not sufficient on their own to provide an understanding of silent film acting, they are nevertheless valuable social documents that offer 'insight into the social history and social hierarchy of an occupation still seeking to establish itself as a respectable profession'.[5] They also offer insight into the way in which dreams of stardom could solidify into active career ambitions. With the multiple meanings of instructional literature in mind, this chapter examines a number of surviving British guides to film acting written in the silent period. It begins by placing instructional guides in the context of what has been described as the culture of participation that grew up around cinema in the 1910s and 1920s. It then examines the content of early instructional guides in detail, exploring the variety of advice given to prospective film actors as well as the skills and requirements deemed most crucial for success on the silent screen.

Silent cinema and participation

Despite worries voiced by critics of the cinema since the silent period that watching films is a largely passive experience, early audiences were strongly encouraged in various ways to adopt an active role in relation to film culture.[6] Studies of audiences in Britain in the 1930s to 1950s show that cinemagoers engaged routinely, and sometimes creatively, with films and film stars both inside and outside the cinema auditorium.[7] Although there are fewer firsthand accounts of cinemagoing in the 1910s and 1920s, the material that does survive suggests that the concept of participation was as important to audiences of silent film as it was to later generations, if not more so. There were inevitably limits as to how far the film industry in Britain was prepared or able to sanction audience involvement. But, rhetorically, at least, film viewers were frequently invited to interact with the raw materials of the cinema, variously as consumers, dedicated fans, expert critics and contributors to the filmmaking process.

Popular film magazines, or fan magazines, were crucial to the early emphasis on participation. Discussing what she calls the 'interactive fandom' of American cinema in the 1910s to 1920s, Marsha Orgeron argues that fan magazines trained cinemagoers to take an active interest in film culture by 'repeatedly asking their readers to move out of the somewhat passive role of spectatorship to pursue a wide range of activities'.[8] Whereas the earliest film magazines were filled with short fiction (chiefly retellings of the plots of new film releases), publishers quickly moved to a more eclectic format that centred on stars and details of their lives.[9] Within this format, there was more room for competitions, quizzes and polls, as well as contributions from readers in the form of letters, poetry, drawings and star appreciations. For young people growing up with cinema, the fan magazine became, in Kathryn Fuller's description, 'a lively colloquium for the sharing of movie fans' knowledge and creative interests'.[10]

Fan magazines continued to proliferate in the interwar years. Fuller suggests that the character of American fan publications altered somewhat in the late 1910s, as titles such as *Motion Picture Magazine* dropped many of the features that allowed fans to contribute directly, while influential new titles, such as *Photoplay*, omitted them from the outset.[11] However, as Orgeron notes, interactivity remained an important organising principle of American fan magazines throughout the 1920s, evident in letters pages, advice columns and a wide range of contests.[12] Moreover, the concept of participation had also become part of the economic logic of the American film industry, with fan magazines and publicists encouraging audiences to invest, both financially and emotionally, in Hollywood stars and products.[13]

During the silent period, an equivalent film culture emerged in Britain, which was also closely tied to fan magazines. The first British popular film magazine, *The Pictures*, was launched in 1911. A rival title, *Illustrated Films Monthly*, appeared in 1913. Both magazines began as vehicles for short stories designed to summarise and advertise new films. But, by the early years of World War I, British fan magazines, similar to their American counterparts, had developed a mixed format 'based around a proliferation of film stars and their lives'.[14] The typical fan magazine format at the end of the 1910s included film publicity and studio gossip, letters pages and advice columns, reader polls and contests, as well as star interviews and collectible photographs. As Jane Bryan notes, at a material level, fan magazines were 'designed to be dismantled', with editors repeatedly inviting readers to remove and frame star portraits, cut out vouchers and competition forms and fill in quizzes and reader surveys.[15]

In their tone, British popular film magazines also cultivated a sense of participation and inclusivity around the cinema. To this end, they drew heavily on the editorial strategies of contemporary periodicals for young working-class and lower-middle-class women, such as *Peg's Paper*, which sought to achieve a close identification with its readers by addressing them informally as friends.[16] Crucially, in the case of fan magazines, the promise of inclusivity extended not just to film fans, but also to the film celebrities who featured in the magazines. The first issue of the British fan magazine *Film Flashes* in 1915 declared that its aim was 'to establish a strong bond of friendship' between the editor and readers, and between readers and stars. 'We are going to make this the picture-theatre-goers' very own paper,' an opening editorial explained. 'You will find in the paper each week all the latest news about the best films, and intimate and chatty items about all your screen favourites.'[17] Elsewhere, the sense of intimacy between readers and stars was nurtured in regular features, such as Gertrude Allen's 'Little Chats with British Film Favourites' in *Pictures and the Picturegoer*, or the 'Fay Filmer's Film Chat' and 'Letter from Dorothy' items in *Girls' Cinema*, both of which were attributed to young British women supposedly reporting firsthand on events in Hollywood.[18] British fan magazines remained invested in the concept of participation throughout the interwar years, and fans seem to have taken their message of inclusivity to heart. Newer magazines, such as *Picture Show*, continued to run contests and make space for readers' submissions, and at the end of the 1920s, the letters pages in *Picturegoer* could still be imagined, in the words of one correspondent, as 'a delightful debating society, open to all readers'.[19]

If the participatory film culture that grew up around the silent cinema was centred on fan magazines, it was expressed in other ways, too. Notably, the silent period saw a popular interest in screenplay, or 'scenario', writing. In America, as Kathryn Fuller remarks, scenario writing reached 'the level of a national pastime' in the 1910s.[20] During the early days of filmmaking, amateur and freelance writers frequently sent film scenarios to production companies. Frank Woods, the scenario editor at American Biograph, claimed to have received some 7,000 unsolicited manuscripts over a period of just a few months in 1913.[21] Some producers, such as the Thanhouser Film Company, actively encouraged amateur submissions by sponsoring contests for original stories.[22] At the same time, a sizeable instructional literature emerged to cater to amateur scenarists. At least 80 advice books and pamphlets on writing scenarios were published in America between

1910 and 1922.[23] After this point, the American film industry seems to have been less willing to sanction fan participation in screenwriting. Fuller attributes this not necessarily to a lack of demand, but to a combination of factors, including the increasing professionalisation of the studio system in Hollywood, the rise in lengthier feature films, legal concerns over copyright and, at the end of the decade, the advent of synchronised sound.[24]

There was comparable popular interest in scenario writing in Britain. From the 1910s, numerous guides to writing scenarios appeared in Britain, promising to help novices establish themselves in the industry. Early titles included C.E. Graham's *How to Write Picture Plays* (1913) and Harold Weston's *The Art of Photo-Play Writing* (1916), and similar publications appeared throughout the interwar period.[25] Searches for original scripts, such as the competition launched by the Ideal Film Company to devise a scenario for their film *Whoso Is Without Sin* in 1916, and later schemes supported by B&C and British Instructional Films, also blurred the gap between cinema audiences and professional filmmakers.[26] While the opportunities for non-professional screenwriters seem to have dissipated in America during the 1920s, the British market for amateur scenarists remained open, and may have actually expanded. Producers in the late 1920s and 1930s continued to accept unsolicited scripts, a significant number of which made it to the screen.[27] In the same period, there was a fresh wave of scenario manuals, as publishers attempted to capitalise on the optimism generated by the passing of the 1927 Cinematograph Films Act and responded to the general reassessment of screenwriting conventions in the era of sound.[28]

Like early handbooks on scenario writing, the instructional guides to film acting first published in Britain during and after World War I can be seen as part of the broader ethos of interactivity. The earliest British film guides appeared around 1914, and at least 20 titles written before 1930 have survived.[29] In addition, many American titles were readily available in Britain through trade magazine advertisements or booksellers.[30] Guides ranged from short pamphlets, such as the anonymous *Film-Land: How to Get There* (1921), to lengthier volumes such as Lilian Bamburg's *Film Acting as a Career* (1929).[31] Throughout the silent period, there was a close connection between the advice given by editors and actors in the pages of fan magazines and the content of screen acting manuals. Many of the anecdotes of studio life circulated by magazines made it into instructional guides, and some fan magazines even published their own handbooks. William Elliott's *How to Become a Film Actor* (1916) began life as a series of articles in the magazine *Picture Palace News*.[32] Although fan magazines sometimes made fun of aspiring stars and often warned readers of the difficulties involved in entering the film industry, they continued to relay the advice of celebrity film performers on screen acting technique and to advertise advice books and acting lessons. By the 1920s, guides to film acting were, on one level, highly specialist texts. But they were also part of the general texture of British popular film culture.

How to become a film artiste

To get a sense of the information and opinions available to would-be film actors in Britain, it is helpful to focus on a sample guide; *How to Become a Film Artiste* (1921) offers itself up as a useful example.[33] Published at what might be thought of as the height of the 'craze' for film acting at the start of the 1920s, it continued to be advertised throughout the silent period and was still available at the start of the 1930s.[34] Its authors, Fred Dangerfield and Norman Howard, were connected in various ways to the British cinema. As the editor of the magazine *Pictures and the Picturegoer* between 1913 and 1920, Fred Dangerfield was closely involved in the popularisation of film and film stars in Britain.[35] Before that, he had edited several theatrical magazines, including *Playgoer* and *Play Pictorial*, and this had given him a front row seat for observing changes in popular taste in both film and stage performance.[36] His co-writer, Norman Howard, was an actor in British stage plays and films, and thus one of the few authors of early instructional guides to have demonstrable experience of film acting. Under Dangerfield's editorship, he was also a regular contributor to *Pictures and the Picturegoer* as a fiction writer, translating the plots of new film releases into short stories – a job that involved regular visits to cinemas and private film trade screenings.[37]

Dangerfield and Howard's guide to film acting was thus in a position to draw on both anecdotal evidence and publicity stories circulated in fan magazines, and firsthand knowledge of films and the workings of the film industry. According to its authors, *How to Become a Film Artiste* was intended for 'all sorts and conditions of men and women who aspire to play before the camera'.[38] In particular, though, it spoke to existing film fans. Published by Odhams, the same firm responsible for *Pictures and the Picturegoer*, it was clearly aimed at the readership that had been built up for Dangerfield's fan magazine over the previous decade. The illustrated front cover, with its depiction of a pair of actors closely resembling the Hollywood couple Mary Pickford and Douglas Fairbanks, further announced its connection to popular film culture and invited readers to imagine themselves taking the place of well-known stars (Figure 2.1). The final chapter, entitled 'Stars Speak for Themselves', which comprised snippets of interviews with leading actors and producers, offered a further attraction to dedicated film fans and may have contained much that was familiar to *Pictures and the Picturegoer* devotees.

In between, the guide spanned a range of topics that would be recognisable across other instructional guides to film acting published during the silent era. The book combined practical advice about seeking employment, acquiring costumes and 'making-up' for the screen with more thoughtful discussions about the art of film performance. Among other things, Dangerfield and Howard's guide was interested in the practical and artistic differences between film and theatre acting, the value of screen 'types' and the importance of portraying character and emotion primarily through gesture and facial expression. These subjects were central to many other British instructional guides to film acting, although, as the following sections show, they often prompted markedly different opinions and advice.

Stage experience not essential

The question of whether or not actors with stage experience made the best film actors was the cause of considerable debate in Britain during the silent period. While there was significant traffic in actors between British theatres and film studios by the 1920s, many commentators argued that the cinema required very different skills and acting styles from those that pertained to the stage. Dangerfield and Howard remarked on the general consensus that 'to become a recognised cinema star, a certain amount of stage experience is absolutely essential'. But, they continued, in actual fact, 'a gulf exists between the speaking and silent stage'.[39] Similar to the author

Figure 2.1. Front cover of Fred Dangerfield and Norman Howard, *How to Become a Film Artiste: The Art of Photo-Play Acting* (London: Odhams, 1921). Courtesy of Cambridge University Library.

of *Cinema Acting for a Profession* (1915), who suggested that, in many respects, 'amateurs make much better Cinema artistes than those who have long been before the public on the boards', Dangerfield and Howard argued that theatre actors must effectively relearn their craft when making the transition to films.[40]

> On taking up picture work, our friend the stage 'pro' must realise the manifold differences of the two arts, and must be prepared to master the technique of the new profession [...] otherwise he will be scarcely of more use to the picture producer than the veriest novice, and will find only too soon that there is little room for him in the strenuous crowded life of the first-class studio.[41]

As evidence, the writers noted that the 'recognised qualifications' for the stage – 'the voice, elocution, articulation' – were irrelevant for film work.[42] In addition, they said, stage actors would undoubtedly miss the atmosphere of the theatre, being unable in the film studio to rely on the immediate response of a live audience to guide and validate their performance.[43]

While Dangerfield and Howard's observations may well have been based on firsthand experience, they joined in the broader tendency – notable from the early 1910s – to focus attention on cinema's unique properties in order to differentiate it from other media.[44] In addition, there was undoubtedly something reassuring for Dangerfield and Howard's intended readership of film fans in the suggestion that stage experience was 'not essential' for success on the screen.[45] Other writers, including those with connections to the stage, were more inclusive in their discussion of the relationship between theatre and film. Agnes Platt, a sometime theatrical producer and agent, argued in her *Practical Hints on Acting for the Cinema* (1920) that film producers invariably preferred people with acting experience over 'novices'.[46] But, along with Dangerfield and Howard, she agreed that stage actors would have to adapt themselves to the different conditions of film work. Moreover, she suggested that some theatrical performers might be better suited to the screen than others. Actors who were known to 'under-act' on the stage were often successful in films, Platt thought, whereas the actor 'who riots in facial play and rapid gesticulation' was liable to turn into a self-caricature on the screen.[47] Platt's assessment represents one strand of popular opinion about the theatrical acting styles best suited to film, although opinions over how successful individual stage stars were as film performers varied, and continued to differ throughout the period.[48]

The most fundamental difference between theatre and film work, according to Dangerfield and Howard, was found in the role played by technology. A first-time film actor from any background, they said, needed to learn to work successfully with the camera. 'Never forget that the "stage", they warned, 'is only that portion of the ground or floor commanded by the lens.'[49] Actors should never walk into the camera's line of sight directly (or risk looking 'gigantic' if they did), nor should they ever look straight into the camera (a cardinal rule of most 'serious' fiction filmmaking since the early 1910s).[50] Because of the amount of equipment and expense involved in producing the average fiction film compared to that required to mount a play, there was also less room for error or ego on the set, and actors were told always to defer to the will of the producer. Dangerfield and Howard wrote:

> If you are a stage actor and play for pictures, you must forget the former fact. You're not a stage actor. The success or failure of the picture play depends wholly on its producer. No matter how big your stage reputation, you are nothing more or less than a puppet.[51]

Although less brutal in her description of the actor's status in the studio, Agnes Platt agreed that, because of the cost of film stock and the size of the crew, the financial stakes involved in film production were especially high, saying that 'the old adage "Time is money" applies with practical force, for time in the studio is translated into so many feet of film'.[52] William Elliott reminded his readers that, whether they were theatre-trained performers or novices, spoiling a length of film would be viewed as 'the most serious crime an actor could commit'.[53]

Screen types

Just as there was debate over the relative value of stage experience for actors in silent films, there was also disagreement over the importance of screen 'types'. In general, the identification and parody of distinctive types of film characters were consistent sources of humour throughout the 1910s and 1920s. This was the case not only in satirical journals such as *Punch*, which included numerous spoofs of stock film characters, but also in specialist film trade journals and self-reflexive films.[54] *So This Is Jollygood* (1925), Adrian Brunel's short 'burlesque' of popular fiction filmmaking, parodied the conventional portrayals of a range of screen types, including 'vamps', Mexican bandits, Germanic villains, matinee idol heroes and 'coy, innocent, beautiful, appealing' heroines.[55]

In their instructional guide, Dangerfield and Howard were more pragmatic about the necessity for recognisable character types. The film producer responsible for casting, they said, needed to maintain versatility among the regular studio stock company in much the same way that actors in nineteenth-century theatrical repertory companies were expected to adopt different 'lines of business', such as comedian or villain, in order to minimise rehearsal time.[56] Other film acting guides agreed, advising actors to decide on their preferred screen type and concentrate on finding engagements along that line. In his booklet on 'The Value of Specialisation', Stewart Rome argued that actors could increase their chances of employment by specialising in this way.[57] Rome provided lists of some of the most common screen types that British studios typically required, which spanned (and closely reflected) demarcations of class and gender. For men, the choices included butlers, waiters, clergymen, policemen, sailors, 'smart City men', 'well-tailored society men', solicitors, judges and doctors, while for women the most popular types, according to Rome, were domestic maids and cooks, nurses, typists, 'smartly clad society women', 'the mother or aunt type', village gossips, country girls, 'the sporting masculine type', dancers, society hostesses, the 'grande dame' and the 'demi-mondaine'.[58] In her contribution to the same British collection of instructional guides, Mary Pickford argued that film actors should behave like businessmen (or women) and survey the job market to identify the demand for different part types. Actresses should select their choice of, for instance, vamps, mothers or young girls, she said, and then 'set about in a methodical way to learn all about it'.[59]

For Dangerfield and Howard, there was a limit to the extent to which a film performer could learn to act as a particular type. Film's underlying photographic realism and its different formal conventions, they said, made it more difficult for actors to adopt disguises or theatrical make-up in order to portray a character. Comparing film to theatre again, they argued that, in contrast to the stage actor, 'the cinema player must not only act but look the part'. In practice, this meant:

> A young man cannot make up to take an old man's part – it must be taken by an old man. A woman of middle-age, though she may succeed in a young girl's rôle on the stage, cannot play the part before the camera. Because of the enormous mass of detail which the camera absorbs, an old 'make up' on a young face would look unusual, odious and ridiculous when it reached the 'close up' views, if not before.[60]

Not everything on the screen appeared as it did in real life, they conceded. For dangerous stunts, producers sometimes had to find 'doubles' to take the place of regular actors. But, in all other cases, they wrote, 'the parts are cast as far as possible in accordance with the natural adaptability of the artiste for the part'. One of the incidental benefits of this system for actors, they noted, was that 'an obscure player' with little experience could nevertheless get an opportunity in films 'by being possessed of some peculiarity' that was required for a role.[61]

The belief that the camera's objectivity made it impossible, or at least much harder, to alter or disguise an actor's appearance was widespread and had been voiced for many years. Pointing to the practice of filming outdoors, away from the scenery and lighting effects of the stage, the cartoonist and scenarist Harry Furniss wrote in 1914 that film work was 'bald, matter-of-fact reality', as contrasted with the 'make-believe' of the theatre.[62] This belief persisted in spite of celebrated cross-racial performances by Hollywood stars such as Constance Talmadge and Richard Barthelmess, and the many transformations of British character actors and stars such as Moore Marriott and Matheson Lang, who reprised his 'Oriental' stage make-up for the film *Mr. Wu* (Maurice Elvey, 1919).[63] Writing at the end of the 1920s in her guide to *Film Acting as a Career*, Lilian Bamburg acknowledged that an experienced film actor such as Lon Chaney, well known for his elaborate use of make-up and prosthetics, could adopt 'various wonderful disguises' with success. But she maintained that, in general, 'no facial change of type or personality is possible for screen work'.[64] In essence, this is the same conclusion reached by the Soviet filmmaker and early theorist of film performance V.I. Pudovkin, whose lectures to the Film Society in London in 1929 argued that 'one cannot "play a part" on the film; one must possess a sum of real qualities, externally expressed'. For this reason, he said, producers should expect to 'discover', rather than artificially 'build up', the type of actor required for a film.[65]

While it was widely accepted that producers preferred to cast according to type, the system also had its opponents. The film critic Iris Barry blamed the Hollywood star system for encouraging typecasting and limiting the quality of film performance. 'Stars cannot act,' she said bluntly. 'It has never been required of them'.[66] Instructional guides pointed out that the belief in types also presented problems from the actor's point of view. Dangerfield and Howard remarked that 'the successful impersonator may be forced into a groove and looked upon as being only able to portray such characters as he or she may have been originally associated with'. One film actor in London, they said, 'rarely plays any other rôle than that of an old butler, because he *walks like an old butler* and is permanently round shouldered'.[67] It was not only the rationalising tendency of the studio casting and production processes that was seen to force actors into types, but also the mechanisms of film publicity. In his instructional guide *The Way to the Studio* (1926), Russell Hallen agreed that actors could benefit from building up a reputation for playing particular types, but warned that 'once you become known as a specialist in a certain part, that role and only that role will be yours'.[68]

Speech, gesture and movement

Even in the absence of recorded sound, silent film actors were expected to deliver dialogue in order to make scenes appear lifelike, either working from what was written in the script or, as the British scenarist Harold Dickinson remarked in 1916, speaking words 'which they make up as they go along'.[69] Dangerfield and Howard advised actors to learn their lines, if they were given any, and to 'not necessarily stick to a prepared and rigid dialogue but know your theme – so perfectly that you accurately improvise your part'.[70] In general during the period of silent cinema, however, it was assumed that bodily gesture and movement would do most of the actor's share of characterisation and storytelling. 'The story of the film,' Dangerfield and Howard wrote, 'is told by natural movements of the eyes, hands, lips, and the entire body in accord with the emotions to be portrayed.' The camera, they continued, recorded any 'inharmony' or 'inaccuracy' of movement, even if the producer failed to notice it on the set. Because of this high level of scrutiny, the writers reminded film actors that their gestures should always be 'balanced, round and free from any traces of hurry'.[71]

The importance of avoiding inharmonious or hurried movement when acting for the camera was reiterated in other instructional guides. Agnes Platt thought that, in the past, stage actors working in film had tended to overcompensate for the lack of audible dialogue by amplifying their movements, without appreciating that the camera was liable to make 'a springy, bounding gait' look like 'a series of jumps'.[72] William Elliott told his readers to 'be always slow and deliberate'.[73] Even though slowness was said to be more important for serious drama than for comedy, actors were advised to employ graceful movements in all cases. 'There are of course scenes in which hurry must be shown,' wrote E. Camiller in the guide *How to Get Film Work* (1922), 'but even then the artist should endeavour to avoid jerkiness.'[74]

Across different guides, the need to make action smooth for the camera was weighed against the recurrent suggestion for British (and specifically English) actors to make their movements sufficiently pronounced. Dangerfield and Howard cited the Danish actress Asta Nielsen, who apparently doubted whether English people could ever make truly successful film actors. 'The average Englishman and Englishwoman,' she was quoted as saying, 'has not the temperament for acting on the stage, let alone before the camera.'[75] The idea that the reserved English or 'Anglo-Saxon' temperament was a barrier to effective performance in a wordless medium, and that actors from other national or ethnic backgrounds, especially the more expressive 'Latin races', were better equipped for films, features in some of the earliest writings on film acting in Britain.[76] At the start of the 1920s, Agnes Platt repeated the claim, arguing that English actors would first need to overcome an in-built tendency to be undemonstrative. 'We have about us,' she wrote, speaking on behalf of English people, 'just that ineradicable touch of self-consciousness which belongs to our natural reserve.'[77] In Platt's opinion, while Italian actors sometimes appeared 'more than natural' in their actions, Dutch and Scandinavian actors (who shared the 'English self-control') might serve as a useful model for British actors seeking to adapt their conventional behaviour for the screen.[78] Similarly, Russell Hallen wrote that, because English actors were not used to employing gestures, they had to work harder in front of the camera, adding: 'The French and Americans have a great advantage over us herein, as they are continually gesticulating with their limbs in every-day conversation.'[79]

Cultural stereotypes such as these were pervasive and fairly consistent in discussions of film acting styles in early instructional guides. But there was little consensus on whether or not the English 'natural reserve' was a benefit or a hindrance. Optimistic about the future of the British cinema, Dangerfield and Howard thought that the 'best English film-players' turned their native temperament to their advantage, and mastered 'the portrayal of emotion through restraint'. They explained the process whereby deliberately restricting actions could make their emotional meaning more powerful:

> To attempt restraint for the sake of restraint would mean impersonations that ended without animation. They would be wooden. It is necessary to start with the emotion, realise it completely, and then hold the full force of the emotion in leash; put it through a refining process.[80]

As Jon Burrows notes, this idea, sometimes called 'reserved force', originally gained currency in descriptions of new styles of British theatre acting in the late Victorian and Edwardian periods, when it was seen to mirror upper-class forms of behaviour and notions of good breeding and propriety.[81] But it continued to offer critics a useful framework for understanding and evaluating British film performances in the 1920s, even if, as Christine Gledhill shows, the 'power of restraint' was often more appreciated in men than in women, who ran the risk of being labelled 'inexpressive' if they were not outwardly emotional in their performances.[82]

The art of facial expression

Similar to movement and gesture, facial expression was assumed to be especially important for communicating character and narrative in silent film, and a 'film face' was consistently cited in instructional guides as the most valuable asset a film actor could possess. Agnes Platt gave her readers a detailed description of what constituted the ideal face for the cinema. Conventional beauty was an advantage, she said, but versatility and mobility were considered equally important. 'You have to be good-looking in the right way', she wrote, with clear-cut features, lips that were not 'too thick', and dark eyes that were not 'too large and round', in order to photograph well.[83] Lilian Bamburg agreed, disabusing readers of the common assumption 'that, to be a successful cinema star, all you need is to be pretty or handsome'. In fact, she said, the essential requirement was 'an *expressive* face – one that can look sad, elated, thoughtful, or a dozen other emotions all in the space of a few seconds'.[84]

In Dangerfield and Howard's guide, the ability to express emotion through facial expression, alone, was particularly associated with the close-up. Close-up shots, showing an actor from the chest up, had been a feature of dramatic films since the late 1900s, and, although still relatively rare, extreme close-ups, showing only the actor's face, had become more common in Hollywood feature films by the 1920s.[85] For Dangerfield and Howard, the need to perform in close-up represented another point of difference between acting in film and theatre.

> With the 'legitimate', the average member of the audience is too far away to perceive the changes of 'fine expression'. He has a distant view, and it cannot be observed.
> On the screen it is quite the reverse. The actor depends exclusively upon his expressing fine shades of character work and his actions.[86]

This was especially true, they continued, in scenes 'where the actor's face is enlarged almost to the size of the entire screen', meaning that 'the slightest movement of each muscle shows'. The film actor, they concluded, 'must be a master of facial expression' in order to succeed.[87] In studio terminology, the ability to express emotion through facial expression in this way was known as the skill of 'registering'.[88] As the actor Aurèle Sydney explained in his 1919 guide, successful registering involved not only producing facial expressions on cue, but also retaining them for the benefit of the camera.[89] Such skills were said to be especially important for the efficiency of the film production process, because scenes were usually taken out of narrative sequence and often involved multiple camera set-ups. Agnes Platt told actors that, for some films, 'an expression may have to be held for well over two minutes while the camera is being readjusted'.[90]

Along with screen types, 'film faces' were a regular source of humour in the silent period. Fred Dangerfield's *Pictures and the Picturegoer* was not alone among fan magazines in parodying conventional facial expressions. A representative cartoon by the magazine's resident artist mocked a range of 'familiar faces', including stunned villains and women cross-eyed with terror.[91] Writing in the 1930s, the actor Robert Donat joked that what constituted acting in the cinema of his childhood was little more than 'face-pulling' and 'conventionalised grimaces'.[92] In their instructional guide, Dangerfield and Howard acknowledged that the portrayal of the 'fine shades of expression' was difficult and prone to misunderstanding: 'An expression for dismay, for instance, might be taken for despair, disgust, distress, grief, fear, pain, and so on.'[93] But by the 1920s, the ability to convey subtle differences in emotion with a look, a shift of the eyebrow or a turn of the lip had become a central part not only of the advice contained in acting handbooks, but also of the publicity surrounding film stars. Trade advertisements for dramatic actresses such as Norma Talmadge and Alla Nazimova presented their 'many faces' and 'thousand moods' as selling points to exhibitors and audiences.[94] In fan magazine editorials and star appreciations, including the regular 'The Expressions of...' feature in *Picture Show*, an actor's skill in registering was held up as the sign of his or her seriousness as a screen artist (Figure 2.2).[95]

In popular fiction, too, registering had become synonymous with the skill and appeal of the film actor. Vanna George, the star of the newspaper serial *The World's Best Girl* (1919), was said to have an unremarkable face in ordinary life, 'but once faced by the camera it registered every emotion in just the exact degree to stir men and women'.[96] As Vanna's ability to 'stir' her viewers suggests, the emphasis on fine shades of expression in accounts of film acting also speaks to the intimacy between actor and audience that the camera's closer view seemed to create. In *The World's Best*

GERALDINE FARRAR
The Screen Star Who is Also a Famous Prima Donna

GERALDINE FARRAR, celebrated actress of the screen and prima donna, shares her time between the Royal Opera House and the Goldwyn studios.

From the first she was a screen success.

Her first appearance was in a hair-pulling scene in a picture version of "Carmen," which scene she later transferred to the stage, and again made a sensation.

A Dramatic Artiste.

ALL her pictures are dramatic, even melo-dramatic, and her most successful parts have been when she played opposite her husband, Lou Tellegen.

She tells of the time when the directors of the Opera House frowned upon the screen. They were particularly angry with her because she had received a tempting offer to act for the films, and told them that she was going to accept it.

"How can you?" they asked her. "You have already made a reputation as the greatest American prima donna. When people can see you on the pictures for a few coppers, they will not want to pay notes to hear you sing."

A Successful Experiment.

BUT Geraldine said she was willing to experiment and take the consequences, and the consequences have been satisfactory—even for the opera, for many a movie admirer has become an opera convert, and many an opera devotee has become a lover of picture shows.

Some of the films in which you may remember having seen Miss Farrar are "Maria Rosa," "The Woman God Forgot," "The Turn of the Wheel," "The Devil's Stone," "Joan of Arc," "The Stronger Vow," "Shadows," "The World and its Woman," "The Flame of the Desert," and "Carmen."

The Secret of a Happy Marriage.

SPEAKING of her marriage, Geraldine Farrar says that she found the fairy prince of whom every girl dreams almost as soon as she was old enough to play with dolls.

"Lou Tellegen and I have many interests in common," she says, "and I think that is the secret of successful marriages, a true and perfect comradeship.

"We are both interested in the theatre, but fortunately in different branches of it, apart from our screen work. Mr. Tellegen loves the opera, and he attends every one of my performances at the Metropolitan whenever he is not playing himself, and when he was playing in New York last season I believe I attended his performances at least twenty times. So, you see, we enjoy each other's work without the least feeling of jealousy. We are interested in the same things, Mr. Tellegen paints and writes and sculptures, and I like to watch him and talk with him about his work."

If You Would Look Tall.

MISS FARRAR is five feet six inches in height. But her experience of the stage has taught her how to dress to appear even taller. She uses shoes, collars, combs, earings, and a hundred other little dress accessories to get an effect for her different character roles. She says that one can even arrange one's hair to give a different aspect to the character introduced on the screen. She tells of one part, for instance, when she took the role of a cowgirl. It was essential that she should wear low-heeled shoes to obtain the free easy walking movement, but to gain the height lost by wearing low-heeled shoes, she wore a tall Spanish comb in her hair, which was quite in keeping with the character.

She has one little fad in frocks; on no account will she wear a high collar, for she says that low-necked frocks give height and gracefulness.

If you want to write her, address your letter:

GERALDINE FARRAR,
Metropolitan Opera House,
New York City,
U.S.A.

GERALDINE FARRAR.

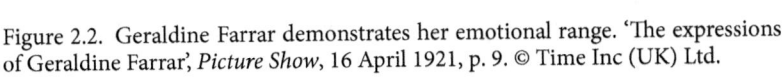

Figure 2.2. Geraldine Farrar demonstrates her emotional range. 'The expressions of Geraldine Farrar', *Picture Show*, 16 April 1921, p. 9. © Time Inc (UK) Ltd.

Girl, Vanna's fiancé first falls in love with the star when he sees her on screen, as does the impressionable young hero of the magazine serial *The Fellow Who Loved Violet Hopson* (1919–20).[97] The narrator of Elizabeth Bowen's short story 'Dead Mabelle' (1929) elaborates on the romantic and erotic possibilities that close-ups of film actors (and especially actresses) conjured up in the popular imagination, describing the first encounter between a British cinemagoer and a fictional Hollywood star named Mabelle Pacey:

> The film had begun; with a startled feeling he had walked down the tilted gangway towards Mabelle's face and the dark-and-light glittering leaves behind. A caption […] then a close-up: Mabelle's face jumped forward at him […]. He stood for a moment, feeling embraced in her vision.[98]

Close-up views, such as the fictional one described by Bowen, were strongly associated with the evolving dynamics of stardom. In learning how to register, would-be actors were preparing themselves not just to communicate meaning, but also to stir emotion in ways that were increasingly expected of stars.

An imaginary camera in your sitting room

Instructional guides weren't there only to explain the fundamentals of film technique. They also offered practical advice for new actors who wanted to learn the skills required for film performance. The amount of practical tuition differed significantly between handbooks. An anonymous guide from 1920 offered a whole course of training, including individual exercises for speaking, walking, moving in the dark and eating on screen.[99] Other guides told readers to focus their efforts on perfecting the basic tools of movement and expression, and on adapting to the conditions of the studio. But the exercises themselves were invariably scaled down for a domestic setting, encouraging readers to make use of the spaces and objects around them. 'Set up an imaginary camera in your sitting-room,' wrote William Elliott, suggesting to his readers how they might become accustomed to the strict limits imposed by the angle of the lens, 'and practice diligently entrances and exits, gestures, and other motions.'[100]

Several guides provided similar exercises for learning to move smoothly and expressively, or for overcoming the English 'natural reserve'. Agnes Platt told readers to practise the movements involved in hailing and boarding a bus, while a friend guessed the content of the scene.[101] Lilian Bamburg recommended that film actors 'stand in front of a full length mirror [...] and practice movements of all sorts for half an hour each day'.[102] Almost every guide contained exercises for mastering facial expression. In order to gain control of the facial muscles, actors were advised by one writer to look at their face in a mirror without blinking or moving any part of the body for two minutes; the author added: 'Any twitching of the face or uncontrollable movement is a sign of nervous defect, and should be remedied.'[103] Like other writers, Dangerfield and Howard gave their readers a list of 'common expressions' to practice registering, ranging from admiration to craftiness, disgust, fury, joy, surprise and worry. 'To the aspirant for screen acting,' they wrote, 'mirror rehearsals should become a daily study, for the practice of the facial muscles is more than a mere help, it is absolutely essential.'[104] Other guides provided readers with photographic guides to facial expression, designed as both illustrations of basic screen technique and templates for students to follow in their daily routines in front of the mirror (Figure 2.3).

In addition to mirror exercises, a number of guides featured short scenes that combined a variety of technical skills and resembled short film plots in their own right. Scenes involving conversations, telephone calls or letters were popular, as in a scene recommended in a 1920 guide:

> You enter your room, having just returned from an enjoyable evening, start to remove your gloves, glance towards the table, there is a letter, you have taken off one glove, but leave the other and pick up the letter, open it and read. It contains very bad news, and your face must tell the audience before the letter is thrown on the screen. Do not make the mistake of changing your expression before you have opened it.[105]

The actress Violet Hopson provided a sample letter for film actors in her 1919 guide, annotated with numbered points that signalled the different emotions that readers should attempt to convey, 'giving the audience some idea of the text of the letter'.[106] Other writers offered more active scenarios.

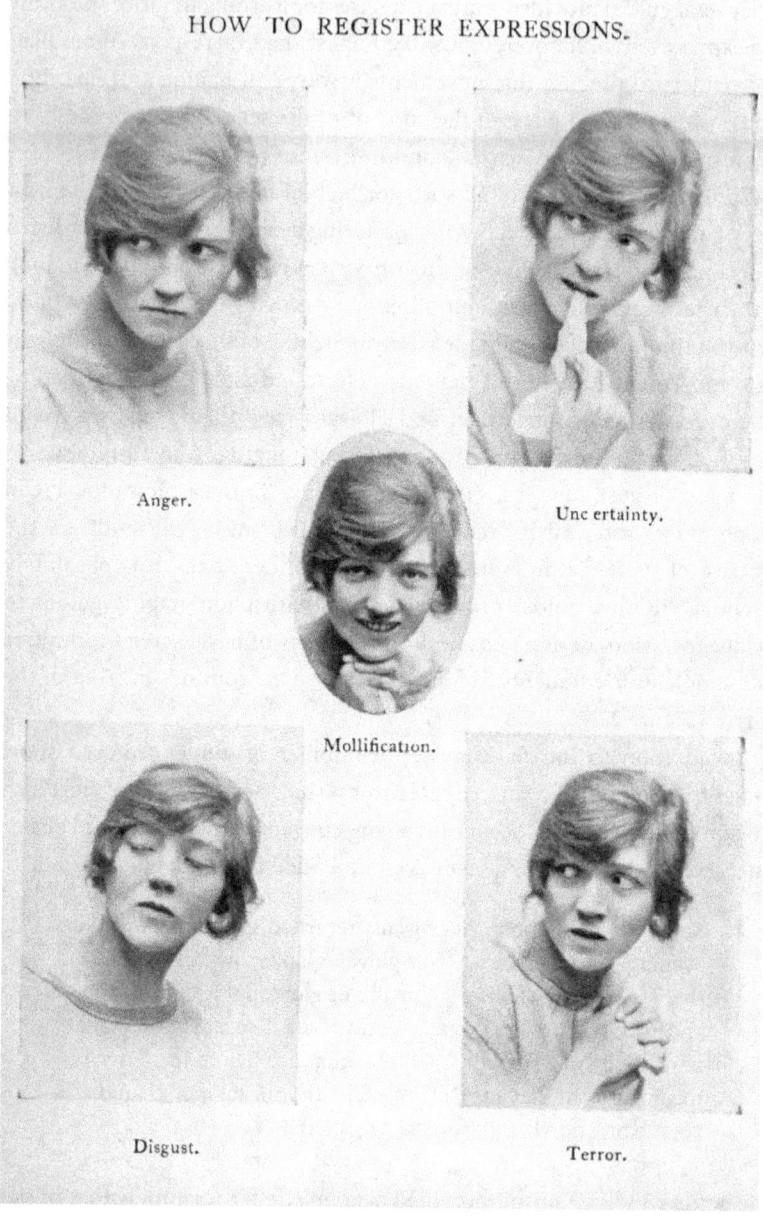

Figure 2.3. 'How to register expressions'. Violet Hopson, 'Hints for the kinema actress', in *Cinema Acting as a Profession: A Splendid Course in 10 Lessons* (London: Standard Art Book, n.d. [c. 1919]), Lesson 9. Courtesy of the Bill Douglas Cinema Museum, University of Exeter.

Russell Hallen asked his readers to imagine themselves as wanted criminals, being chased by police, hiding behind furniture and, finally, being shot dead.[107]

According to Hopson, exercises such as these were designed to prepare readers for entry to the film industry by reflecting the typical screen tests that new actors would be put through in British studios.[108] There is some evidence to suggest that this was the case. A vocational handbook from the period said that, before engaging actors, producers would often ask them 'to enact a particular dramatic situation' or to ' "register" contrasting emotions, such as fear, anger, joy, love, hate, or the like'.[109] Mabel Poulton, who prided herself on her ability to shed tears on command, was asked to perform an 'emotional crying scene' when she auditioned for the producer George Pearson.[110] At the same time, the invitation to act out film scenes in private mirrored the rhetoric of participation and interactivity that was central to other aspects of popular film culture. It also potentially tapped into emerging or ongoing fan practices. Later studies of cinema audiences in Britain showed that many film fans needed little incentive to act out scenes inspired by particular films or genres at home or at friends' houses, making such role-play a regular part of their leisure activities, whether as children or young adults.[111] In acting handbooks, the advice to turn a living room into an imaginary film set was presented as part of a commitment to professional film acting, but it may have also reflected how thoroughly a part of everyday domestic life film culture was becoming for a growing number of people.

A cheap course of star study

Several instructional guides took the invitation to re-enact scenes at home further, suggesting that readers treat the cinema as a space for learning and perfecting their craft. William Elliott told actors to develop their skills as film critics in tandem with their performance technique.

> Study your chosen profession closely and continually. Go to the picture houses and watch keenly the pictures in which actors of repute are taking part. Study their methods; note how they handle certain situations, and do not be afraid to use your critical faculty in coming to an estimation of their effectiveness.[112]

A guide from 1920 told readers that they should go to the cinema often 'with the full intention of learning all you can', drawing on the films later in domestic rehearsals.

> Watch very carefully the movements and facial expressions of every artiste; take special interest in the star of the leading picture, memorize as much as you can of the story, and when you get home, put yourself in the part of the star and go through what you consider to be the most difficult part of the plot.[113]

Violet Hopson framed this practice as an economical way to combine business with pleasure, telling her readers to give themselves 'a cheap course of "star study" at your local cinema theatre' by watching and emulating 'the screen star who makes the biggest appeal to you'.[114]

Again, the evidence provided by later studies of British audiences would suggest that the invitation to watch the performances of film stars closely, to borrow from their mannerisms and behaviour and to re-enact scenes from their films at home anticipated or reflected existing fan practices.[115] The recollections of people who were regular cinemagoers in the 1920s add weight to the idea that role-play and re-enactment were not limited to those aspiring to be professional actors, and that it was not only young women who attempted to put the lessons of their 'star study' into practice. Several of the men and women who responded to the sociologist J.P. Mayer's call for cinema memories in the 1940s remembered imitating their favourite stars as children. A male fan of Douglas Fairbanks wrote that he 'tried to imitate his personal mannerisms and emulate his athletic prowess' in order to 'achieve extra strength and self-reliance'.[116] Another man who came of age in the 1920s said that the films of Rudolph Valentino made a particularly formative impression on him as an adolescent boy: 'Every little detail was observed and noted, the play of his hands, the movement of the lips and eyes, and carriage of the body'.[117] The formal structure of Hollywood feature films encouraged this kind of close attention to, and identification with, the performances of stars. As the *Kinematograph Weekly* complained in 1919, film narratives were invariably organised around the performance of 'the "featured" player', and film posters and other promotional materials, such as those advertising an actor's 'many faces' or 'moods', also cultivated the careful observation of stars among viewers.[118]

Learn to act for the cinema in your own home

Instructional guides to film acting written by, or at least attributed to, famous actors offered their own form of engagement with stars. Like the celebrity 'how-to' books on subjects such as cookery, housework, exercise, religion or sex discussed by Amelie Hastie, acting handbooks by British or Hollywood film actors extended the amount of contact a film fan could have with their favourite performers outside the cinema, and gave them another way in which to encounter and consume film stardom.[119] Advertisements for guides played on this idea, telling readers that 'famous film stars' would teach them to act in their own home.[120] In a very literal sense, too, guides written by film stars presented readers with the opportunity 'to perform as the stars performed', by promising insight into their rehearsal methods, acting techniques and attitudes towards the job.[121] By the 1920s, film stars were regularly acknowledged not only as talented and charismatic performers, but also as experts on modern living.[122] Guides to film acting acknowledged and elaborated on this belief, even if they remained predominantly vocational in their outlook. In guides to film acting by Mae Marsh, Mary Pickford, Stewart Rome, Violet Hopson, Aurèle Sydney, José Collins and Gladys Brockwell, readers could find advice not just on acting, but also on the value of professionalism, hard work, discipline, success, confidence, adaptability, and the virtues and dangers of fame.[123]

Just as earlier guides to theatre acting often concluded with words of wisdom from stage stars, the final chapter of Dangerfield and Howard's *How to Become a Film Artiste* was given over to famous film actors and producers.[124] Several stars stressed the 'variety' and 'charm' of film acting. The American actress Marguerite Clark spoke of the job as 'good, healthy, hard work', while the comedian John Bunny told actors that they would be working 'in the open air a great portion of the time on the country side, or by the river or the sea'.[125] Such depictions of film acting, drawn from nearly a decade of fan magazine interviews, would look increasingly out of date in the era of big studio production in the 1920s, but the impression that film acting was somehow more 'natural' than other forms of performance remained important throughout the years that followed. Other actors quoted in Dangerfield and Howard's guide talked optimistically about the increasing respectability of screen performance. Dorothy Gish, for instance, looked forward to the time when 'the photo-play will have so highly educated its public that there will be much art for Art's sake'.¹²⁶ The British producer George Pearson also believed that film artistry was advancing, giving some of the credit to a new generation of actors who were 'making a sincere study of the strange art of picture language' and who were able to use all the tools at their disposal to convey meaning efficiently and accurately to audiences.¹²⁷

For those aspiring film actors who had gleaned all they could from instructional guides, the next step was to make concerted efforts to look for work in the film industry. While there was no single school of film performance style in the 1920s, there was much more consensus in British handbooks when it came to the best way for newcomers to find a job. The best plan, according to Dangerfield and Howard, was to address a letter to 'The Producer' at 'the firm of your fancy', submitting details of age, height and 'athletic attainments', together with recent photographs – 'one full face, the other profile'.¹²⁸ To help readers, they provided a nine-page list of British production firms, together with another six pages of producers in America, Italy, France, Belgium, the Netherlands and Spain.¹²⁹ Other writers, such as William Elliott, recommended that aspiring film actors see British producers in person.¹³⁰ To do this, actors would need to travel into London to the area known commonly as 'filmland' – the commercial and administrative centre of the British film industry, where the majority of film production offices and casting agencies were located. The next chapter follows applicants for film work on this route and examines the response they met with from the film industry and the public.

3

The common round: Finding film work in interwar London

In Katherine Mansfield's 1920 short story 'Pictures', an unemployed singer named Ada Moss leaves her Bloomsbury lodging house to visit a succession of West End employment agencies and producers' offices in the hope of finding work as a film actress. Already that day, she has received a polite but firm rejection letter from the Backwash Film Co., prompting an ultimatum from her unsympathetic landlady that she must pay the rent by eight o'clock that evening, or else. The nagging feeling of hunger and her landlady's enigmatic threats heighten the stakes of Ada's job search. Yet she finds nothing 'doing' at the firms of Kig and Kadgit's and Beit and Bithem's, nor at the offices of the North-East Film Company. Another rejection from the Bitter Orange Company forces Ada to retire to a nearby café in defeat, where she consoles herself with a coffee and fantasises about being miraculously discovered by a concert manager. Instead, she finds herself sitting opposite a 'stout gentleman' who takes a shine to the ribbon in her hair and buys her a brandy. After a short while, Ada agrees to follow the man to his home.[1]

The action of Mansfield's story, which was originally published in 1917 as a dramatic dialogue called 'The Common Round', takes place during World War I and draws on descriptions of the typical routine of an unemployed actress that go back to at least 1914.[2] It may also draw on Mansfield's firsthand experiences of working for British film companies as an extra in several productions in the 1910s.[3] But, while the story's tone of escalating desperation harks back to the war years, the route it maps through the offices and waiting rooms of London's West End was still recognisable in the 1920s, when it was taken by a significant number of people. According to one newspaper, making the daily journey round London's film agencies had become common enough by 1922 for it to be known among jobseekers as 'looping the loop'.[4]

Mansfield's narrative remained recognisable in the 1920s in another sense, too. The link between would-be film actresses and sexual exploitation or prostitution that is alluded to in Ada's assignation with the nameless gentleman at the end of the story was a connection made repeatedly in the interwar press and trade papers. Like the American figure of the 'extra girl', whose search for fame in the Hollywood studio system was the source of much anxiety in Los Angeles during this period, the apparently sizeable presence of women in London's 'filmland' prompted concern among journalists and self-appointed moral guardians, eventually leading to intervention from the local and national authorities, who set out to regulate the capital's film employment agencies and training schools.[5]

This chapter begins by looking at the places that Ada Moss and her real-world counterparts would have encountered on their journey through London's West End. The first part of the chapter explores the network of commercial agencies and training schools that emerged to mediate between aspiring stars and British producers. The chapter then turns to investigate the moral panic surrounding women in London's 'filmland'. As with other depictions of 'screen-struck' young women between the wars, the media attention given to female aspirants reveals as much about the fascination with changing patterns of women's employment and public behaviour as it does about the realities of the British film industry at that time. Stories featuring the sad plight of women who had come to London in search of film work had a basis in fact, but they did not capture the full picture. The last part of this chapter examines the case of one of the most notorious fraudsters to come into contact with London's film business in the 1920s. Her brushes with the law over a series of bogus training schools and employment agencies not only shed light on the underside of the 'craze' for film acting, but also provide a record of the identities and personal experiences of some of the individuals trying to find success as actors in the British cinema.

Waiting rooms

As the outlines of the early careers of Clive Brook, Brian Aherne, Mabel Poulton and Chili Bouchier in Chapter 1 indicate, there were multiple paths into the British film industry in the silent period, not all of them predictable. But, in general, readers of fan magazines, film trade papers and instructional guides to film acting would have known that London, as the centre of British film production, was the most logical entry point. In the 1920s, the London suburbs and the surrounding Home Counties contained almost all of the production facilities in the country.[6] Within central London, the majority of film producers also had offices in the West End, especially in the region of Soho around Wardour Street, a place that became synonymous with the film business in the interwar years.[7] The appropriately titled *Film-Land: How to Get There*, in common with other guides to film work, provided the names and addresses of a long list of 'Companies making pictures in and around London' for readers to write to or call upon in person.[8] The influx of applications from would-be actors was a running joke among producers. Discussing what he described as the most recent wave of 'filmania' to grip the British public, Walter West of the Broadwest Film Company said that the 'victims' of this mania 'await me at the studio every morning of the week', and that 'every mail brings me shoals of letters from people in every walk of life who have become possessed of a "desire to act for the films".[9] Frederick Earle, the casting director at Stoll Picture Productions at Cricklewood, claimed that, between 1 March and 1 June 1921, he had personally interviewed 1,235 people who wanted to act for the company.[10] In magazines and book-length guides to filmmaking, details of the variety of 'types' to be found in producers' waiting rooms became popular features and spoke to the enthusiasm for the cinema across all sections of society.[11]

William Elliott prepared readers of his instructional guide to film acting for a typical interview with a producer. Would-be actors, he said, should be ready on arrival at the producer's office to state their screen 'type' – 'juveniles, heavies, comedies, *ingénues*', or 'whatever you think you are most suited to' – and to leave a set of portrait photographs with the company for their files.[12] The key when dealing with a film producer, Elliott explained, was persistence. 'Don't be content with just one call and then leaving him alone,' he wrote. 'Call round on an average once a week, and just remind him that you are still alive and looking for a shop. If you persist in this method you are almost certain to get a call sooner or later.'[13] As with other advice aimed at would-be film actors, Elliott's words were optimistic. In a novel about life in the British film industry written in the 1940s, and based partly on his time as a producer at the Ideal Film Company, Elliott gave a very different description of the same scenario, this time from the producer's point of view. Describing an interview with the fictional Miss Montmorency, Elliott's alter ego recalls the 'direfully depressing job' of auditioning applicants and 'handing out the same time-dishonoured dope': 'Sorry, Miss Montmorency, but nothing doing to-day – or the rest of this week, I'm afraid. But keep in touch – keep in touch...!'[14] For many people, the producer's office was the place where their ambitions met with the stark realities of the film job market and the continually beleaguered nature of the British production sector.

By the 1920s, more of the work of casting for films was being done not by producers, but by agents. Employment agencies for film work were partly an outgrowth of London's theatre and variety industries. Theatrical agents had been operating in London as early as the 1820s, and they had grown in number and importance during the nineteenth century.[15] By 1910, when the London County Council (LCC) began to license employment agencies, there were at least 136 agents in the capital representing stage actors and variety performers.[16] Over the following decade, several agencies began to expand their remit to include film work. Whereas in 1910, none of the agents registered with the LCC mentioned film actors in their applications for licences, in 1920 there were 23 registered theatrical employment agencies that listed finding work for film actors (or 'cinema artistes') among their duties, and a further six agents who specialised exclusively in placing actors in the film industry.[17] At the end of 1930, the number of specialist film acting agencies had gone down to three, but there were 52 registered agents who dealt with film actors in some capacity.[18] Despite the note of caution sounded by some film commentators about the existence of fraudulent film agencies in London that charged their clients registration fees without ever finding them work, most agents seem to have conducted themselves according to accepted theatre practice, taking a cut of around 10 per cent from their clients' wages for each engagement.[19]

A few London agents established themselves as major suppliers of actors to British studios, and thus as major destinations for would-be actors. At the start of the 1920s, Sidney Jay was one of the best-known film employment agents in London. It was to Jay that the aspiring film star from Leicestershire, Winifred Hopcroft, had written to ask for work, and it was at his offices that she had called when she arrived in London.[20] Jay, whose real name was Sydney Friedman, began his agency shortly after having been demobilised from the army.[21] His background before World War I is unclear, although his sister, Terry Friedman, also worked in the entertainment industry as a dance instructor and counted the dancer and film star Jessie Matthews among her pupils. Indeed, Matthews later credited Jay with beginning her in film work.[22] Starting in 1919 with an office on Oxford Street, Jay soon moved his premises to Wardour Street before relocating again to an address on Shaftesbury Avenue, in the heart of the existing theatrical 'Agency-land'.[23] By 1921, Jay was advertising that he had booked his clients over 10,000 engagements with film companies since he had opened, as well as having found work for upcoming stars including Lilian Hall-Davis, Lionelle Howard and Warwick Ward.[24] His reputation extended to America, where trade journals recommended him as a reliable source of actors for Hollywood companies considering making films in Britain.[25] He travelled to America himself in 1922 to persuade the Hollywood actress Mae Marsh to act in the Herbert Wilcox production *Paddy the Next Best Thing* (Graham Cutts, 1923).[26] Around this time, *Motion Picture Studio* magazine dubbed Jay 'the uncrowned King of Studiodom', and he was still influential at the end of the decade, claiming (slightly improbably) to have between 20,000 and 30,000 people on his books.[27]

Another important agency was Bramlins, which opened at 241 Shaftesbury Avenue in May 1920.[28] This was the initiative of the filmmaker Adrian Brunel, the screenwriter Benedict James and the former solicitor, cinema owner, film actor and producer John Payne. According to Brunel, who had met Payne in the last year of World War I as 'a large, bald-headed soldier', the company was conceived as a way to get Payne 'out of khaki' once the war was over.[29] The name Bramlins was a composite of Brunel and James's surnames, together with a family name of Payne's, and the office itself was furnished with items taken from all three founders' homes. Brunel joked that 'the effect was of a respectable Victorian house in which the children had gone Fabian'. But he was apparently being serious when he recalled that everything in the waiting room had disappeared within a year, taken by 'enterprising collectors posing as extras'.[30] Bramlins soon acquired a reputation as an agency run 'by film-men for film-men'.[31] As well as finding work for actors, the agency also represented screenwriters, producers and cameramen, and offered the services of an in-house location manager and stills photographer. According to Brunel, Clive Brook passed through the agency's doors early in the 1920s, while the actress Joan Morgan recalled that Bramlins supplied all the actors for her father's studio in Shoreham.[32] Payne maintained control of the company until his death in 1941, by which point it could claim to be the oldest surviving film agency in the country.[33]

As well as hosting agencies, London's West End contained a number of places that would-be actors might regularly pass through, if only in the hope of hearing news of new job opportunities. Reprograph on Long Acre was a well-known supplier of cheap professional portraits for actors, and screen make-up could be purchased at Willy Clarkson's theatrical costume shop on Wardour Street.[34] There were also more formal meeting places for film actors. The Kinema Club was founded at the end of 1921 with the aim of forming 'a bond of union between all connected with the production of good British pictures'.[35] In principle, it was open to anyone working in the film industry, and members had access to its premises on Great Newport Street. Inside, the club was equipped with separate clubrooms for men and women, a bar, a writing room and a kitchen, all of which the film pioneer J. Stuart Blackton, speaking at the opening ceremony, hoped would instill a 'family atmosphere' among British film workers.[36] However, the Kinema Club had an ambivalent relationship with would-be actors. Its chief purpose, as set out at the inaugural meeting, was to ensure that the cinema was recognised by the public and among its own workers as a legitimate cultural institution. Because of this, it decided to admit only 'recognised screen actors' – a term that was defined by a committee on a case by case basis, in order 'to make the Club as exclusive as possible, and to prevent undesirables, either amateurs, supers or screenstruck, getting in'.[37] Yet, while the club barred its doors to unproven film aspirants, it also spoke up for them against bogus employment agencies and fraudulent producers as part of its larger mission to defend the film industry's professional reputation.[38]

More inclusive than the Kinema Club, although less enduring, was the Motley Club, founded in 1928 on Dean Street in Soho as a meeting place for performers in the film and theatre professions. Working along more commercial lines, it modelled itself after the Central Casting Bureau in Los Angeles (the employment agency established in 1925 as a centralised source of extras and supporting actors for the major Hollywood studios), and sought to become a place where 'producers in a hurry for a crowd' could find film actors at short notice.[39] More radical was the agency established by the Film Artistes' Guild in April 1928 on Shaftesbury Avenue.[40] The Guild had been founded as a professional body for the film industry the previous year by A. Coulson Gilmer, with the support of established actors including Brian Aherne, and it was subsequently registered as a trade union.[41] Film actors were already eligible to become union members through the Actors' Association, which admitted film actors from 1918, and the Variety Artistes' Federation, which established a 'cinema artistes' section in 1920.[42] They would also soon be able to join the new theatrical trade union, the British Actors' Equity Association, formed at the end of 1929.[43] But, as Geoff Brown notes, the formation of the Film Artistes' Guild represented the continuing growth of a separate professional identity for film actors, even if the union's membership and aims were allied closely with workers on the stage.[44] The Guild opposed the practice of charging commission for finding film extras work, and strongly supported moves to abolish all commercial employment agencies.[45] Accordingly, the agency it ran for its own members did away with the 10 per cent fee usually taken from actors' wages.[46] At the end of the 1920s, then, the 'common round' for would-be actors in London had grown larger than it was at the start of the decade, and was also increasingly regulated and professionalised.

Cinema schools

While employment agencies were seen as exploitative by some British film actors and producers, even more contentious were the places known commonly, and often disparagingly, as 'cinema schools'. These were training establishments that offered lessons in film acting and sometimes other branches of film work, such as projection or screenwriting. Schools that taught film acting were operating in London as early as 1912.[47] However, unlike employment agencies, which were mainly found in London's West End, cinema schools were not only concentrated in the capital. At various points in the silent period, cinema schools opened in cities and towns across Britain, including Manchester, Birmingham, Glasgow, Southsea, Liverpool, Plymouth and Hull.[48] Several of these establishments had links to the British film industry. Some schools, such as the Pavilion Cinema Studios in Esher, hired working studio facilities, while others were staffed by professional film actors or producers.[49] Harry Lorraine, a former member of the Clarendon Film Company, was advertising his services as an acting tutor at the start of World War I.[50] After the war, the Hepworth actor Lionelle Howard served as a 'professor in a school of kinema acting' in Southsea.[51] However, as the trade press was quick to point out, the proprietors of cinema schools often exaggerated or fabricated their involvement with actual film production. In 1920, *The Bioscope* reported on a case in Hull in which a woman had been promised that her tuition would guarantee her a role in an upcoming film starring the Broadwest stars Violet Hopson and Gerald Ames.[52] Ames himself appeared in court to testify that he had no knowledge of the scheme. After this, *The Bioscope* banned cinema schools from advertising in its pages.[53]

One of the few cinema schools that retained any credibility with the British film industry during the 1920s was the Victoria Cinema College and Studios in London's West End. This was founded around 1914 by Edward Godal (the professional name of Eleazor Godalski), with premises at 47 Bedford Street near the Strand.[54] By the end of the following year, the school had moved to rooms at 36 Rathbone Place, off Oxford Street, an address it shared with a tailor, a goldsmith and a piano dealer, where it stayed for the next decade and a half (Figure 3.1).[55] During his time as proprietor, Godal was a vociferous defender of the Victoria against accusations of fraud. He worked hard to differentiate it from other 'bogus self-styled "Cinema Schools"', and he published information about his successful students and the companies who had employed them in fan magazines and trade papers.[56] A prospectus from around 1917 compiled some of the positive

The common round: Finding film work in interwar London

In the Main Office.

Figure 3.1. The main office of the Victoria Cinema College. *Victoria Cinema College and Studios: A Guide to Cinema Acting* (London: Victoria Cinema College, c. 1917). Courtesy of the Bill Douglas Cinema Museum, University of Exeter.

press notices that the college had received, together with testimonials from satisfied pupils and letters of recommendation from filmmakers including Benedict James (then at Ideal) and George Pearson (at Gaumont).[57] The prospectus claimed that many Victoria graduates had gone on to obtain leading film roles, while Godal told *The Era* that, in some films, 'practically the whole cast, from leads to crowds, are College students'.[58]

The training offered at the Victoria Cinema College gives some indication of how cinema schools sought to prepare their students for the screen. At the time of the prospectus, the Victoria offered individual tuition or classes six times a week, in the morning, afternoon and evening.[59] Evening continuation classes were fairly common in other fields at this time, especially at business or commercial colleges offering tuition in practical skills such as typing and shorthand.[60] Film acting was sold as a

The College Studio.

Figure 3.2. The studio at the Victoria Cinema College. *Victoria Cinema College and Studios: A Guide to Cinema Acting* (London: Victoria Cinema College, c. 1917). Courtesy of the Bill Douglas Cinema Museum, University of Exeter.

similar vocational skill, and, as the Victoria's prospectus made clear, the school's flexible schedule was designed to attract working people 'whose occupation prevents their attending in the day time'.[61] There was also the option of 'correspondence lessons' for students living outside London.[62] No details were given of the type of tuition this would involve. However, the materials provided by another school offering 'postal instruction in cinema acting' used exercises similar to those included in contemporary instructional guides. These were based around a system of cards (presumably illustrating different emotions), which pupils were told to place 'one at a time, in the left-hand corner of the mirror, and *practise* each until you are able to assume the *exact* expression without reference to the cards'.[63] Unlike most other schools, the Victoria also offered students direct experience of film acting in the college's own studio – a small room equipped with cameras, lighting equipment and basic props (Figure 3.2).[64]

Students at the Victoria were given more opportunities to take part in filmmaking when, in 1918, Godal took over the management of the production firm B&C after its previous head, J.B. McDowell, left to become an official war cameraman on the Western Front.[65] Following this, Godal seems to have regularly used Victoria pupils as extras in B&C productions. In July 1919, a writer for the *Kinematograph and Lantern Weekly* found Godal supervising a nightclub scene on the set of the B&C film *A Sinless Sinner*. The writer was told that a large percentage of the extras in the scene consisted of students from Godal's college, and that '[t]he would-be "stars" frequently get such opportunities of getting used to the actual atmosphere of the real working studio'. Sidestepping the issue of whether Godal's clients were effectively paying to be extras, the writer added: 'To have such a well-dressed capable crowd at his command must be a great help to the producer.'[66] However, another journalist saw this practice as a cynical way of guaranteeing students 'one day's work' and thus avoiding recrimination from licensing authorities.[67]

One actress who passed through the doors of the Victoria, and who was cast as an extra for B&C, was Mabel Poulton. While working in the press office at the Alhambra Theatre around 1919, Poulton confided in her mother her fear that, 'if I didn't do something I should be a typist all my life'.[68] With birthday money from her mother, she chose a nearby acting school, 'not far from the Alhambra', and went after work to arrange her lessons.[69] In a loosely fictionalised novel based on her silent film career (in which she describes her experiences in the third person), Poulton picked up the story of her lessons: 'Actually the College was not as helpful as she thought it would be and only taught the stage struck youngsters to make faces expressing happiness, sorrow etc etc.'[70] However, the school did get Poulton work as a crowd player in a professional film, in which she played a schoolgirl in a pillow fight scene set in a girls' dormitory. The star of the film, she wrote, was 'an American long past her first youth'.[71] This was most likely a reference to Marie Doro, whom Godal had brought over from Hollywood in 1919 to feature in a series of B&C films, in an early instance of an American star being used to add international appeal to British features.[72] Poulton's first experience on a film set was not a pleasant one, however. Having apparently entered into the spirit of the pillow fight with so much enthusiasm that she knocked the American star to the floor, she was placed in the background of the scene.[73] But Poulton did concede that her tuition at the cinema school had at least given her useful experience in applying screen make-up.[74]

Poulton's contemporary, Chili Bouchier, also seems to have graduated from the Victoria Cinema College towards the end of the 1920s, by which point Godal had transferred the business to new management. When Bouchier was working at a department store in Kensington, she responded to a newspaper advertisement and attended a school in 'a ramshackle street off Oxford Street', which charged £3 3s for a course of training.[75] Her description of the experience in her memoirs gives a further impression of what lessons at cinema schools involved:

> He [the receptionist] showed me into a large bare room [...]. In a short while a man strode in dressed in the typical garb of a silent film director – riding breeches, high boots and a peaked cap worn back to front. [...] He made his way to the end of the room to a dummy camera made of wood and cardboard and picked up a makebelieve megaphone. Shouting through the megaphone he put us through our paces while he cranked the dummy camera. We played love scenes, murder scenes and horror scenes. I thoroughly enjoyed myself although it was beginning to dawn upon me that this was a phoney setup.[76]

While Bouchier was dismissive of her training, it did introduce her to a producer of advertising films, who, in turn, arranged a meeting with Max Rosher, John Payne's junior partner at Bramlins, who secured her further professional work.[77] Both Poulton and Bouchier's recollections suggest that the film trade press certainly had good reason to be sceptical of the claims to professionalism made by many cinema schools. But their experiences also show that the line between reputable and disreputable points of entry to British studios in the interwar period was not always as clear-cut as representatives of the industry would have liked to admit.

Girls who haunt Filmland

In the 1920s, there were various avenues for people seeking film work in London. Equally, there was much concern from commentators inside and outside the film industry, who circulated news or rumours about the exploitation of would-be actors. The vast majority of public concern centred on the fate of young women. This was especially notable in discussions of the 'craze' for film acting in the immediate post-World War I years, but the safety of women in London's film business remained an inflammatory issue throughout the decade that followed.

Part of the issue for many commentators was the familiar argument that people looking to enter the film business were wasting their energies attempting to break into a profession that was already overcrowded.[78] But the most sensational accusation was that women, in particular, were making themselves vulnerable to morally corrupting forces, and that many women were being sexually exploited by fraudulent agents or producers. In his exposé of *The Night Haunts of London*, a book that went through ten editions between 1920 and 1923, the journalist Sydney Moseley attacked what he saw as the deplorable morals of the 'cinema stage', which, 'as a channel of ruin for girls', he said, went 'one better than either the music-hall or legitimate stage'. He warned 'the girl who is cinema mad' to avoid film work at all costs, if she 'values her own true self', and alluded to a number of established stars in British film companies who were 'known beyond question in cinema circles as being the mistress of either producers or proprietors'.[79] The trade press rushed to defend the industry against such attacks on its reputation, arguing that Moseley's accusations were entirely unfounded.[80] But the negative characterisation of London's acting employment agencies and film studios persisted.

Warnings to would-be film actors in London were not only issued by people outside the film world. Writing in 1922, G.A. Atkinson, the film critic for the *Daily Express*, lamented the fate of 'the hundreds of screen-struck women and girls who haunt Filmland in the vain quest for employment'.[81] He described 'the anxious procession of unemployed beauty' that 'wanders in and out of the agency waiting-rooms, sits on the staircase when the waiting-room is full, which it usually is, or trails up and down Filmland thoroughfares'. This wasn't just an inconvenience, however, but a social danger, as Atkinson went on to explain:

> There is a sinister side to this great drift of unemployed beauty. Some unscrupulous producers find in it scope for a certain latitude of conduct, and the girl who is unwilling to forego her ambition may be forced to agree to disagreeable bargains.[82]

Atkinson expanded on his assessment of the situation, stating that would-be actresses were increasingly being pressured into being 'nice' to producers – that is, in the euphemistic terminology of 'filmland', trading sexual favours – if they were to stand a chance of obtaining work.[83]

Whatever truth there was in Atkinson's picture of immorality in the British film industry, such accusations emerged out of a complex climate of uncertainty about public order and women's place in the public sphere. Present in Atkinson's account of the 'great drift of unemployed beauty' into London's production offices and film agencies was an acknowledgement of the larger economic situation that Britain found itself in at the time. National unemployment levels reached an early interwar peak of 2 million people in 1921, or 17 per cent of the insured workforce, a figure that had been unheard of before the war.[84] Industrial strikes, public demonstrations and hunger marches focused attention on the extent of the problem and led many people to speculate about what the long-term social and political effect of mass unemployment might be.[85] While employment levels were higher in London than elsewhere in the country, there were still a significant number of people in search of work.[86] And while the proportion of women in paid employment was actually lower in 1921 than it had been ten years earlier, with many women workers being dismissed or withdrawing from the labour market once the war ended, the threat posed by women apparently taking prospective jobs away from unemployed men could still cause friction.[87] Sally Alexander recounts the experiences of one young woman who was heckled with shouts of 'Girls taking men's jobs' when she started work at a cable factory on the outskirts of London in 1922.[88] Although women in the film industry were not necessarily competing directly with men for the same roles, the image of a 'procession' of women seeking work in film studios sat alongside other contemporary signs of social change, and must have resonated uneasily with some people's sense of the proper social order.

Attitudes towards would-be film actresses in London were also caught up in discussions about 'women's place' in modern life in ways that extended beyond the immediate economic situation. The melodrama of sexual danger that Atkinson and others claimed was being acted out daily in the streets and offices of London's 'filmland' reworked older cultural narratives that figured London as 'the city of dreadful delight'.[89] But it also borrowed some of its features, and much of its urgency, from the series of scandals that shook Hollywood at the start of the 1920s. Most prominent among these were the alleged rape and murder of the actress Virginia Rappe by Roscoe 'Fatty' Arbuckle in 1921 and the mysterious death of the director William Desmond Taylor the following year, both of which generated lurid portraits in the British popular press of the material and sexual excess that supposedly characterised the American film star lifestyle.[90] Indeed, Atkinson's view of London's film industry echoed his depiction of Hollywood in the wake of the Arbuckle scandal, when he labelled Los Angeles the 'Gomorrah of the Golden West' and described the city as being home to 'a host of women of loose character and men of no character at all'.[91] Scandals in the London entertainment world may have further informed attitudes towards women seeking entry into the British film industry. When the young stage actress Billie Carleton died of a drug overdose in 1919, the subsequent inquest revealed links between the illegal traffic in drugs and members of the film business, including the film actor Lionel Belcher, who admitted to supplying Carleton with cocaine.[92] Responding to the news of Arbuckle's arrest in 1921, the *News of the World* connected the deaths of Rappe and Carleton, noting that American moral reformers saw them both as 'examples of the misery, disgrace, and death that follow the breakdown of customs which once protected women'.[93]

As Hilary Hallett says of the American media's response to the death of Virginia Rappe, stories about sexual danger in London's interwar 'filmland' formed part of 'an ongoing debate about the relationship between motion pictures and the rise of sexual modernism'.[94] Women's public visibility in the streets of Soho, and their alleged behaviour behind the scenes in studios, echoed accounts elsewhere in British popular culture that linked the cinema to the self-possessed modern woman, or 'flapper'.[95] A newspaper editorial in 1920 associated cinemagoing with modernity in its description of the typical 'new' woman of the post-World War I era: 'She is confident. She is "all there." She fears neither mice nor men. She can combine the gentle gaze of the dove with the strategy of a field marshal. She can face facts. She has been to cinemas.'[96] While, as Adrian Bingham has shown, the interwar media was by no means universally hostile to the idea that women now had more freedom and opportunities than before, there were still voices that vented anger at changing notions of femininity or, more moderately, expressed discomfort with the rate of change in gender relations.[97]

Attacks on the character of both 'screen-struck' aspirants and predatory film workers did not only appear in the news. More elaborate narratives of women being preyed upon in London's film agencies and studios appeared in the early 1920s in several novels that set out to reveal the depths of the film world's moral decline. In the racy novel *The Kinema Girl*, written around 1920, the young Nancy Jones is eager to escape the restrictions of her suburban, deeply religious home life and decides to 'go in for kinema-acting'.[98] After enrolling in a cinema school near Wardour Street, she finds work with a film company on the outskirts of London. Nancy soon embarks on an affair with the director and is promoted to a starring role. But, when her affair grows complicated, she begins to take opium, while another actress in the stock company becomes addicted to cocaine. The novel ends with a nightmarish journey to Limehouse, home of London's Chinese community and the reputed centre of the drug trade, after which Nancy retires from acting for a quieter life in the countryside.[99]

With its obvious parallels to the Billie Carleton scandal, Nancy's story dramatised the assessment of Moseley and others that film work was an effective 'channel of ruin' for young women. Adolphus Raymond's 1923 novel *Film-Struck*, which follows another young woman in her efforts to become a film actress, presented this view of the film industry even more explicitly.[100] At the start of the novel, Nora Brown, similar to Nancy Jones, is bored of her parochial and sheltered life. Leaving her rural village for London, she takes lessons at a London cinema school, the 'Patricia College School for film-acting' (an allusion, presumably, to the Victoria Cinema College).[101] However, on completing her tuition, she is told by a producer that her qualification is useless – a verdict that mirrors the advice given by a number of real-world producers and casting directors, who declared that they would never knowingly employ a cinema school graduate.[102] Unperturbed, Nora registers with a West End agent, who is later exposed as a 'shark' and 'a white slave dealer'.[103] By the end of the novel, Nora has found herself caught in an illegal gambling den with prostitutes and trapped in a hotel room with the kind of unscrupulous film producer that Atkinson and other commentators warned about. Like most other fictional film actresses of the period, Nora eventually leaves the film profession to return to the safety of her domestic life. Raymond's novel clearly tapped into the larger atmosphere of moral panic surrounding film work, and the publisher's description of the book as 'a revelation of the moving power behind the scenes in Filmland', together with the cast of 'shattered' film actresses that Nora encounters in the book, suggested that such experiences were widespread and inevitable.[104]

If the stories circulated by journalists and fiction writers reflected the complicated attitudes towards young women in the post-World War I era, they also had a direct impact on the regulations surrounding the British cinema. In 1919, police reports about the victims of bogus cinema schools reached the LCC's Public Control Department, the local government body responsible for licensing employment agencies in central London. Having no official mandate to regulate training establishments other than those also operating as employment agencies, the department set about asking for greater powers to deal with this new threat to public safety. In a letter to the LCC executive, the Public Control Committee made it clear that the protection of young women was their major concern, explaining:

> The majority of the students are girls with little or no experience of the career they seek to enter. [...] Pitiful cases have been instanced of girls who have been attracted to London from the provinces by the specious and glowing advertisements, and who, having fruitlessly spent their savings in undergoing training and in hotel expenses, found themselves stranded, with no hope of redress.[105]

The department's concern over the 'pitiful cases' of vulnerable 'girls' attracted to cinema schools was no doubt partly influenced by its longstanding belief that employment agencies and other establishments aimed mainly at women workers were easy covers for prostitution rings.[106] Several years earlier, the department had made a similar request for an extension of their powers in order to deal with massage parlours in the West End, which police suspected were being used as fronts for 'disorderly houses', or brothels. This suggestion was taken so seriously that the department was eventually granted the ability to inspect any premises in London that its committee suspected of being used for 'immoral purposes'.[107] Given its track record, it is reasonable to assume that, in cinema schools, the Public Control Department saw another potential cover for the sexual, as well as the financial, exploitation of young women. The LCC concurred, and they successfully petitioned Parliament for an extension of the London County Council (General Powers) Act at the next session, allowing the Public Control Department to incorporate cinema schools into their licensing system from December 1920.[108] The trade press welcomed this development, and *The Bioscope* hoped that 'before long the wheat will be sorted from the chaff, and the stage and screen-struck will be safeguarded'.[109]

The increased vigilance of the London authorities to film agencies and training establishments, and the continuing animosity of the British film trade press, shows how women jobseekers in London's film industry could be treated at once with suspicion – as examples of a more self-assured, modern femininity – and with a more traditional paternalism, which sought to protect supposedly naive and innocent 'girls' from predatory forces in the city. To explore this ambivalent response and its basis in fact in more depth, the remainder of this chapter examines the career of Marion Quigley, a woman who was the proprietor of a string of bogus cinema schools and employment agencies between 1919 and 1923. Quigley represented the worst fears of trade representatives and moral guardians about the potential for fraud and exploitation among the businesses that sprang up to cater to would-be stars. But the trail of court cases she left behind her also constitutes a particularly rich source of evidence about the people searching for work in the British film industry in the post-World War I years. Although by no means conclusive, the news stories and witness depositions that Quigley's activities generated allow us to look beyond the moral panic and ask whether the popular portrait of would-be actors as screen-struck young women that emerges from other accounts is a fair or comprehensive representation. Her story also offers an illuminating snapshot of a city readjusting to life in peacetime, and responding to the new preoccupations of the postwar world.

The most troublesome woman in London

Marion Jessie Quigley, otherwise known as Jessie Wilding, Mrs Welding, Mrs Glanville, Louisa Granville, Lady Granville Roberts, Mrs Robinson, Mrs Harriet Maria Thomas, Miss Marsh and Madame Luck, was a confidence trickster active in London at the start of the 1920s. Born around 1897, she may or may not have been the daughter of an Irish peer. She was educated, possibly, in a French convent, and claimed to have been the widow of a doctor killed in World War I. In the interwar years, she described herself variously as a dance instructor, film actress and cinema school proprietor.[110]

Quigley's appearances in the British press began around the start of 1920, when she was summoned, aged 23, to Bow Street Police Court alongside Oxford Welding, an older man of around 41, who gave his profession as film producer. Welding seems to have been Quigley's partner or husband, and he was certainly her accomplice in several schemes. On this occasion, Quigley and Welding stood accused of obtaining money under false pretences by running a fraudulent film acting school and employment agency known as the Kinema Production Company on New Oxford Street. Quigley had allegedly told one student that she was the American film star Mae Marsh, while Welding had posed as an acting teacher called Mr Wilson.[111] The case was sent to trial at the Central Criminal Court a few months later, where the couple denied all charges.[112] Quigley scoffed at the suggestion that she had ever worked as a barmaid, claiming instead to have a respectable, upper-class background. Welding claimed to be a successful actor from a theatrical family, known professionally as Stanley Ross.[113] However, evidence of duplicity mounted as the trial progressed. According to the police, the school had been active since around the time of the Armistice in November 1918, and had made as much as £2,482 profit from 400 pupils in the intervening year and a half.[114] At the end of March 1920, both Quigley and Welding were found guilty of fraud, but only Welding was given a nine-month prison sentence. At one point in the proceedings, Quigley fainted while on the stand, and had to be attended by

87

a doctor. Taking Quigley's apparent ill health into consideration, the judge allowed her to leave the court with a lighter sentence, adding that the older man was doubtless the driving force in the partnership.[115] Welding may indeed have had a history of running bogus cinema schools, but a police officer who was present at the Old Bailey and who gave evidence in a later trial, had little doubt that Quigley's fainting fit was a 'put-up collapse', and accused her of doing 'a little bit of acting in the dock'.[116]

A year later, in March 1921, Quigley was back in court for breaking the terms of her sentence by operating another film acting school and employment agency – the London Academy of Cinema Acting on Shaftesbury Avenue – with another, unnamed man. The same judge reiterated the terms of Quigley's sentence and gave her a further warning.[117] However, despite the judge's intervention, Quigley continued to operate cinema schools in the West End. In August that year, she appeared at Marlborough Street Police Court accused of having reopened the unlicensed London Academy.[118] Quigley had, in fact, applied to the LCC for a licence the previous December, when the Public Control Department's new licensing powers came into force, but was refused because of objections from Detective-Inspector Gillard, who had uncovered the extent of Quigley and Welding's operation earlier that year.[119] Quigley claimed that she had never guaranteed her students employment. But a sign placed over the stairway leading up to the school stating 'This is not an employment agency' was not enough to convince the magistrate that Quigley had been acting in good faith, and she was issued a £50 fine plus 13 days' imprisonment.[120]

The same magistrate encountered Quigley again in December 1921, reunited with Oxford Welding and running yet another school, this one advertised as the Cinema Academy of Acting and Dancing, also on Shaftesbury Avenue. The school had collected another £2,000–3,000 over the space of ten months.[121] As news of the arrests spread, more witnesses came forward, including one woman who had paid the substantial sum of £42 for a screen test with Stoll Picture Productions. Maurice Elvey, then a director with Stoll, and Joseph Grossman, Stoll's studio manager, were called into court to testify that they had never been connected with the school in any way.[122] At the start of 1922, the case was eventually referred to the Central Criminal Court, where Welding was sentenced to 15 months' and Quigley to 9 months' imprisonment for conspiracy.[123] The judge found them both guilty of 'deliberate, systematic, and cruel frauds', although, as before, Welding was said to be the worse offender, who had, 'like a coward, remained in the background and put Quigley forward'.[124]

A more complex case the following year, in 1923, saw Quigley back in court and revealed the extent of her deceptions. In previous trials, it had emerged that Quigley had assumed various identities besides that of film acting tutor, including a peeress – Lady Granville Roberts – and the fiancée of a young officer, before disappearing.[125] It seems that, in October 1922, more or less as soon as she had been released from prison, Quigley had approached a woman called Emily Wells with the idea of setting up the Empire Studios of Kinemaphotography, a film production company and training school. Wells had been a pupil of Quigley's before her arrest, yet was somehow persuaded to invest money in the new venture, to rent rooms on Baker Street as a space to conduct lessons and to apply for an LCC licence in her name. Quigley also told Wells that her fellow investors would be Lord Leverhulme (supposedly an old admirer of Quigley's) and Lord Willoughby – both entirely fictitious.[126]

Quigley disbanded the Empire Studios in July 1923, leaving Wells worse off by a total of £1,670.[127] Soon after Quigley absconded, she began posing as Mrs Harriet Maria Thomas, the owner of a house in Pinner that she was renting with Oxford Welding, now also out of prison, and a young man, who was possibly Welding's brother. On the basis that she owned the house, she convinced a loan and investment company to lend her £100.[128] However, another moneylender she approached became suspicious and eventually accused her of giving him false information. In a dramatic encounter, Quigley broke down in tears in the moneylender's office, then hit him and wrestled her way out onto the street.[129] A policeman on duty nearby saw Quigley running in front of traffic on Piccadilly, amid cries of 'Stop her! Stop her!', and watched as she fell to the ground while attempting to board a passing taxi outside the Ritz Hotel. Taken into custody by the policeman, Quigley (who gave her name as Jessie Wilding) asked what was to become of her two children, one 5 years old, the other 10 months, who were both apparently waiting for her at home.[130]

This sensational scene fuelled press attention. 'Baby in Prison' and 'Dash for Taxicab' were the headlines in the *Daily Mirror*.[131] After Quigley's trial at the Old Bailey, in which she was found guilty of all charges and was sentenced to 12 months' imprisonment, the *News of the World* ran detailed stories about her under the headings 'Swindler Unmasked', 'Beauty Who Duped Film Aspirants' and 'A Menace to London' (Figure 3.3).[132] Despite the fact that Oxford Welding was complicit in the fraud, and despite the previous suggestions in court that Quigley had been a victim of his pernicious influence, it was Quigley who now received the blame and the credit for perpetrating such an elaborate scheme. Her youth (she was 27 in 1924) and flair for the dramatic was well suited to the tastes of the interwar press, which, as Matt Houlbrook and Angus McLaren have noted, was especially concerned with sensational crime stories involving reinvention and disguise, and which colluded in celebrating new kinds of criminal celebrity.[133] As Houlbrook argues, a rash of 'crook' life stories serialised in the popular press in the 1920s and 1930s repackaged the activities of confidence tricksters and thieves as 'more entertaining than threatening'.[134] In the process, they drew sympathetically on the 'rags to riches' narratives of social mobility made popular in romance novels and serials – and also in the cinema – even as they revealed anxiety about the erosion of stable class boundaries.[135] Quigley's treatment in the press reflected the interwar media's ambivalent attitudes towards criminal self-fashioning. The newspaper *John Bull* spoke of Quigley's 'appalling record and character' and demanded that the authorities show her the full force of the law.[136] But the *News of the World*, which labelled Quigley an 'adventuress' and a 'swindler', also proclaimed her as 'one of the most audacious and accomplished female criminals' of recent years, promising readers that '[h]er latest exploits form an entertaining chapter of an amazing life'. Her capacity to frustrate the detectives of Scotland Yard, whom the paper said would surely name her as 'the most troublesome woman in London', together with her 'charming manner', 'vivacious disposition' and her decision to defend herself ('with considerable ability') in court, placed her in a line of women 'crooks' who were able to use their apparently feminine resourcefulness and magnetism to manipulate the less 'nimble-witted'.[137]

The victims of the story, the 'would-be stars' who were repeatedly 'fleeced' by Quigley (as the *News of the World* put it), were presented in terms ranging from tragic to comic. Here, the media's uneasy fascination with the blurring of social boundaries was also a factor. If press reporting on Quigley packaged her performances and deceptions as entertainment, accounts of

THE NEWS OF

SWINDLER UNMASKED.

BEAUTY WHO DUPED FILM ASPIRANTS.

A Menace to London.

"News of the World" Special.

Notorious as an adventuress, a woman described by the police as one of the most audacious and accomplished female criminals who had been in their hands for years, was sentenced to 12 months' imprisonment by Mr. Justice Greer, at the Old Bailey, for a series of frauds on moneylenders.

She was convicted in the name of Mrs. Jessie Wilding, but is better known as Jessie Quigley, the proprietress of many bogus cinema agencies.

In the course of her career she has swindled thousands of would-be film artists. Her latest exploits form an entertaining chapter of an amazing life.

LURE OF THE CINEMA.

HOW WOULD-BE STARS WERE FLEECED.

RETRIBUTION FOR MANY OFFENCES.

If Scotland Yard officials were asked to say who was the most troublesome woman in London, there is little doubt that they would name Jessie Wilding. Decidedly pretty, with charming manners and a bright, vivacious disposition, she has been known to the police for over five years as a clever, nimble-witted adventuress who has secured thousands of pounds by various frauds. The licensing officials of the L.C.C. know her particularly well as a person who conducts bogus employment agencies and so-called film schools, where aspiring cinema artists are induced to pay heavy fees on the supposition that they will be found employment. Wilding has appeared in the courts on many occasions, and, with the exception of a sentence of nine months in the second division imposed upon her at the Old Bailey on February 14, 1922, has hitherto been fortunate enough to escape richly merited punishment. She is undoubtedly exceedingly clever and gifted, with a specious tongue, and unlimited audacity, easily calculated to deceive. She was charged at the Old Bailey with

Attempting to obtain £500 by false pretences from Newton Thomas, moneylender, of Premier House, Dover-street, W.;

Obtaining £100 by false pretences from T. C. Reeve, secretary to the Watford Loan Investment Co.;

Obtaining by false pretences from Mrs. E. G. Wells sums totalling £725 10s.; and Conspiring with a man not in the dock to obtain sums of money from anyone who would become pupils in the Empire Studios of Kinema Photography.

There were half a dozen other charges of obtaining small sums from women who wanted to become film artists, in addition

method of fraud was only one of many Wilding employed in order to obtain money. In January, 1923, she rented a furnished maisonette in Alma-square, St. John's Wood, for 5gns. a week. In June the owner of the place discovered to her astonishment that the occupant had vanished, and had taken with her furniture which was subsequently found at Baker-street, the headquarters of the Empire Studios. The property was recovered, but other and more valuable things disappeared altogether. When Wilding went she owed over £30 for rent, £15 for gas and £2 10s. for electric light. She entered another maisonette at Marlborough-hill, St. John's Wood, for which she was to pay 5gns. a week, but left about four weeks later, taking with her all the linen and plate. About the end of July she took Elm Leigh, Hatch End, Pinner, and while in possession of this place attempted to negotiate the loan with Mr. Thomas. The owner of the house was Mrs. Lillian Thomas, and Mrs. Wilding pretended to Mr. Thomas that she was the proprietress of the place. From Mr. T. C. Reeve Mrs. Wilding secured £100 by posing as Mrs. Thomas, and she made a good many further attempts to obtain sums from other moneylending concerns. Wilding's husband, it appears, was a soldier who died during the war, and it is thought that the name from Devonshire to find employment in London in the early days of hostilities. After her husband died she got into touch with a man named Oxford William Wilding, and with him worked a great many frauds through the medium of bogus employment agencies. Her age

Mrs. Wilding.

is 27, and she has two pretty children, one about a year old, the other about five years. On March 24, 1920, she was bound over at the Old Bailey for obtaining money by fraud in conjunction with the man Wilding. It was then stated that something like

SIXTY PEOPLE HAD BEEN DEFRAUDED

in a bogus cinema agency, and that close on £2,000 had been obtained. Twelve

Figure 3.3. Marion Quigley, also known as Jessie Wilding. 'Swindler unmasked', *News of the World*, 13 January 1924, p. 6. © News Corp UK & Ireland Ltd.

her clients were both sympathetic and scornful of their desire to reinvent themselves in order move up the social ladder. 'Most of her victims are in poor circumstances,' the *News of the World* sympathised, 'and parted with their money on the promise of lucrative employment.'[138] However, other newspapers emphasised the gullibility of Quigley's clients and poked fun at the lessons they had paid for. Details of the tuition offered at the London Academy of Cinema Acting in 1921 were reported as 'Amusing Evidence at the Old Bailey' by the *Pall Mall Gazette*. Mrs Jessie Ogden, a 'middle-aged woman', according to *The Times*, told the court that 'she had to pose and march about in a chalked-off space and "do a lot of nonsensical work"'. One scene, which prompted laughter in the courtroom when it was described, involved Ogden brandishing a pistol and 'trying to shoot imaginary people off the wall'.[139]

Lessons in facial expression, closely resembling those recommended in contemporary handbooks to screen acting, were another subject of humour in the press, and were often taken to imply a degree of narcissism on the part of would-be actors. 'Woman's Story of Making Faces at a Mirror' was how the *Daily Mirror* introduced the testimony of Katherine Paterson, who was taught 'to make expressions denoting joy and sorrow' by Oxford Welding.[140] The *Pall Mall Gazette* recounted how another pupil was made to repeat one of his lessons in court, reading out a letter informing him that he had inherited a fortune as an exercise in 'expressing pleasure'.[141] *The Times* reported on the laughter that accompanied the testimony of another former student, who had been told that his ability to fly a plane, drive a car and swim made him a suitable candidate for the screen.[142] For the trade press, who followed Quigley's career closely, the appropriation of popular film culture and the accepted tenets of screen acting for criminal ends was a particular source of embarrassment, and hardened their opposition to the cinema school industry.[143]

Schools for the screen-struck?

The response to Quigley's crimes highlights the ambivalent attitudes towards those seeking work in the British film industry in the 1920s. The media's role in both promoting and critiquing narratives of social mobility and reinvention will be discussed more in the next chapter in relation to interwar 'star search' contests. But the documents generated by Quigley's various bogus cinema schools also provide a unique record of who the people 'haunting' the peripheries of London's film industry in the immediate post-World War I years actually were. The details provided by newspaper reports and witness depositions suggest that young women did indeed form a significant proportion of cinema school pupils, although several of the young women who called on Quigley did so with the encouragement of hopeful, older relatives. Older women were also among the people who answered Quigley's calls for film actors, as were a number of men who were either seeking work after being demobilised or more generally looking to improve their lot.

As the LCC's internal communications highlight, young women or 'girls' were thought to be the biggest clients for interwar cinema schools. Autobiographical and fictional accounts of cinema schools also support this view. In the waiting room of the Patricia College School in the novel *Film-Struck*, Nora Brown encounters 'little nurse-girls, typists who had scraped together a few pounds, seamstresses' and other women, while at the fictional school attended by Nancy Jones in *The Kinema Girl*, all but one of the students is female.[144] Chili Bouchier remembered her fellow students at the Victoria Cinema College as 'lots of girls in homemade dresses and some pimply youths'.[145] Young women were certainly well represented among the witnesses in Quigley's numerous trials. An early victim who had visited one of Quigley's schools on Shaftesbury Avenue in 1919 was 20-year-old May Shepherd, who had recently been dismissed from her role in the Women's Auxiliary Army Corps and was looking for alternative employment. Her testimony gives some credence to the narratives of sexual danger circulated in popular discourse in relation to film work. Having paid £6 6s for a course of lessons, she had been told by Oxford Welding that she might be eligible for film work were she to 'let her hair down and shorten her skirt'.[146] The newspapers also recounted the case of another, unnamed young woman, who had travelled to London from Scotland in search of a job. After paying Quigley and Welding a total of £76 for tuition, the woman apparently found herself 'walking the street practically destitute'.[147] At least one other woman had travelled even further before arriving at Quigley's door. Mademoiselle Daubignae, who described herself as an Italian cinema actress, paid around £12 for a course of lessons and was promised a film contract in New York.[148]

Several more young women testified against Quigley. Ethel Evans had been persuaded to pay for extra lessons to learn 'Egyptian dances' for an upcoming film role.[149] Sybil Collins, 'a prepossessing and vivacious young woman', according to *Motion Picture Studio*, had travelled into London from Sussex for her lessons.[150] However, many of Quigley's students proved less easy to cast in the role of 'film-struck girl'. Jessie Ogden, the 'middle-aged woman' who had been told by Welding to shoot imaginary people with a pistol during her tuition, was one of several older women who had visited the cinema school with younger female relatives, when she had attended lessons with her young niece.[151] Mrs Beatrice May Ross from East London had also gone with her niece, Daisy Baker, to visit Quigley after she had seen an advertisement in a London Underground station.[152] Mrs Violetta Derry had responded to a newspaper notice for Quigley's Baker Street school on behalf of her young granddaughter, while Mrs Dora White from Stepney Green had arranged tuition in film acting for her 13-year-old daughter, Tina.[153] In attempting to prepare her daughter for the labour market, Mrs White had followed the example of many mothers in the interwar period, who took responsibility for finding work for their young girls and often accompanied them to labour exchanges and job interviews.[154]

There were also several older or married women who had undertaken film training on their own or with relatives of their own age. Mrs Phyllis King had gone to see Quigley with her sister, and ended up paying additional money for riding lessons and the cost of hiring horses, having being promised a part in an upcoming society drama.[155] Matilda Sutherland, a 'spinster' from Earls Court, had been told that, after her training, she would be playing 'the part of an Aunt' in a new British feature.[156] Older women may, of course, have been more likely than teenage girls to read news of Quigley's various arrests in the papers, and so may have been overrepresented as witnesses in Quigley's trials. But other sources suggest that their cases were probably not unique. A journalist for *Motion Picture Studio* thought that unmarried, middle-class women who had been widowed in the war were particularly vulnerable to the claims of cinema schools, being 'handicapped by having had no professional training', and yet 'having to provide a living for themselves and for others, too, perhaps'.[157]

It was not only women who had brought young relatives to see Quigley. Giacomo Dall Oste, an immigrant Italian artisan from South London, had paid more than £94 for film acting classes for his two young daughters, one of whom had been promised the part of an 'Indian Princess' in another of Quigley and Welding's imaginary productions.[158] Several men had also attended lessons. Albert Root, a builder and former Royal Air Force pilot from Lewisham, who had visited Quigley and Welding for film acting lessons in 1919, had been told that he would make the perfect athletic leading man in their new stock company.[159] Like Root, Reginald Saville, who had visited Quigley the same year, had also recently been demobilised, in this instance from his duties as a ship's quartermaster.[160] The presence of demobilised men in London's 'filmland' at this time is not surprising, given the sheer number of ex-servicemen returning to civilian life and attempting to find work in the years after the war. Charles Bennett, best known for his collaboration with Alfred Hitchcock as a screenwriter (beginning with the adaptation of his stage play *Blackmail* in 1929), remembered his own experiences of looking for work as a film actor a decade earlier, after he had been 'demobbed'. 'All of us,' he said, 'used to go flocking to Sidney Jay's office hoping to get jobs, just a day's work in the movies.'[161] Men, as well as women, could view the transition from wartime to peacetime roles as an opportunity to pursue their ambitions. John Oldham, an ex-soldier from the Gordon Highlanders regiment, got a job as a railway porter on leaving the army, but he soon left Scotland to take up tuition in a cinema school and to look for film work in London.[162]

In the 1920s, as more workers found themselves unemployed or struggling to earn a living, Quigley's schools attracted other men, who thought that film acting might offer them a way to a more prosperous life. Victor Nathan, a salesman and importer from Shepherd's Bush, had paid £20 for acting tuition in 1921.[163] In the same year, John Dobson from Kensington had paid nearly twice that amount for film and dancing lessons.[164] William Moss, a travelling salesman from Manor Park, had given Quigley more than £10 for film acting lessons and costumes, in the hope of joining a studio company as a salaried employee. 'The prospect of regular work at 2 guineas a day appealed to me,' he said in his deposition before Quigley's last known trial.[165] The same prospect evidently appealed to many more people.

While the range of would-be film actors who fell victim to Quigley and her accomplices' fraudulent cinema schools is not necessarily representative, it is at least suggestive of the variety of people seeking work in the British film industry. Despite the almost exclusive focus of the local authorities and film industry representatives on the fate of 'girls', the evidence from contemporary court reports suggests that older and married women constituted a significant part of the clientele for London's cinema schools. The reports also suggest that men formed a sizeable presence in the waiting rooms and stairways of London's 'filmland', and were equally vulnerable to the claims of people such as Quigley, who offered a quicker or more certain route to the studio.

As with other moral panics, the public anxiety over women's exploitation in the film industry died down somewhat as the 1920s progressed. But it did not disappear completely. In 1927, the problem of London's cinema schools once again became a matter of national concern. As Parliament debated the new Cinematograph Films Bill in March of that year, Harry Day, the Labour MP for Southwark and the proprietor of his own London theatrical agency, asked the Home Secretary William Joynson-Hicks if he was aware of the 'many bogus self-styled cinema schools' operating in London and the larger provincial cities.[166] Although, after investigating the matter, the Home Office was satisfied with the LCC's existing licensing arrangements, Day continued to cite the apparent rise in cinema schools as an argument against the Bill, using it as an example of the unregulated financial speculation in the film industry that he believed the legislation would cause.[167] In his 1929 novel *Vile Bodies*, Evelyn Waugh elaborates on this idea, describing the activities of the fictional National Academy of Cinematographic Art, in which pupils' fees are used to subsidise the salaries of professional film actors while the pupils, themselves, are used as extras – a situation that echoed the workings of the Victoria Cinema College some years earlier.[168]

The Victoria Cinema College, itself, was also a source of concern at the end of the decade. In December 1927, Patrick Mannock, the editor of *Picturegoer*, wrote to the LCC to oppose the renewal of the Victoria's training school licence on the grounds that its managers were not qualified to teach film acting, and that the school was 'entirely discredited by the production industry'.[169] For Mannock, this was part of a longstanding campaign; he had raised similar objections to the LCC against other cinema schools earlier in the decade.[170] In January 1928, at a special meeting of the Public Control Department, witnesses assembled against the college's new proprietor, Thomas Hugh-Jones. The assembly included the agents Sidney Jay and Max Rosher, as well as some of the students who had passed through the college's doors – all of them, on this occasion, women.[171] Defending himself against Mannock's charges, the owners of the college told the Public Control Committee that, out of the 1,368 students who had come to them for tuition in the last three years, 906 had obtained engagements. On inspecting the college's books, however, an official from the LCC disputed these figures, telling the committee that there were more than 100 students registered at the college during one two-month period alone, suggesting a higher turnover of clients than the owners cared to acknowledge. Hugh-Jones also admitted that he encouraged students seeking work to tell producers that they had experience of acting at professional studios in Esher, despite never having been there. 'We have been forced to use these methods,' a lawyer said, 'to defend ourselves against the unfair prejudice and attacks made against us by the Trade.'[172] Despite these admissions, the LCC decided to let Hugh-Jones off with a caution. However, similar objections were made later in the year and the LCC warned that, if they received any further complaints, the Victoria's training school licence would be revoked.[173] Perhaps influenced by this decision, the company behind the Victoria Cinema College wound up their operations shortly afterwards.[174]

Although the hostility expressed towards cinema schools at the end of the 1920s was ostensibly directed at defending the professionalism of the British film industry, the perceived problem of 'screen-struck' women was never far from the surface. Shortly after the LCC decided to renew the Victoria Cinema College's training school licence, the *Picturegoer* issued its own thinly veiled attack on the Victoria's reputation by parodying the college's inflated publicity claims in an article called simply 'That Film School'. Picking apart a cinema school prospectus, the writer, Victor Hilton, dismissed the glowing testimonies from 'unknown' or 'defunct' producers and laughed at the photograph of the college studio: 'quite a big room – three times, at least, the size of my sitting-room'.[175] Next to the article, the magazine's resident illustrator depicted what was imagined to be the typical cinema school pupil and her motives for pursuing film work in the form of a young, unmistakably modern woman reading a cinema school prospectus, with pound signs dancing above her head (Figure 3.4). Fraudsters and

Figure 3.4. A would-be film star, as imagined by *Picturegoer*. Victor Hilton, 'That film school', *Picturegoer*, May 1928, p. 50. Courtesy of the British Film Institute Reuben Library.

charlatans may have been the chief enemies in the film industry's ongoing pursuit of respectability, the *Picturegoer* implied, but young women's ambitions and their dreams of stardom continued to threaten not only their own best interests, but also the good name of the British cinema. The next chapter leaves the streets of London's 'filmland' behind to follow the treatment of would-be actors in the interwar media more closely. In particular, it explores a number of highly publicised national contests to find new British film actors, which both fuelled the 'craze' for film acting and tested the limits of Britain's interwar fascination with film stardom.

4

Stand forth, Mary Pickford the second! Searching for British stars

At the start of Edgar Wallace's novel *The Avenger* (1926), Jack Knebworth, an American film producer working at a studio in Britain, orders his leading lady off the set. Stella Mendoza, whose real name is Maggie Stubbs, has been causing problems for Jack ever since she returned from Hollywood with, he complains, 'nothing [...] but a line of fresh talk'.[1] With Stella out of the picture, Jack addresses his remaining cast, 'sardonically' conjuring up a replacement from the crowd:

> This is where the miracle happens. [...] This is where the extra girl who's left a sick mother and a mortgage at home leaps to fame in a night. If you don't know that kinder thing happens on every lot in Hollywood, you're not students of fiction. Stand forth, Mary Pickford the second![2]

The miracle of overnight film stardom was, as Jack reminded his cast, a common trope in interwar popular culture. In novels and short stories, the immediate celebrity seemingly offered by the cinema was variously celebrated and critiqued.[3] British fan magazines circulated real-life stories of famous actors, including Rudolph Valentino and Gloria Swanson, who had at some point 'lined up for pay' as extras before being promoted to stardom by a producer or casting agent.[4]

From the end of World War I, a series of national 'star search' contests, in which winners were offered cash prizes and roles in feature films, gave the British public a more tangible and potentially more accessible reference point for studying the opportunities for instant fame. Between 1918 and 1928, there were at least eight nationwide star searches in Britain. These ranged from small-scale collaborations between specialist film magazines and British film companies to large schemes involving mass-circulation newspapers, newsreels, cinemagazines, Hollywood studios and consumer brands. Although they have attracted relatively little attention, star searches were by no means marginal to popular film culture in Britain.[5] During the interwar years, they attracted tens of thousands of women, among them Marjorie Hume, Miss June and Mabel Poulton, who all entered star search contests before establishing themselves as film actresses.[6] Contests, and the narratives of success that accompanied them, also fuelled public debate about the impact of cinema on British society. The winners of these contests – women such as Alice Lee, Tommy Sinclair, Phyllis Nadell, Winifred Nelson, Margaret Leahy, Sybil Rhoda, Eugenie Prescott and Kathleen Joyce – had varying and mostly limited success as film performers. But their involvement in star searches arguably put them at the vanguard of new constructions of celebrity and social mobility in Britain, brought about by the rise of the cinema and its convergence with other forms of mass media.

This chapter explores the development of star search contests in Britain from World War I to the end of the 1920s. Whereas previous chapters have viewed events from the perspective of film actors and would-be film actors, this chapter begins by examining star searches from the point of view of their promoters. It asks who the promoters of star search competitions were, and how they attempted to use the popular appeal of film acting and film stardom to attract people as both performers and consumers. Viewing the treatment of would-be actors from the vantage point of interwar newsrooms, film production companies and advertising agencies sheds new light on the 'craze' for film acting in the 1920s and reveals how popular film culture in the silent era was shaped and increasingly appropriated by a variety of forces beyond the national – or even international – cinema industry. The chapter ends by following the experiences of Margaret Leahy, the winner of the most high-profile and contentious star search of the decade, as she made the journey from Britain to Hollywood and back again.

Fan magazine readers get their chance

In Britain, national film star searches reached their height during the interwar period, but they had their roots in wartime and pre-World War I practices. Competitions for would-be film actors had existed in Britain since the 1910s, forming part of the repertoire of promotional schemes used by cinema exhibitors to attract and engage audiences. Contests in Bristol and Torquay, which invited audience members to re-enact scenes from recent film releases for the amusement of other cinema patrons, were held up as examples of the 'advertising tips and wrinkles' that successful cinema owners should adopt.[7] The same kind of showmanship was evident at the first International Cinematograph Exhibition at London's Olympia in 1913. Designed to raise the profile of the British film industry, the event featured a contest in which members of the public were invited to perform in a short film scene, judged by a panel of leading producers including Cecil Hepworth and G.H. Cricks of Cricks and Martin. According to the organisers, more than 3,000 men and women from across London and its suburbs entered the contest during the week of the exhibition, attracting large crowds of spectators.[8] It was deemed successful enough that a similar competition was repeated at the following year's trade exhibition in Glasgow.[9]

During World War I, larger contests were organised by British fan magazines, alongside the other reader competitions and interactive features that were increasingly becoming part of popular film culture.[10] In September 1916, the *Picture Palace News* (later shortened to *Picture News*) launched what might be considered the first national film star search contest in Britain. Unlike later contests, this was open to both men and women, and was intended to provide 'budding Charlie Chaplins or Mary Pickfords' with a chance to make themselves known by sending in photographs that would be assessed by fellow readers.[11] But, while the competition clearly tapped into the rising popularity of film acting as a profession, there was little sense that the winners would automatically become stars themselves. The first prize, shared by a young man and a young woman from London, was not a role in a film, but a course of lessons at the Victoria Cinema College.[12]

More ambitious was the contest launched by *Pictures and the Picturegoer* in the summer of 1918, which aimed itself more firmly at female readers. The editor, Fred Dangerfield, claimed to be responding to letters asking why there was no British equivalent of the international stars who dominated British screens.[13] Open exclusively to women, the contest further stipulated that only British-born contestants would be eligible. They also had to be young (aged 15–25), and without prior stage or studio experience. Rather than receiving training, the winner would receive a supporting role in a British feature film to be made by the Broadwest Film Company, with the possibility of a longer contract.[14] In a format that would be replicated numerous times over the next decade, the 8,000 entrants were whittled down by an 'expert' panel to 14 finalists, who were then given screen tests at the Broadwest studios in Walthamstow.[15] After more than six months of magazine coverage, the winner, Alice 'Lavender' Lee from Yorkshire, was finally announced in March 1919.[16] In May, she was said to be rehearsing for a part in a Broadwest horseracing drama, and she was still being promoted by *Pictures and the Picturegoer* that July.[17] It is unclear whether her performance ever made it to the screen, but it is certain that the magazine's stated hope of launching a national rival to Mary Pickford didn't come to fruition. Nevertheless, the publicity generated by the contest fitted well with Broadwest's efforts elsewhere to promote itself as a forward-looking production company, with a commitment to building up a British film star system. Writing in the trade press soon after the '*Pictures* Girl' contest had concluded, the company's co-founder Walter West regretted the lack of well-known film actors in Britain, but shared his determination to find talent anywhere he could – 'in trains, 'buses, tubes, and restaurants' – in order to create films that would attract domestic audiences and could be marketed around the world.[18]

Fan magazines continued to host star searches in the post-World War I years. Towards the end of 1919, the short-lived magazine *Picture Plays* joined forces with another ambitious British production firm, the Alliance Film Corporation, which had recently been launched with much fanfare as the country's 'million pound' film company.[19] For this contest, the magazine (published by Walter Hutchinson, who also sat on the Alliance board of directors) offered three aspiring stars training in the Alliance studios.[20] In the 1920s, there was at least one further fan magazine competition, launched in the magazine *Picture Show*. In the summer of 1925, Edith Nepean, a novelist, publicist and regular contributor to the magazine, invited women readers to take a 'sporting chance' by sending in their photographs for the judgement of T.C. Elder, the joint managing director of Stoll Picture Productions.[21] Images of 'sporting chance' girls became a regular feature of Nepean's *Picture Show* column, and, after several months, 15 women were invited to attend screen tests at the Stoll studios in Cricklewood. Sybil Rhoda, the winning 'sporting chance' girl, was subsequently given a role in Stoll's *Sahara Love* (Sinclair Hill, 1926), and went on to act in several more British features, including *Downhill* (Alfred Hitchcock, 1927).[22] The Stoll screen tests themselves resulted in a two-reel film, *Starlings of the Screen* (1925), which was released commercially in cinemas.[23] The opening sequence, featuring the 'sporting chance' contestant Nancy Baird, dramatised the popular appeal of the star search contest. In it, a young *Picture Show* reader, introduced as 'One of the Three Thousand' entrants, sees Stoll's call for 'British girls' in the magazine, leaps to her feet and runs to her writing desk to dash off an application. In the next scene, she is at the Stoll studios getting ready for her screen debut. The ability of fan magazines to usher their readers into the world of film celebrity, already implicit in the chatty familiarity with which magazines spoke about stars, was further illustrated in the cover image celebrating Sybil Rhoda's triumph, in which her portrait seemed to burst through the paper, beside the heading 'A *Picture Show* reader gets her screen chance!' (Figure 4.1).[24]

Newspaper contests

While the star search was still a feature of post-World War I fan magazines, the film competitions that attracted the biggest numbers of entrants and generated the most discussion were connected to the national popular press. The first of these was launched in the *Sunday Express* in 1919 and took place against a background of changing newspaper readerships and fierce 'circulation wars'. While national newspapers in Britain grew in importance during the interwar years, finally outstripping the combined circulation levels of the provincial press in 1923, the market remained dominated by a small number of titles.[25] This led to intense competition

Figure 4.1. Sybil Rhoda, the winner of *Picture Show*'s 'sporting chance' contest. 'A *Picture Show* reader gets her screen chance', *Picture Show*, 10 October 1925, front cover. © Time Inc (UK) Ltd.

between rival newspaper groups, in which editors became reliant not only on eye-catching headlines and images, but also on reader contests, special offers and giveaways designed to boost readership.[26] The newspaper historian Harold Herd commented in 1927 that the modern mass-circulation newspaper was 'always on the alert for fresh ways of bringing itself to the public attention – attractive competitions, novel advertising schemes, new features and so on'.[27] The aim of these schemes was not simply to sell more copies of newspapers, but also to increase their value for advertisers, who now formed a crucial part of the press's financial calculations.[28]

From the perspective of newspaper proprietors, women were an especially underexploited, and therefore desirable, source of readers. In 1903, Lord Northcliffe, owner of the *Daily Mail*, launched the *Daily Mirror* as Britain's first national newspaper marketed explicitly at women. Although it was soon rebranded as a more general 'picture paper', it retained its emphasis on attracting a female readership.[29] The paper's decision in 1907 to launch the country's first national newspaper beauty contest for women can be seen as part of this editorial strategy.[30] The following year, the paper organised two more contests aimed exclusively at women to find chorus girls for London's Gaiety Theatre and its touring company.[31] A much bigger scheme, which began as a search for the most beautiful woman war worker, ran in the same paper from 1918 to 1919 and was followed by similar competitions to find beautiful 'Sports Girls' and 'British Girl Workers' in the 1920s.[32] As well as inviting participation from women, such contests were also designed to attract the attention of male readers, giving newspapers licence to fill their pages with images of attractive 'girls' and, in the process, contribute to the increasing sexualisation of women in the popular press.[33]

Newspaper proprietors soon became aware of the rising popularity of the cinema in Britain and took note of the potential to use film-related news to attract new readers. Lord Northcliffe wrote to the *Daily Mail*'s editor in 1919 to express his desire for 'more film matter with pictures', adding: 'I had no notion the topic of public conversation among all classes films have become.'[34] With or without such internal pressure, editors were quick to respond to changes in popular taste. Miriam Sabbage, the winner of the 1918–19 *Daily Mirror* beauty contest, became only one of numerous points of contact between the British popular press and the film industry when she reportedly made the transition from newspaper beauty queen to 'film star', following in the footsteps of the winner of the same paper's 1907–8 contest, Ivy Close.[35] By the 1920s, national newspapers routinely gave space to film reviews and cinema listings, along with coverage of visiting stars and news of events in American and British studios. The interest in incorporating more 'film matter' into newspapers reflects the broader role that the popular press took on in the interwar years in mediating between the British public and new forms of mass culture.[36]

The *Sunday Express*'s decision to launch a film star competition in 1919 can be understood as a further expression of the popular press's interest in courting film fans. Private correspondence between Lord Beaverbrook, the owner of the *Express* group, and his staff sheds light on the specific context in which Britain's first national newspaper star search took place. The Canadian entrepreneur Beaverbrook (formerly Sir Max Aitken) had taken over the *Daily Express* in 1916, expanding the company's operations to produce a Sunday edition of the paper from December 1918.[37] His aim in doing so was to make up for the poor sales of the weekday edition, but he found that the circulation figures for the new title were also low.[38] A letter sent to Beaverbrook in January 1919 advised that simply spending more money on advertising the paper would not be sufficient to remedy the situation, and suggested instead that the paper publish better quality content and 'something special to advertise and boom'.[39] A report from the company's circulation manager agreed, arguing that the *Sunday Express* needed to differentiate itself from its weekday counterpart. 'The public look for something different on Sunday,' the report explained, 'such as new writers, news of the week, songs, competitions, etc.'[40] Beaverbrook himself placed particular emphasis on the new title's appeal to a female readership, reportedly patrolling Hyde Park on Sundays to look for women reading the paper.[41] Over the coming months, the example of the *Pictures and the Picturegoer* contest, which reached its conclusion in March 1919, and the success of the *Daily Mirror*'s latest beauty contest, may have presented themselves as useful models for a paper in search of ways to generate publicity and attract female consumers. By the end of March, the *Sunday Express* was running a contest for film scenario writers, and at the start of April one of Beaverbrook's staff wrote to inform him that the details of another 'Cinema Competition' were nearly worked out.[42] The plan, the letter said, was 'to guarantee a two years' contract to the winner' and 'to get some producing firm to do this', noting that the Stoll Film Company had been approached already and was in favour of the idea.⁴³ Stoll evidently consented, and the competition was announced in the next edition of the *Sunday Express*, just four days later.⁴⁴

Similar to the *Pictures and the Picturegoer* contest, the *Sunday Express* scheme was open only to women. The eventual prize on offer was £200 cash, along with a role for the winner in a new Stoll feature film based on a popular novel.⁴⁵ In this way, the contest served as publicity both for the newspaper and for Stoll's production activities, which had begun on a modest scale the previous autumn.⁴⁶ While Stoll had not yet begun the concerted attack on American films that it would embark upon later in 1919, the company was already committed to a policy of adapting literary works by British authors as a means of distinguishing its output from the Hollywood products that dominated British screens.⁴⁷ The promotional rhetoric employed by the *Sunday Express* presented its Cinema Star Competition as a further contribution to strengthening the national film industry. 'Why is it that the majority of the film stars today are Americans?' the newspaper asked. 'We believe it is because many likely English girls have never had the opportunity.'⁴⁸ The contest also offered personal benefits to the woman who won. The job of the film actor, the paper said, meant an enviable salary and the chance of 'travelling and seeing the world'.⁴⁹ The contest apparently attracted so many entrants that the paper was forced to take on emergency staff to sift through the photographs.⁵⁰ As it drew to a close, 20 finalists chosen by a panel of journalists, artists and representatives from Stoll were taken on a 'cinema joy tour' of London, where they were treated to trips to West End theatres, cinemas and restaurants and to novelties such as river cruises and aeroplane flights, before being given screen tests by the director Maurice Elvey at the Stoll studios (Figure 4.2).⁵¹ As Rebecca Conway remarks of later British beauty contests, what was held out to women participating in the *Sunday Express* star search was not only fame and money, but also the chance to experience a previously inaccessible way of life that was dramatically different to their own.⁵² The contest also promised women the possibility of reinventing themselves. The winner, Tommy Sinclair, a former chorus girl from London, spoke of using the prize money to establish herself not only as a film actress, but also as a scenarist and songwriter.⁵³

Figure 4.2. Finalists in the 1919 *Sunday Express* Cinema Star Competition. 'On the first rung of the ladder of fame', *Sunday Express*, 29 June 1919, p. 2. © Sunday Express/N&S Syndication.

The *Sunday Express*'s involvement in a national star search scheme further highlights the British press's ambivalent and often contradictory attitude towards both film fans and young women in the post-World War I years. Throughout the 1920s, newspapers continued to voice criticisms of 'foolish', 'film-struck' girls and to repeat calls from film producers or concerned readers for anyone dreaming of film stardom to give up their 'ridiculous' and 'futile' ambitions.[54] At the same time, newspapers offered tips on 'acting for the "movies"', suggestions on the 'film faces' and types best suited to the screen and advice and encouragement from well-known stars.[55] Different attitudes towards film stardom could exist side by side or be expressed by the same journalists, depending on the context. Sydney Moseley, the writer who railed against the immorality of the film industry and the threat that studio work posed to young women in his 1920 exposé of *The Night Haunts of London*, was also the competition editor at the *Sunday Express* during its 1919 star search contest. Indeed, he later remembered making the arrangements for the final screen tests himself, and personally escorting the 'bevy of lovely girls' around the West End as part of their 'cinema joy tour'.[56] Such conflicting sentiments were not unusual in a popular press that thrived on turning the ambiguities of modern life into controversial 'talking points'.[57] In the right circumstances, papers could just as easily celebrate the lure of film stardom as they could warn of the dangers lurking behind studio gates.

Cinemagazine beauties

Along with fan magazines, film production companies and national newspapers, the makers of newsreels and cinemagazines were also involved in early star search contests in Britain. Newsreels, comprising short films of current world events, had been regular items in British cinema programmes since 1910.[58] Cinemagazines, so called because they imitated the general interest format of the print magazine rather than the current affairs focus of the newsreel, were a later addition, gaining in popularity during the interwar years, especially with women viewers.[59] Several star search competitions during this period played out across print and cinema platforms at the same time, illustrating the increasingly interconnected nature of media organisations as well as the concentration of news companies in a relatively small number of hands.[60]

For instance, in 1920, Lord Beaverbrook was indirectly involved in another star search. In this case, the impetus came not from the *Express*, but from one of his newer acquisitions. Beaverbrook became one of the first of the British 'press barons' to involve himself in the film business, when he invested considerable amounts of money in several cinema chains in 1919. The following year, he purchased a controlling interest in the British subsidiary of the French-owned film company Pathé Frères.[61] The company, which had once been a major fiction film producer, was now focusing its efforts on newsreel production, along with its distribution and exhibition arms, and it was reported that the main purpose of Beaverbrook's investment was to secure Pathé's 'topical reviews and news pictures' for his cinemas.[62] By this point, Pathé's news pictures included the long-running newsreel *Pathé Gazette* and the newer series *Pathé Pictorial*. Launched in 1918, this second title is generally regarded as the first cinemagazine in Britain, and it would go on to become one of the most enduring.[63] However, as Frank Smith, Pathé's general manager in Britain, explained in a letter to Beaverbrook, the *Pictorial* was originally conceived as a way of grouping together, and thus increasing the value of, Pathé's scientific and educational films, which had previously been booked by cinema exhibitors only as cheap 'fill-up' items to pad out their programmes.[64] But the cinemagazine soon developed its own identity. By 1920, a typical instalment, according to Smith, comprised a 'Pathécolor' travel film, an animal scene, novelty slow-motion footage, scenes of the latest fashions and dances, and films of celebrity 'artistes of every description', recorded in Pathé's small Wardour Street studio.[65]

At the start of 1920, Pathé was making a modest 25 prints of the *Pictorial* each week (compared to 220 copies of the twice-weekly *Gazette*), but it was already planning ways to increase circulation.[66] In February, Smith wrote of the company's intention 'to run a cinema Beauty Competition, in conjunction with the Press'. The competition apparently drew directly on a recent newspaper beauty contest in France, although Smith would doubtless have been aware of the earlier initiatives in the *Sunday Express* and British fan magazines.[67] The difference would be that, as part of the competition, Pathé would make screen tests of the entrants for inclusion each week in the *Pictorial*, and the public would then be asked to vote for their favourite contestants. Smith suggested that there could even be two contests, one for women and another for children. Films relating to the competition, he said, 'should be advertised in such a way as to force the exhibitors' hands'.[68] Presumably, as news films were booked on a monthly basis, this meant generating enough public interest in the contest over an extended period to ensure that cinemas would feel obliged to book the title for months at a time. When the contest was launched in March, cinema owners were reassured that there would be 'countless ways' to 'turn the Competition to account for their own advantage' by making use of newspaper marketing to attract patrons or by running their own tie-in publicity campaigns.[69]

Perhaps as a further fillip to exhibitors, entrants in the contest were asked to submit their photographs in person at participating cinemas.[70]

The Pathé Screen Beauty Contest, as it was known, ran until December 1920. It was advertised extensively in the popular press, with lengthy editorials appearing in Beaverbrook's *Express* newspapers. Although, in contrast to previous star searches, the winner was not promised a film contract, the competition was nevertheless presented as a way of 'giving every one a chance' of film stardom, and of redressing the balance in the world film market.[71] In the past, 'American girls [...] had the greater opportunity', said one editorial in the *Daily Express*, but now 'British girls with beauty and ability' would be able to demonstrate their talent on the screen, too.[72] Opportunities were also being extended to cinemagoers, newspapers claimed. Much was made of the central role played by public voting, which writers promised would both empower cinemagoers and ensure that the winner was selected on her merits, alone. 'Movie enthusiasts,' an editorial in the *Sunday Express* claimed, 'would just as soon see an English star as any other, provided she were equally appealing.'[73] Another article remarked that 'no fairer method' could be devised than introducing potential stars to the public via the screen. 'If a girl has possibilities, if she has talent, the screen will reveal them.'[74] In preparation for the public judging, it was said that more than 2 million voting cards were distributed to cinemas around the country.[75] The scale of audience involvement heightened the sense that cinemagoers were being given a democratic choice, with one newspaper headline dubbing the contest the 'Grace and Beauty Election'.[76] In this case, it was an election whose primary constituency – young women – was still excluded from the national political sphere.

From July 1920, screen tests of selected contestants, including several filmed on the picturesque grounds of Cherkley Court, Beaverbrook's Surrey estate, were shown in weekly instalments in the *Pathé Pictorial*.[77] More films of the six finalists were shown in October.[78] According to the 'exclusive' announcement in the *Sunday Express*, Phyllis Nadell, a 19-year-old hairdresser from Glasgow, won the popular vote with a majority of more than 13,000.[79] Surviving footage of Nadell performing in the Pathé screen tests, with her hair cropped and lipstick accentuating her cupid's bow mouth, suggests that British cinema audiences preferred a distinctly modern-looking type of feminine screen beauty.[80] But, although

Nadell was subsequently given professional screen tests by several film companies, the promise of a successful acting career for the winner failed to materialise.[81] In contrast, Pathé's plan to boost sales of its cinemagazine appeared to work. After the screen tests came to an end, staff at the company noticed a 'slight falling off' from the thriving sales figures that the *Pictorial* had enjoyed over the summer months, which they planned to rectify by embarking on another competition.[82]

Pathé was not the only firm to orchestrate a cross-media star search in 1920. Running simultaneously with the Screen Beauty Contest from March was a rival scheme for would-be actors, known as the Golden Apple Challenge.[83] The initiative was associated with the film company Gaumont, the cinemagazine *Around the Town*, the Northcliffe press and a group of theatre entrepreneurs. *The Bioscope* credited Northcliffe's *Daily Mail* with organising the scheme, but the idea could just as easily have come from Gaumont.[84] Since December 1919, Gaumont, which distributed *Around the Town*, had been marketing the new cinemagazine as a direct rival to the *Pathé Pictorial*.[85] *Around the Town*, whose motto was 'Beauty and Celebrity Everywhere', was intended as the cinematic equivalent of the newspaper gossip column, and Gaumont aimed its publicity efforts predominantly at attracting female patrons.[86] However, according to Pathé's internal survey of the newsreel and cinemagazine market at the start of 1920, the new title was struggling. 'I should not imagine that this film is a paying proposition,' Frank Smith reassured Beaverbrook, 'and unless it changes in the near future I should not be at all surprised to see it drop out of circulation.'[87] This may have been wishful thinking on Smith's part. But, as Pathé had already calculated, a long-running film star competition with a cinemagazine element could potentially boost Gaumont's bookings while also bolstering *Around the Town*'s intended appeal to women and its modern, aspirational image.[88]

Whether spearheaded by the Northfcliffe press or Gaumont, the Golden Apple Challenge closely shadowed the Pathé Screen Beauty Contest. Details of the competition were announced just days after the launch of the Pathé scheme, and it came to an end a week after the Pathé contest concluded.[89] Its main point of difference was that it sought to attract would-be stars for both the British cinema and the theatre. Gaumont held out the offer of a film contract, while the theatre impresarios Alfred Butt, Edward Laurillard and George Grossmith promised to help the winner find stage engagements. Potentially, said the *Daily Mail*, the 'Golden Apple Girl' could chose to split her time evenly between the two fields, undertaking 'film work by day and stage work by night'.[90] In practice, though, advertisements and editorials focused mainly on the attractions of film stardom, which was said to give British women the chance to be 'international' and to have 'the eyes of the whole world' upon them.[91] The screen tests, comprising short dramatic scenes, were also designed primarily to assess the contestants' film acting skills, including their 'bearing before a kinema camera' and 'the manner in which they express emotions'.[92] Out of a reported 26,000 photographs submitted to the contest, 150 women were chosen by regional panels of businessmen and local dignitaries for screen tests, which were shown in editions of *Around the Town* between July and September.[93] In December, the winner was named as Winifred Nelson, a ballroom dance teacher from Eastbourne.[94] She was later said to be rehearsing for a part in a specially written, although perhaps never completed, film produced by *Around the Town*.[95]

Despite their repeated claims to be looking for talent to strengthen the British film industry, early star searches failed to produce a British film star who could compete on the international stage. What the Pathé and Gaumont contests did provide, though, was a chance for entrants to see themselves not just in print, but also on screen. Newspapers captured the reactions of women watching themselves perform. Madeleine Polyblank, the third-prize winner in the 1920 Screen Beauty Contest, told the *Sunday Express* how nervous she was when she saw her screen test for the first time, adding: 'It was interesting and sometimes amusing to hear the comments of the audience sitting around me when my picture appeared.'[96] Throughout this time, the film trade press remained largely sympathetic towards star searches. Some writers saw them as evidence that British producers were trying to expand the pool of film acting talent beyond established theatre actors, while others argued that they represented a way of dealing fairly and 'generously' with the influx of applicants to British studios.[97] However, the next major star search competition in Britain would test the limits of these arguments, bringing the motives of contest organisers into question and leading to more vocal and often extremely hostile criticisms of the star search format.

A protégée for Norma Talmadge

The competition launched by the *Daily Sketch* in 1922 proved to be the most controversial British star search of the decade. While the exact origin of the contest remains difficult to trace, it involved a collaboration between a national newspaper company, the newsreel *Topical Budget*, the British film distribution company Film Booking Offices, the American company First National and the American film star Norma Talmadge. The first three of these were all owned by the press magnate Edward Hulton. Hulton, who had inherited a newspaper business from his father, founded the *Daily Sketch* in 1908 as a rival to the *Daily Mirror*.[98] Similar to Beaverbrook, in the years after World War I he expanded his financial interests in the film industry, buying a controlling share in the company behind the long-running newsreel *Topical Budget* in 1919, and joining the directorate of the British rental firm Film Booking Offices (FBO) soon afterwards, with the aim of securing a distribution channel for his newsreel series.[99] First National, known officially as Associated First National Pictures, was an American firm that had begun life as a network of exhibitors but had since made moves into the distribution and production sectors by commissioning films directly from well-known stars.[100] The American actress Norma Talmadge, who ran her own production company with her husband and producer Joseph Schenck, signed a deal with First National to distribute her films in 1919, as did her sister Constance.[101] Buster Keaton, the actress's brother-in-law through his marriage to the third Talmadge sister, Natalie, became part of First National's roster of participating stars in 1921.[102] All of these people would play a part in the contest's proceedings.

The premise of the 1922 contest, announced in the *Daily Sketch* in September, was that Norma Talmadge had asked the paper to help her find 'a true, typical British girl' to star opposite her in an upcoming feature film. The winner would be taken to America and transformed into 'a real, worthy star of the screen', who could then return, perhaps to make her own 'all-British production'. The *Sketch* emphasised the novelty of the contest and the magnitude of the prize. 'Never before has a newspaper done such a thing,' it said. 'Somewhere in England, Scotland, or Ireland there is a young woman who, although she doesn't know it to-day, is destined, perhaps, to be Britain's greatest star of the films.'

Talmadge's image presided over the article, and the paper reprinted a letter from the actress, in which she defended the film acting talents of British women:

> I have always said those who argue that British girls are not as good film actresses as American girls are very wrong. [...] I know the British girl has all the talents and the capabilities that go to make the successful screen actress – if only we can teach her to 'come out of her shell,' as we say in America – to escape repression and break the bonds of her fey reserve.

Talmadge's letter promised that the star would nurture the contest's winner as her 'protégée', giving her the benefit of 'the best and most considerate film producers in America', 'the best of its studios' and 'the warmest-hearted and most sincere celebrities of America's screen world'.[103]

Despite these personal touches, commentators and critics identified various ulterior motives behind the *Daily Sketch* scheme in the weeks that followed. The most common explanation, advanced in both the trade and popular press, was that the competition was a 'stunt' designed to publicise the release of Talmadge's latest film for First National, the historical romance *Smilin' Through* (Sidney Franklin, 1922).[104] Earlier in the year, First National had established a British distribution arm, which had been experimenting with new 'exploitation', or publicity, methods for its films, involving live performances, specially composed music and 'tie-ups' with national newspapers.[105] In September, the company's manager in Britain, Ralph Pugh, announced that First National was instituting a new release policy that came to be known as 'direct exhibition' or 'premiere runs', whereby its biggest films would no longer be premiered privately to the trade, but would instead be launched publicly in cinemas, accompanied by elaborate 'exploitation' practices in order, he said, 'to ensure that the picture fan does not stay away through ignorance of the event'.[106] The justification for this change was to allow the public to make up its own mind about new films rather than rely on the opinions of cinema owners or booking agents. But British exhibitors and distributors, who were already disgruntled by the uneven relationship in the Anglo-American film trade, argued that the real effect of this move would be to inflate the market value of 'indifferent' pictures through showmanship and 'purchased applause'.[107]

Talmadge's *Smilin' Through* was the first film released as part of this new distribution policy. The extensive publicity surrounding its release included the publication of souvenir sheet music and gramophone records, a window display in Selfridges department store and a newspaper advertising campaign 'booming both star and picture'.[108] It is possible that the *Daily Sketch* contest was conceived as part of this campaign. Harold Pontefract, Ralph Pugh's director of publicity, had previously held the same role at Pathé and may well have had a hand in its Screen Beauty Contest.[109] The fact that Talmadge was already en route to Europe for an extended promotional tour may have also suggested the possibility of a 'tie-up'.[110] In any case, *Smilin' Through* premiered in London on the same day as the announcement of the details of the *Daily Sketch* contest, and First National encouraged exhibitors booking the film to take full advantage of the publicity this generated.[111] In an echo of the local contests for would-be actors that had been popular a decade earlier, cinema owners around the country organised their own star searches. Some exhibitors gave out awards for the entrants who most resembled Norma Talmadge, while others asked audiences to decide which contestants should put themselves forward to compete for the *Daily Sketch* prize.[112] The manager of the Shaftesbury Pavilion in London invited any woman planning to enter the contest to attend a special screening of *Smilin' Through* at his cinema. Cameramen from the *Topical Budget* were on hand to film the crowd that gathered outside, which was big enough to block traffic along Shaftesbury Avenue.[113]

By the time the *Daily Sketch* competition closed in October, newsreels reported that more than 70,000 women had entered – more than double the number of contestants claimed for the Golden Apple Challenge two years earlier.[114] As with previous schemes, newspaper coverage emphasised the opportunities on offer to British women through film stardom, with a particular stress on the contest's egalitarian nature. The contest offered an 'equal chance for all', explained the *Daily Sketch*'s initial call for British film actresses.[115] 'Class, influence, and beauty are not to be taken into account against any girl,' said another editorial, 'for talent comes before looks or upbringing.'[116] The involvement of Norma Talmadge made such assertions particularly resonant. This was not least because of the various stories circulated about the star's own 'discovery' and rise to fame.[117] But it was also because, to many British film fans, the American cinema and its star system constituted a fundamentally democratic institution in which, as Christine Gledhill argues, social mobility appeared easier to achieve – both for stars and the characters they played – than it did in the class-bound British society of the interwar years.[118] Editorials about the *Daily Sketch* contest encouraged this image of American stardom and celebrated the fact that most of the British women entering were from 'modest walks of life'.[119] The newspaper even vied with Hollywood over the speed with which it could transform the contest winner into a star. 'The lightning leap into the world's arena of some of the American actresses,' the paper said, 'will appear a laborious performance compared to the rise of the lucky girl whose first step to fame will be the dispatching of her photograph to the *Daily Sketch*.'[120] In contrast to contemporary instructional guides to film acting, whose authors typically subscribed to a conventional belief in the value of patience, hard work and perseverance, the promoters of star searches offered a new message of luck, spontaneity and innate (but undiscovered) talent as the keys to success.

The winner of the *Daily Sketch* competition, chosen by Talmadge and announced in November 1922, was Margaret Leahy, a 20-year-old shop worker from London.[121] As a later section of this chapter shows, Leahy was quickly sent on a national publicity tour, before sailing for America. The plan was initially for Leahy to appear opposite Talmadge in *Within the Law* (Frank Lloyd, 1923), an adaptation of a popular stage melodrama, but she was eventually cast as the female lead in Buster Keaton's slapstick feature film *The Three Ages* (Buster Keaton and Edward F. Cline, 1923). When it came to Britain, months before it was shown in America, *The Three Ages* was handled not by First National, but by Hulton's distribution company FBO, who went about selling the film to exhibitors in advance (a practice known disparagingly as 'blind booking'), largely on the strength of Leahy's celebrity.[122] The response in certain sectors of the British film trade to these events was openly hostile. Fuelled partly by ill feeling over First National's new distribution policy, but also by a broader anti-American sentiment, trade journalists accused Talmadge, her distributors and the *Daily Sketch* of obliquely insulting British actors and the entire British film industry. An editorial in the magazine *Motion Picture Studio* complained that, 'while there are talented and experienced screen actresses literally starving' in Britain, the 'Talmadge stuntists' were looking instead for a new star 'behind the counters or in the offices, laundries and factories of this country'. In a backlash against the democratic premise of star searches, the magazine blamed the contest for encouraging 'otherwise sensible girls' to attempt to 'enter a world for which they are not fitted either by training, birth or breeding'.[123] *The Encore*, a specialist magazine for actors and variety performers, also closed ranks against untrained 'amateurs', suggesting that, if Talmadge and the *Daily Sketch* wanted to find a new British film star, they should 'visit the Kinema Club and the film agencies in Wardour Street', where professional actors in their hundreds were waiting for jobs.[124]

Whereas the trade press had been largely tolerant of or sympathetic towards earlier star searches, the involvement of an American star and an American company in such a high-profile British newspaper competition added to existing concerns about the modern 'exploitation' methods associated with Hollywood. In part, this can be seen as a belated recognition that the rapid changes in the world film market that had taken place during the war years, in which American genres and stars had become internationally popular, were not simply a temporary arrangement, and that, as a result, British film companies and film actors were chronically disadvantaged.[125] However, trade commentators went further in their objections by suggesting that 'American' publicity methods were incompatible with traditional British cultural values. 'We agree that exploitation is essential', said *Motion Picture Studio*, 'but not the soulless, conscienceless exploitation' practised by First National and the *Daily Sketch*, which, the article said, represented 'the worst kind of American sensationalism'.[126] In practice, the use of intensive advertising and distribution strategies such as direct exhibition and blind booking was not limited to American firms, just as star searches themselves were already a fixture of British film culture. But, as with other changes to the cultural landscape between the wars, the threat of America and 'Americanisation' became a convenient focus for anxieties over new ideas, standards of behaviour and ways of doing business.[127]

The controversy over the *Daily Sketch* contest partly explains why, when *The Three Ages* was released in the summer of 1923, the trade press dismissed Leahy's performance as that of a 'good-looking "extra girl"' and remarked that the film was essentially 'a "freak" attraction' that was all hype and no substance, relying 'upon publicity and not upon merit'.[128] The news, announced at the start of June, that Leahy herself had been invited to judge a follow-up star search in the *Daily Sketch*, this time to find a co-star for Constance Talmadge, was met with even more anger and bewilderment.[129] 'Could anything be more farcical', *Motion Picture Studio* asked, than a 'raw untrained amateur' recruiting 'yet another of these publicity protégées?'[130] The proposed contest never took place. But the response within the British production sector indicated that the star search format had become increasingly divisive, revealing new levels of antipathy towards Hollywood and the methods of star promotion that it had come to represent. Talmadge's reputation among cinema audiences in Britain, however, does not appear to have been harmed by her involvement in the competition. According to Lisa Stead's study of the magazine *Picturegoer*, in the decade between 1918 and 1928 both Norma and Constance Talmadge remained hugely popular with British fans, with Norma Talmadge being featured in its pages more times than any other female star besides Mary Pickford.[131]

Friday night is Amami night

In the immediate post-World War I years, competitions to find film stars in Britain were presented publicly as ways to revivify the national film industry, to deal fairly with the surplus of actors in British studios and to give young women access to a new and more glamorous life. Privately, they had been seen as ways to attract female newspaper readers, to boost the circulation of newsreels and cinemagazines and to increase the market value of films and film performers through publicity. In the late 1920s, there was a shift to a more internationalist rhetoric in the promotion of two British star search contests. Both were associated with production companies that had emerged as major producers in the wake of the 1927 Cinematograph Films Act. One of them also reflected the increasing convergence of cinema in Britain with other forms of consumer culture.

The two contests were launched within a month of each other early in 1928. In February, weeks after the protective legislation contained in the 1927 Films Act came into force, the Northcliffe newspaper the *Weekly Dispatch* (later renamed the *Sunday Dispatch*) noted that, because of 'the great expansion' in British production, the editors were receiving more letters from younger readers eager to take up film acting, and so had decided 'to institute a search for suitable "film faces"'.[132] Supporting the scheme was British Instructional Films (BIF), an older production company that had used the favourable conditions created by the passing of the Films Act to take a more decisive step into fiction filmmaking.[133] It was one of two contests in the *Weekly Dispatch* that BIF supported in 1928, the other being a competition to find a new film plot.[134] Once made, the newspaper explained, the prize scenario would provide the debut role for the winning British star.[135] The *Dispatch*'s Film Face contest ran until August, apparently attracting more than 30,000 submissions.[136] The panel assembled to judge the contest included BIF's new star director Anthony Asquith, the British artist Lewis Baumer and the Hollywood screenwriter Anita Loos, who ingratiated herself with readers by arguing that Britain 'beat the world for pretty girls'.[137] The winner, 16-year-old Kathleen Joyce, was pictured in the *Dispatch* receiving a cheque for £100 at the London Hippodrome, where she was performing in the chorus of a musical comedy, but neither Joyce nor the winning film plot seem to have made the transition to the screen.[138]

Running side by side with the *Weekly Dispatch*'s Film Face competition for much of 1928 was a competition known as the Amami Film Star Quest. Sponsored by the Amami shampoo brand, the contest aimed to find a 'Great British Film Star', who would be trained by British International Pictures (BIP) for a year and would then be given the chance to act in the company's films.[139] BIP was the biggest of the new firms launched around the time of the Films Act, having begun its ambitious production activities the previous year in a huge new studio complex at Elstree, which was optimistically nicknamed the 'British Hollywood'.[140] The panel assembled to judge the contest included two of BIP's highest profile stars, Carl Brisson and Lilian Hall-Davis, and its leading directors, Alfred Hitchcock and E.A. Dupont, whose mixture of British, Danish and German nationalities reflected the company's commitment to the internationalist 'Film Europe' movement.[141] Screen tests of selected 'Amami beauties' were made in Elstree in May, but the contest reopened in September and the winner, Eugenie Prescott from Cheshire, was finally announced in November.[142] She went on to appear in a number of BIP films, including *The Lady from the Sea* (Castleton Knight, 1929) and *A Romance of Seville* (Norman Walker, 1929).[143]

The background to Amami's involvement in the Film Star Quest, recorded in the pages of specialist advertising magazines, reveals much about the relationship that was developing between the film industry and the makers of consumer products in Britain in the 1920s, and shows how stars were beginning to take on the characteristics of commercial brands. Amami shampoo was widely used in Britain by the late 1920s. The brand's slogan, 'Friday night is Amami night', encouraged users to set aside a portion of their Friday evenings to take pleasure in the process of shampooing and styling their hair. According to women growing up in the interwar period, both the slogan and the Friday night ritual quickly entered into common use.[144] But, as an article published in the trade journal *Advertiser's Weekly* explained, at the start of the 1920s Amami was generally seen as a luxury product, costing twice the price of most shampoos and only popular in 'well-to-do districts'.[145] In 1923, in an effort to expand their business, the makers of Amami, Constance and Prichard, hired the services of an advertising expert, George S. Royds. He advised the company to bring the product to the mass market by 'cultivating the typists, the shop assistants, the factory and mill girls rather than their more prosperous sisters'.[146] Constance and Prichard agreed, and raised its annual advertising budget from £1,000 to £20,000 over just five years.[147] This increase reflected a more general trend in Britain, with national expenditure on advertising nearly doubling over the course of the 1920s.[148]

One of the strategies used extensively by Royds was to solicit testimonials from theatre and film stars.[149] Celebrity testimonials had been a feature of advertising since the late nineteenth century, when cosmetics companies, in particular, had sought endorsements from famous theatre actresses and 'postcard beauties' in order to lend credibility to the claims they made for their products.[150] American film actors, notably Mary Pickford, were paid to endorse products from the mid-1910s, and, by the 1920s, film star endorsements were increasingly common for a wide range of goods.[151] In Britain, Betty Balfour lent her name to brands including LUX soap, Pond's Vanishing Cream, Odol's toothpaste and Kia-Ora lemon squash.[152] The actor John Stuart promoted Ovaltine and 'the fine mellow flavour of Turf Cigarettes'.[153] Amami looked mainly to Hollywood for its early film celebrity testimonials, recruiting stars such as Edna Purviance, Irene Rich, Phyllis Haver and Clara Bow and capitalising on their glamourous and fashionable screen personae.[154]

Running competitions for Amami users was the other main strategy that Constance and Prichard adopted during the 1920s to turn the shampoo into a mass-market brand. In 1924, Royds orchestrated a search for a new stage star in collaboration with the theatre impresario André Charlot. The success of this search, according to *Advertiser's Weekly*, prompted 'nearly a score of contests' over the following years. 'Films and beauty are the basis of all the most successful' competitions, the magazine said.[155] The marketing for the Film Star Quest demonstrated how both subjects could be intertwined as part of fantasies of stardom. Entry to the contest was only possible by sending away for a free 'beauty book', which also contained photographs of 'famous Amami beauties' for contestants to consult and emulate.[156] Newspaper advertisements for the contest offered more striking depictions of media celebrity for women to imagine themselves into. A typical advertisement presented a glamorous woman in an evening gown, poised on a staircase and turning her face to a movie camera, in a scene representing what the text described as 'The magic gates of Filmdom opening for HER' (Figure 4.3).[157] Another advertisement declared: 'You – famous! Think of it. Dream of it. You, a great film star. Your name outside every cinema. Your photograph in all the magazines. The most talked of young lady in the country.'[158]

Through its star testimonials and competitions, Amami appealed to the idea, gaining momentum in the interwar years, that cosmetics and other beauty products, previously associated with 'loose' morals or prostitution, now offered women new and legitimate modes of self-expression and self-fashioning.[159] This idea had much in common with the promise that star searches held out to their contestants, namely that women could realise their full potential or reinvent themselves through participating in the dynamics of celebrity. The identities of the women who won Amami's theatre and film star searches were sometimes literally reinvented to transform them into ambassadors for the Amami brand. Miss Kathleen June Punchard, winner of the 1924 Stage Career Scheme, became Kathleen Amami when she appeared to theatregoers, while the winner of a studio apprenticeship with BIP, Eugenie Prescott, was likewise rechristened Eugenie Amami for the duration of her brief film career.[160] Like established film stars, she was also used by Amami as the basis for more tie-in contests, in which Amami consumers were asked to identify the emotions she was registering in a series of photographs – 'disbelief or teasing', 'surprise or thrill'? – or to choose the Hollywood hero who would look best opposite

Figure 4.3. Advertisement for the 1928 Amami Film Star Quest. 'To some lucky Amami girl', *Weekly Dispatch*, 11 March 1928, p. 9. Courtesy of Cambridge University Library.

her – 'Ronald Colman or John Gilbert? Clive Brook or Jack Holt?' – for the chance of winning cash or luxury goods.[161]

From the perspective of advertisers, the only note of caution about the use of star searches as a marketing tool was the suggestion that the majority of women, who were never chosen for stardom, might harbour feelings of resentment. *Advertiser's Weekly* said, 'it is plausible that every advertisement in which the fortunate winner figures [...] serves to give the unsuccessful competitors a little pang of regret', which, the magazine added, could have a negative effect on sales.[162] But, by the end of the 1920s, the brand's strategy had, in any case, moved away from star searches to smaller monthly competitions, of which the expense for promoters and the stakes for competitors were lower.[163] This shift fed into a larger pattern, which would become more prominent during the decade that followed, in which the desire for film stardom, especially for women, was channelled into forms of consumption both inside and outside the cinema.[164] Women who might have felt excluded from the fame and fortune offered to winners of star search contests could nevertheless hope to partake in the film star 'look' – for instance by wearing fashions or cosmetics popularised in films, or, as one Amami advertisement suggested, by using commercial beauty products to acquire 'film-star hair' and to participate vicariously in the film star lifestyle.[165]

Cinderella of the films: Margaret Leahy

In the correspondence between newspaper and film industry managers and in the reports of advertising men, the winners of film star competitions typically appeared as afterthoughts. At best, they were seen to generate opportunities for further publicity efforts, whether for the films they acted in, the newspapers and newsreels they continued to feature in or the products they endorsed. But star search winners also took on a larger cultural significance. For critics, they became symptomatic of a 'film-struck' populace, while, in the idealised imagery of promoters, they were emblems of opportunity and upward social mobility. Like the winners of other beauty contests in the interwar years, and similar to established British film stars, they were also frequently invoked as symbols of national identity.[166] Examination of the press coverage of Margaret Leahy, the winner of the 1922 *Daily Sketch* contest, shows how early star search contestants could take on multiple meanings at once. The fragments of documentation Leahy left behind also suggest her own attempts to negotiate these different roles.

Margaret Leahy was 20 years old when she was chosen as Norma Talmadge's British protégée (Figure 4.4). She was born around 1903 in Bermondsey, South London, the daughter of a ship's steward.[167] Writing in the *Daily Sketch* shortly after her selection, she described herself as Irish and spoke of her tomboyish childhood, her desire to provide for her parents during the war years and her 'inclination towards fashion work', which led her to find employment in a clothes shop in Brixton.[168] The newspaper made much of Leahy's identity as a shop girl who had been suddenly

Figure 4.4. Margaret Leahy, the '*Daily Sketch* Girl'. Postcard, *c.* 1922. Author's collection.

transported to fame. Elaborating on early coverage of the contest, which had described the fate awaiting the winner as the story of a 'Cinderella of the films', the novelist Olive Wadsley reimagined Leahy's life for *Daily Sketch* readers as the romance of a 'New Cinderella':[169]

> Think of a girl who is twenty going every day in a motor-bus or tube to work, and tapping out typing or adding up numbers or measuring stuffs, or doing something everyone else does. And then one morning she finds that that side of her existence has been swept away. She has been swept utterly out of the humdrum of life into the land of sheer romance.[170]

In the weeks and months that followed, the newspaper continued to refer to Leahy as the 'Cinderella Girl' or 'the world's most famous "Cinderella"', describing Talmadge as Leahy's 'beautiful fairy godmother' and even circulating an anecdote about an admirer who found Leahy's missing shoe aboard her ship to America.[171] Such stories lent themselves easily to parody. Several years later, Bernard Rolt's novel *Cinderella of the Cinema* (1927) satirised the contest and its claims to be a 'fairy tale come true'.[172] In Rolt's version, a newspaper scheme to find a 'Little English Sister' for an American star prompts 'severe attacks of film fever' in 'the brains of the shop-girls, typists' and 'chorus ladies' of Britain, 'making them ruinously dissatisfied with their present spheres in life'.[173] Rolt's novel offered a paternalist corrective to what it clearly saw as the *Daily Sketch*'s distorted definition of success for women. Coming to her senses, his winner eventually gives up her place in the studio and instead decides to concentrate her efforts on becoming 'famous at home' for her new husband.[174]

Whereas other star search winners in the 1920s quickly faded from public view, Margaret Leahy continued to feature in the *Daily Sketch* and in Edward Hulton's newsreel, *Topical Budget*, long after the contest ended. The day after she won, it was announced that Leahy would tour the country in order to satisfy the 'universal desire' to meet the 'Cinderella of the Film' in person.[175] She made her public debut at the Marble Arch Pavilion cinema in London, where her screen test was shown, then travelled to towns and cities including Brighton, Glasgow, Sunderland, Leeds, Manchester, Liverpool, Birmingham and Bristol, dining with local dignitaries and making personal appearances at cinemas and theatres.[176] Throughout her tour, Leahy – or 'Bubbles', as she was familiarly known – was accompanied by Olive Wadsley, who continued to translate her activities into the language of romance, and Percy Phillipson, the British sales manager for First National.[177] She was also closely followed by cameramen from *Topical Budget*, who filmed her visiting hospitals, attending welcome receptions and receiving flowers from crowds of admirers.[178] Luke McKernan notes that, during a nine-week period towards the end of 1922 that also saw the dramatic break-up of David Lloyd George's coalition government and a subsequent general election, the combined coverage of the *Daily Sketch* contest, Norma Talmadge's visit to Britain and Leahy's victory tour made up around a fifth of the newsreel's entire output.[179]

After Leahy sailed for America at the end of November, the *Daily Sketch* continued to follow her progress, printing accounts of her voyage across the Atlantic, her arrival in New York and her cross-country journey to California. In the first of her regular 'week end letters' to the newspaper, Leahy described her initial impressions of America and her meetings with notable film industry figures such as Will Hays and D.W. Griffith.[180] By the end of December, she was with her mother and the Talmadges in Los Angeles, preparing for her role in *Within the Law*. In recording the details of her day-to-day life in the American movie colony, Leahy's letters mediated the glamour of Hollywood in much the same way as Mark Glancy says of British fan magazines, by depicting the stars she encountered as people who are 'very nearly British', but who 'happen to live in a distant utopia of wealth, beauty and fulfilment'.[181] 'Everyone was so kind to me,' Leahy wrote in one of her weekly cables to the *Daily Sketch*, describing Christmas dinner at the Talmadge household. 'They seemed so much like home girls I could hardly imagine so many of them were famous all around the world.'[182] Leahy's stories of life in Hollywood also established her as a transatlantic star in her own right, inhabiting a world in which national identity sometimes seemed to matter less than the shared experiences of celebrity culture.[183]

If Leahy's letters occasionally blurred the boundaries between Hollywood and her home life in Britain, her role as a national representative on the world stage was never entirely forgotten. At the start of 1923, it was announced that Leahy would not be appearing opposite Talmadge in *Within the Law*, but would instead be taking a role in Buster Keaton's comedy *The Three Ages*. According to Keaton's biographers, this was the result of complicated behind-the-scenes negotiations. Talmadge's director, Frank Lloyd, disliked Leahy's performance and threatened to quit the film unless she was replaced. Fearing legal repercussions if the terms of Leahy's prize weren't honoured, Joseph Schenck persuaded Keaton to step in, arguing that Leahy's involvement in the film would, at the very least, increase its earnings on the British market.[184] To the American press, First National's publicity manager explained the decision by saying that Leahy had shown 'a special aptitude for comedy'.[185] In the *Daily Sketch*, it was reported that Leahy had been advanced to a starring role straight away, beating almost 'every actress in America' to the part.[186] As she made preparations to return to Britain for the premiere of *The Three Ages* later in the year, a message printed in the *Daily Sketch* expressed Leahy's desire 'to "make good," not only for myself – but for England'.[187]

The *Daily Sketch* promoted Leahy's homecoming with the same intensity that had accompanied her departure for Hollywood seven months earlier. Editorials reported on her achievement in becoming 'a star of the first magnitude' in record time, calling her (with echoes of Mary Pickford) 'England's Sweetheart' and looking ahead to her next big picture with Buster Keaton.[188] Her daily appearances in the newspaper were closely tied to FBO's marketing campaign for the British release of *The Three Ages*, which was aggressively advertised to exhibitors and audiences. It was said that Leahy was personally transporting the prints of the film with her on the ship from America.[189] 'Never before have managers bought a picture which they have not seen in advance,' the *Daily Sketch* dubiously announced, 'but they have been so besieged by their regular patrons for a sight of Margaret in the "Three Ages" that they have found it impossible to resist the demand.'[190] Having never acted in a feature film before, Leahy, much as her screen debut, was being sold on the promise of greatness. It wasn't only Hulton's businesses that were involved in creating so much advance publicity. Crowds reportedly gathered outside Selfridges the day before her arrival to see the illumination of an electric sign on the front of the store announcing 'Margaret Leahy, the *Daily Sketch* Girl, will arrive in London at 5.56 Friday evening.'[191] In the run-up to her return to Britain, Leahy was also recruited by Constance and Prichard to be the judge of the company's earliest Amami tie-in competition, for which she was tasked with finding an Amami user with 'the hair of a film star'. Advertisements for the scheme referred to Leahy as 'Britain's Ambassadress to Filmdom' and deferred to her expertise as 'the one British girl who really understands what Los Angeles seeks in Beauty types'.[192]

Writers in the trade press were eager to keep Leahy's celebrity status in check. When she eventually arrived back in Britain at the end of June and made her radio debut on the BBC's 2LO service, broadcasting a message of thanks in a show called 'Among the Film Stars in Hollywood', the *Kinematograph Weekly* accused the BBC of airing what amounted to 'the baldest possible Hollywood whitewashing publicity', and protested against the radio announcer's description of Leahy as a 'distinguished British film-star'.[193] The trade paper's objections did little to curb the media hype. After a brief and much-publicised visit to Paris, supposedly to film scenes for her next film, Leahy was feted at a charity concert organised by the *Daily Sketch* at the London Hippodrome, where the song 'Normarose', specially composed in honour of Talmadge's protégée, was performed for the first time.[194] The following day, she was the guest of counts and countesses at the Carlton Hotel and the House of Commons, before finally appearing at the Marble Arch Pavilion for the gala screening of *The Three Ages* that evening. Before the film, Leahy asked the assembled audience of minor royals, journalists, famous beauties and theatre stars to remember that it was only her first production. 'I am, after all, just a Brixton shop girl,' she said. 'But I shall work very hard to be better and better as my career goes on, and then, some day, I hope you will greet me here and say I have done well.'[195] Afterwards, she embarked on another lengthy promotional tour of the provinces, visiting cinemas, making more radio broadcasts and greeting crowds.[196] Despite the negative response to *The Three Ages* in the British trade papers, its producers back in America recorded a successful performance on the international market.[197] Possibly through Schenck's influence, Leahy was named one of the upcoming 'Baby Stars of 1924' by the Western Motion Picture Advertisers (the 'Wampas') in Hollywood.[198] However, *The Three Ages* was to be Margaret Leahy's only feature film appearance.

The details of Leahy's later life are less well documented. The reported second feature film with Buster Keaton was never made. At the end of 1923, the *Motion Picture Studio* reported that Leahy had instructed lawyers to issue a writ against Edward Hulton, the editor of the *Daily Sketch*, Joseph Schenck, and Norma and Constance Talmadge for breach of contract, fraudulent misrepresentation, conspiracy and libel.[199] By 1924, fan magazines were fielding questions from readers asking where Leahy had gone; the following year, editors were able to tell them that she had moved back to Los Angeles to marry a businessman.²⁰⁰ This was presumably Ernest Vogt, the owner of a horse-riding school in Beverley Hills, whom she divorced in 1935, testifying that he had been withholding a fair share of his considerable income from her.²⁰¹ Acquaintances later told Keaton's biographers that Leahy had worked for a time as an interior decorator in a Los Angeles department store, that she had grown to hate the movies and that she had once made a bonfire of her Hollywood scrapbooks.²⁰² Relatives who remained in South London remembered Leahy visiting Britain in the 1960s, by which point her film career was no longer discussed.²⁰³ She died towards the end of the decade, apparently committing suicide by drinking drain cleaner.²⁰⁴

Leahy's story after the release of her first film reads less like the narrative of success scripted for her in newspaper and newsreel coverage and more like one of the growing number of cautionary tales about the Hollywood film industry that purported to reveal 'the hidden dangers of success, ambition, and career'.²⁰⁵ Beyond her weekly letters to the *Daily Sketch*, her experiences of studio life and fame remain largely hidden. But, in spite of the reports that Leahy destroyed her scrapbooks, some personal traces of her time in America have survived in the form of a photograph album and a book of newspaper clippings that have been passed down through her extended family.²⁰⁶ The album contains family portraits, publicity stills and snapshots, capturing Leahy on location in California during the filming of *The Three Ages*. The photographs depict a more relaxed atmosphere than the troubled production recorded by Keaton's biographers (Figure 4.5).²⁰⁷ The album also suggests that, as much as she was in training to become a star, Leahy remained a film fan. Pasted around her own images are souvenir postcards of the homes of Charlie Chaplin, Harold Lloyd, Mae Murray and other people she may have encountered during her time with the Talmadges. The book of newspaper clippings, apparently compiled by Leahy (though it frequently refers to her in the third person), is a meticulous record of the coverage she received in the *Daily Sketch* from the day after she was named Talmadge's protégée to the release of her debut film.²⁰⁸ In the margins, there are glimpses of Leahy's response to the newspaper stories published about her, as she sought to revise or challenge the public version of events. Typed annotations next to press cuttings about

Figure 4.5. Margaret Leahy with Buster Keaton on the set of *The Three Ages* (Buster Keaton and Edward F. Cline, 1923). Images from the Margaret Leahy Collection, courtesy of the British Universities Film & Video Council.

her personal appearances and statements to journalists and broadcasters remark 'unsure she ever said this', 'untrue', or simply 'This story is a complete fake'. Interspersed throughout the scrapbook, these notes represent Leahy's small but ongoing attempts to keep a true account of her day-to-day life in the face of the increasingly elaborate mechanisms of star publicity.

In the late 1910s and 1920s, film star search contests offered a condensed but powerful version of the stories of overnight success circulated in studio press releases, fan magazines and fiction. Looking at the development of star searches in Britain from popularity contests in specialist fan magazines to sophisticated media events offers a fuller picture of a number of aspects of British film culture during the silent period, including the relationship between cinema and the popular press, attitudes towards film marketing and the relationship between the British and American film trades. Following the experiences of people who took part in star searches, such as Margaret Leahy, can provide evidence of how the celebrity culture taking shape during the interwar years impacted on individual lives, and how its dynamics were interpreted by contemporary observers. Leahy's role as a marketing tool, not only for her own films, but also for other consumer products, demonstrates an awareness on the part of actors and producers of the commercial potential of film stardom outside the cinema. By the 1920s, leading film actors could increasingly expect to trade on, and be traded for, their value as recognisable brands.[209] Leahy's experiences in Britain and Hollywood were unique, but the status ascribed to her in newspapers, newsreels and film publicity as a representative of national identity was also one shared, to a greater or lesser extent, by all British performers who appeared in front of the movie cameras. While the international flow of images through cinemas, newspapers and fan magazines allowed for new kinds of transatlantic or global celebrity in the 1920s, the pressure on British actors and would-be actors to 'make good' for the sake of Britain and its film industry was still strongly felt.

Epilogue: From silence to sound

I began this book by following a young woman, Winifred Hopcroft, in her attempts to become a 'second Mary Pickford' in the post-World War I British film industry. Looking back from the vantage point of the early twenty-first century, the world she encountered appears both strange and familiar. The moral panic and derision that would-be film stars provoked in the pages of interwar newspapers and novels can be seen as part of the larger fascination with young women, and especially with changes in women's public behaviour, fashions and career expectations, that now seems characteristic of the 1920s.[1] Yet, women's aspirations and the role of celebrity culture in shaping those aspirations are still the subject of much debate in Britain today, as journalists, politicians and educators attempt to understand, and in many cases assuage, young people's seemingly unhealthy appetite for fame.[2] There is a history of ambition and fantasy surrounding media celebrity in Britain that stretches back from modern-day talent shows such as *The X Factor* to the film star quests of the interwar years, which remains unexplored. The men and women growing up in Britain in the 1910s and 1920s surely occupy an important place in that history. They were part of the first generation to imagine themselves on screen, the first to witness the glamour of the Hollywood star system and the power of its international publicity machine in action, and the first to find themselves at the centre of a wide range of marketing campaigns that promised them that their dreams of stardom were not only reasonable, but also attainable.

While there are significant continuities between the early fascination with film acting as a profession and contemporary cultural preoccupations, the end of the 1920s also saw important changes in the way film acting was practised and perceived in Britain. Some of the changes stemmed from new institutional structures that followed the passing of the 1927 Cinematograph Films Act. These included the formation of several British film companies into vertically integrated 'combines' and the increased involvement of American studios and distribution companies in British production.[3] But the most dramatic developments in the film industry, and the actor's place within it, undoubtedly resulted from the introduction of sound technology. There had been attempts to synchronise films with spoken dialogue since the cinema's first decades. But these early initiatives ultimately failed because of the lack of suitable amplification. In an average-sized cinema, Cecil Hepworth later recalled of his 1908 'Vivaphone' sound system, the sound of accompanying speech or song from an ordinary gramophone 'was like a bee trying to make itself heard in the Albert Hall'.[4] The decisive shift from silent cinema to sound cinema in Britain began towards the end of the 1920s, about a year later than in America. The Warner Brothers musical *The Jazz Singer* (Alan Crosland, 1927), which has been seen as a turning point in the history of film sound, had its British premiere at the Piccadilly Theatre in London on 27 September 1928, a year after its debut in New York.[5] It was closely followed that October by another Warner Brothers production, the 'all-talkie' crime film *The Terror* (Roy Del Ruth, 1928).[6] Despite the interest generated by these releases, the spread of sound films outside London's West End was relatively slow. Feature-length sound films did not arrive in Glasgow or Birmingham until December 1928, while audiences in smaller cities such as Nottingham waited until the following summer for their first experience of the new talking pictures.[7] Although filmmakers and commentators would soon look back on the coming of the talkies as a radical break with what had come before, in reality the period of transition from silent to sound films in the exhibition sector was gradual and uneven, lasting until at least 1931, and in some cases as late as 1933, when a handful of British cinemas had yet to be wired for sound.[8]

Epilogue: From silence to sound

During this transitional period, it was not immediately clear what the impact of sound technology would be on film production. Some commentators, such as Lionel Collier in *Picturegoer*, envisaged a future in which silent films and sound films would co-exist. Cinema had become too international, Collier argued, and the flow of film personnel around the world too free to be suddenly 'restricted by dialogue'.[9] Other journalists suggested that dialogue sequences would remain a novelty, similar to the use of colour or sound effects, within otherwise silent films. In the spring of 1929, R.J. Whitley in the *Daily Mirror* thought that dialogue would be used sparingly 'to emphasise the dramatic high spots' of a film, while G.A. Atkinson in the *Daily Express* wrote that in most films 'talk will dwindle to not more than 30 per cent of the average running time'.[10] For some time after the arrival of sound films, the implications of the new technology for film actors in Britain were also uncertain. In her 1929 guide to *Film Acting as a Career*, Lilian Bamburg predicted the rise of a new type of film performer, the 'Talkie actor', who would be distinct from counterparts in either theatre or silent film. Over the next few years, she said, 'there is going to be a big demand for Talkie actors'; meaning, 'if you can talk pleasantly, in a cultured voice, you stand a very excellent chance of securing a small part'.[11]

British companies had travelled to America to record synchronised dialogue sequences by the end of 1928, but changes in British studios only began in earnest during 1929.[12] By March, British International Pictures (BIP) had constructed the first of its sound studios at Elstree. This was a small, temporary structure, built within the walls of an existing building and lined with heavy drapes and other sound-absorbing materials. To avoid excess noise, the camera was encased in a wooden, lead-lined box, with a larger booth concealing the sound-recording equipment and its operators.[13] Other British producers soon followed suit. In June, the glass roof of the earliest of Gaumont's studios at Shepherd's Bush was permanently sealed and covered over in order to eliminate echo, while a 'cathedral calm' descended on the Gainsborough Pictures studios in Islington later that month, when the usually loud atmosphere was muffled by more layers of drapes and insulation material.[14] By the end of 1929, a number of other firms had installed sound-recording equipment, and BIP alone had produced 16 feature length talkies or 'part-talkies'.[15]

For actors in British film studios, the advent of sound brought with it some notable short-term effects on working conditions. It was initially planned that production at BIP's temporary sound stage at Elstree would take place mainly at night, when there was less chance of outside noise.[16] But the production diaries of the assistant sound recordist David Cunnynghame for 1929 show that the studio instituted both day and night shifts for its workers, in an attempt to get maximum use of the expensive sound equipment.[17] In June 1929, production at Twickenham was also said to be going on 'round the clock', with two casts at work on separate talkie versions of the same film, *At the Villa Rose* (Leslie S. Hiscott/ Louis Mercanton, 1930) – one in English, the other in French.[18] The practice of making multiple-language versions of films was a response to the challenge of international distribution posed by synchronised dialogue. Noting this development, Lilian Bamburg suggested that, for the would-be 'Talkie actor', 'some slight knowledge of French or German will be valuable in securing your advancement on the Screen'.[19] British companies collaborated in a number of multilingual film productions, notably *Atlantic* (E.A. Dupont, 1929), which was filmed in German, French and English. However, the practice effectively stopped by 1932, as improvements made in dubbing and subtitling processes ultimately resulted in fewer international employment opportunities for British actors beyond America.[20]

There were other long-term effects of the transition to sound on the professional prospects of film actors. The 'terror of the microphone' experienced by silent film stars in Hollywood, who worried that their voices might not suit the demands of the talkies, has been well documented in histories of the American film industry and mythologised in fictional accounts of the movie business such as *Singin' in the Rain* (Gene Kelly and Stanley Donen, 1953).[21] In Britain, many actors and commentators actively welcomed the introduction of sound. Perhaps inevitably, given the heightened sense of what Mark Glancy calls 'film nationalism' surrounding the passing of the 1927 Films Act, the advent of sound at the end of the 1920s was seen in some quarters as precisely the boost that British production needed to secure its status on the domestic and international markets.[22] The release of early Hollywood talkies in Britain prompted much comment among film reviewers about the voices of their American stars. To many ears, the unfamiliar accents emanating from cinema loudspeakers sounded jarring and incongruous. Surely, it was thought, audiences in Britain and its Empire would much prefer to hear British English spoken than what one reviewer called the 'metallic Americanism' of Hollywood dialogue.[23] Lilian Bamburg agreed, noting that, while 'Americans were the pioneers of the Talking films', they had 'overlooked the fact that the American voice was the last thing suitable for reproduction purposes on the screen'. The accents of British actors, she suggested, would be more familiar and more palatable to audiences than the 'national nasal twang' of the Americans.[24]

There were also practical reasons for some actors to celebrate the microphone's presence in the film studio. Brian Aherne, who had resented the noise and interference of the directors and crew in his silent film work, remembered the very different atmosphere on the set of his first sound feature, *The W Plan* (Victor Saville, 1930), which had been filmed in Elstree:

> [W]e, the actors, did all the talking just as we had been trained in the theatre; the director, the cameramen, and their technical retinues were all deprived of their megaphones and huddled into small glass-fronted, unventilated booths in which they crouched miserably with cameras, able only to make signs at us, when we bothered to look at them.[25]

For Aherne, sound technology freed film performers to be more attentive and expressive. Without the distractions of hammering and 'mood music', he said, 'we could think at last about our lines and pay attention to our acting'.[26] Chili Bouchier was more circumspect about the changes that sound recording brought. 'I arrived on the set,' she wrote, remembering the experience of shooting her first talkie sequences in *The City of Play* (Denison Clift, 1929), 'to find my lover, my beloved camera, confined to a padded cell.' Although she found the microphone restricted her movements around the set, she adapted relatively quickly to the new production methods, having gained experience of delivering lines in amateur dramatics and having already been made self-conscious enough about her non-standard 'Fulhamish' accent during her silent film days to alter her speaking voice.[27] In contrast, Mabel Poulton fared less well in front of the microphone. The problem, as she remembered, was her East London accent, which proved resistant to elocution lessons and which went against the emerging conventions of 'proper' film speech, as informed by existing theatrical and radio practice.[28] 'No actor was allowed to have regional accents in those days,' Bouchier wrote, 'and everyone had to speak BBC posh.'[29] In the British cinema of the 1930s, sound would bring to the fore new issues of class and regional affiliations, as well as national identity, which, in time, would alter the ways in which a film actor's public persona was crafted and understood by audiences.[30]

In some respects, the introduction of sound brought studio conditions for actors closer to those of the stage. The British-based director Alberto Cavalcanti later remarked that, at the start of the sound period, 'actors from the theatre poured into the studios', bringing with them different styles of acting, which, as in the period of early cinema, had to be adapted 'all over again' to make them suitable for the screen.[31] Certainly, many British producers invested in the screen rights to stage plays, or recruited entire theatre companies, in the rush to utilise the new technology. Herbert Wilcox at British and Dominions, for instance, engaged players from the Aldwych Theatre in 1929 to film a number of their popular stage farces, and other production companies formed close links with the theatre world in the years that followed.[32] It could be argued that this was simply an extension of the close links between British film and theatre formed during the silent period. Moreover, any increase in the overlap between stage and screen may have had as much to do with other changes to the post-Films Act industry, in which makers of the so-called 'quota quickies' (cheap films made to fulfil the terms of the Act's quota legislation) often turned to experienced stage talent in order to find actors who could take on a role with minimal rehearsal time.[33] Nevertheless, it is true that, during the 1930s, sound opened the studio doors for many theatre-trained actors, as well as singers, dancers and music hall performers, such as Stanley Lupino, Jessie Matthews and Gracie Fields, who would become important additions to British films.[34]

Sound also had an effect on the popular understanding of film acting as a profession. As the 1920s came to an end, the assumption that sound films required a 'cultured' speaking voice, as Lilian Bamburg put it, became a significant barrier to entry for many people who might otherwise have imagined themselves in a film career. Whereas ten years earlier a working-class girl such as Mabel Poulton could be advised by an acting school to choose film over theatre work because her 'slight Cockney accent' would matter less in the silent medium, this argument carried less weight in the era of the talkies.[35] A woman who responded to the sociologist J.P. Mayer's survey of cinema audiences in the 1940s remembered how, as a teenager during the transition to sound, she 'often dreamed how lovely it would be to be a famous star in films'. But, she added, 'I never went to any lengths to study Dramatics or Elocution, or anything that might have helped.'[36] Other people did pursue training to prepare or reinvent themselves for the demands of the microphone. Acting tutors, similar to actors, had to adapt to the times. Just as 'cinema schools' thrived on the popular enthusiasm for film acting in the early 1920s, a number of schools for '"talkie" voice production' emerged at the end of the decade, offering classes in elocution.[37] Similar to their earlier counterparts, such cinema schools continued to be seen largely as ways for crooks and confidence tricksters to exploit gullible aspirants.[38] In a more reputable context, the Royal Academy of Dramatic Art, apparently for the first time, became involved in film actor training in 1929. In a joint effort with the Federation of British Industries, the Academy, which had been giving lessons in microphone technique for radio broadcasting since 1926, organised a series of lectures led by British producers designed to give students a full course in acting for the screen.[39]

As the emergence of schools for 'talkie' actors suggests, the culture of aspiration surrounding film acting by no means disappeared in the 1930s. But it was altered in some important ways. Historians of the American cinema have argued that, by the end of the 1920s, popular film culture was centred less on the idea of participation and more on acts of consumption. Samantha Barbas writes that, in their ongoing attempts to capitalise on the enthusiasm of fans, American 'film studios, fan magazines, manufacturers, and advertisers encouraged women to experience the Hollywood dream vicariously, through consumption'. In the 1930s, she continues, films 'were no longer seen as a potential way to *earn* money, but an excuse to *spend* money'. Audiences were invited to purchase not only cinema tickets and magazines, but also film memorabilia, products endorsed by film stars and outfits explicitly marketed as affordable versions of the latest Hollywood fashions.[40] We might see this transformation from participation to consumption largely as a shift in emphasis. In the popular film culture of the silent period, the rhetoric of interactivity and the principles of consumerism were always closely intertwined. Discussing Hollywood, Marsha

Orgeron argues that 'the discourse of ambition, participation, and emulation' characteristic of early fan magazines was so prevalent because it 'proved economically successful for the industry as a whole'.[41] The promise of participation provided powerful encouragement to audiences to invest in the Hollywood system, but actual work in the film industry could only ever be possible for the few.

In many respects, a similar shift in emphasis from participation to consumption can be traced in British popular film culture during the 1920s and 1930s. Although interwar Britain was not a consumer society on the scale of America, much of the burgeoning culture of consumption was aimed precisely at those young men and women who were also likely to be the most active film fans and aspiring stars.[42] As demonstrated by the Amami shampoo brand's involvement in star search contests from the mid-1920s onwards, women were especially targeted as the chief consumers of films and film stars, and were shown ways to use film performers to cultivate their own public image and sense of self. Studies of British cinema and society in the 1930s suggest that the convergence of cinema with other forms of consumer culture continued to have important effects on women's relationship with films and film actors.[43] As Annette Kuhn persuasively argues, by the end of the decade, women's interest in looking or acting like film stars was no longer a niche subject limited to the pages of fan magazines, but was instead becoming more and more integral to constructions of British femininity.[44] The hopes and ambitions of 'screen-struck' would-be actors still prompted comment in Britain in the 1930s.[45] But the interest in film acting and screen stardom that had once been widely understood as a 'craze' was now an accepted, if still contentious, aspect of British popular culture.

Approaching the early history of cinema in Britain from the perspective of the people who acted or dreamed of acting in front of the cameras, as this book has done, sheds light on the institutional structures that constituted the British film industry, from the working conditions of the studio to the activities of employment agencies and film publicists. It also shows how attitudes towards film performance and stardom were often caught up in efforts to promote a national cinema that could compete with Hollywood on the world stage. Attending to individual stories of actors and would-be actors in the British cinema challenges the contemporary view of aspiring stars, put forward forcefully in newspaper scare stories and fictional narratives, as gullible and irrational. Although many people were undoubtedly naive or over-optimistic about the extent of the opportunities available for actors in the beleaguered British production sector, there were many reasons why film acting, especially in the era of silent films, appeared as an attractive and relatively accessible career option for people eager to improve their lot. Asking why and how people set out to reinvent themselves as film stars in this period, and who encouraged them in this pursuit, is crucial for understanding the development of popular film culture between the wars and its impact on the changing shape of British society.

Notes

Introduction: Winifred Hopcroft's story

1 'Missing girl in London', *Daily Express*, 15 July 1920, p. 5.
2 'Film fame lure', *Daily Mirror*, 15 July 1920, p. 2; 'Cinema agency clue', *Dundee Evening Telegraph*, 16 July 1920, p. 4.
3 'The film lure', *Daily Mirror*, 16 July 1920, p. 1.
4 'Missing girl in London', *Daily Express*, 15 July 1920, p. 5.
5 'Cinema agency clue', *Dundee Evening Telegraph*, 16 July 1920, p. 4.
6 Ibid.
7 'Film fame lure', *Daily Mirror*, 15 July 1920, p. 2.
8 Ibid.
9 'The cinema lure', *The Times*, 27 September 1915, p. 13.
10 'Miss Marie Lohr robbed', *The Times*, 19 April 1920, p. 9.
11 'Wanted cinema acting', *Hull Daily Mail*, 25 February 1918, p. 4.
12 'Page's film craze', *Daily Mirror*, 3 May 1920, p. 2.
13 'Cinemaitis', *Daily Mirror*, 10 November 1919, p. 8.
14 'Lady Diana Cooper', 13 November 1920, p. 1; 'Lady Diana Manners as a film star', *Kinematograph Weekly*, 18 November 1920, p. 65.
15 Philip Ziegler, *Diana Cooper: The Biography of Lady Diana Cooper* (Harmondsworth: Penguin, 1981), p. 147.
16 'The craze for "getting on the films"', *Daily Mirror*, 20 January 1922, p. 5.
17 Shelley Stamp, *Movie-Struck Girls: Women and Motion Picture Culture after the Nickelodeon* (Princeton: Princeton University Press, 2000), pp. 37-9.
18 Andrea Haller, 'Diagnosis: "flimmeritis": Female cinemagoing in Imperial Germany, 1911-18', in Daniel Biltereyst, Richard Maltby and Philippe Meers (eds), *Cinema, Audiences and Modernity: New Perspectives on European Cinema History* (London: Routledge, 2012), pp. 130-41.
19 Andrew Horrall, *Popular Culture in London, c. 1890-1918: The Transformation of Entertainment* (Manchester: Manchester University Press, 2001), p. 4.
20 For jazz music and dance steps, see Mark Hustwitt, '"Caught in a whirlpool of aching sound": The production of dance music in Britain in the 1920s', *Popular Music*, 3 (1983), 7-31; and Ross McKibbin, *Classes and Cultures: England 1918-1951* (Oxford: Oxford University Press, 1998), pp. 390-6. For

psychoanalysis, see Dean R. Rapp, '"Better and better–": Couéism as a psychological craze of the Twenties in England', *Studies in Popular Culture*, 10/2 (1987), 17–36. Robert Graves and Alan Hodge discuss the craze for crossword puzzles, along with other 1920s amusements, in *The Long Weekend: A Social History of Great Britain, 1918–1939* (London: Faber & Faber, 1940), pp. 130–2.

21 'Film-struck girl', *Daily Mirror*, 14 July 1926, p. 2; R.J. Whitley, 'Finding new stars', *Daily Mirror*, 4 June 1928, p. 23.

22 Nicholas Hiley, 'The British cinema auditorium', in Karel Dibbets and Bert Hogenkamp (eds), *Film and the First World War* (Amsterdam: Amsterdam University Press, 1995), p. 162.

23 'Mary Pickford joy scenes', *Daily Mail*, 23 June 1920, p. 2; 'Mary Pickford as a popular idol', *The Times*, 23 June 1920, p. 13.

24 '"Prince Charlie" home', *News of the World*, 11 September 1921, p. 1; 'Charlie Chaplin in tears', *Sunday Express*, 11 September 1921, p. 1.

25 *Cinema Acting as a Profession: A Splendid Course in 10 Lessons* (London: Standard Art Book, n.d. [c. 1919]).

26 See Chapter 4.

27 'The Romance of a Movie Star', *The Bioscope*, 12 August 1920, p. 25. The film was scheduled for release in October 1920: see 'The Romance of a Movie Star', *Kinematograph Weekly*, 12 August 1920, p. 68. It was based on the novel *The World's Best Girl* by Coralie Stanton and E. Heath Hosken, serialised in the *Evening News*, 10 February 1919–26 June 1919.

28 Graves and Hodge, *Long Weekend*, p. 130.

29 Roberta E. Pearson, *Eloquent Gestures: The Transformation of Performance Style in the Griffith Biograph Films* (Berkeley: University of California Press, 1992); James Naremore, *Acting in the Cinema* (Berkeley: University of California Press, 1992), pp. 99–130; David Mayer, 'Acting in silent film: Which legacy of the theatre?', in Peter Krämer and Alan Lovell (eds), *Screen Acting* (London: Routledge, 1999), pp. 10–30; Andrew Klevan, *Film Performance: From Achievement to Appreciation* (London: Wallflower, 2005), pp. 19–25; Cynthia Baron and Sharon Marie Carnicke, *Reframing Screen Performance* (Ann Arbor: University of Michigan Press, 2008), pp. 89–112; Gaylyn Studlar, *This Mad Masquerade: Stardom and Masculinity in the Jazz Age* (New York: Columbia University Press, 1996); Patrice Petro (ed.), *Idols of Modernity: Movie Stars of the 1920s* (New Brunswick: Rutgers University Press, 2010).

30 Jon Burrows, *Legitimate Cinema: Theatre Stars in Silent British Films, 1908–1918* (Exeter: University of Exeter Press, 2003); '"Our English Mary Pickford": Alma Taylor and ambivalent British stardom in the 1910s', in Bruce Babington (ed.), *British Stars and Stardom: From Alma Taylor to Sean Connery* (Manchester: Manchester University Press, 2001), pp. 29–41; Michael Williams, *Ivor Novello: Screen Idol* (London: British Film Institute, 2003). See also

Geoffrey Macnab, *Searching for Stars: Stardom and Acting in the British Cinema* (London: Cassell, 2000).

31 Michael Sanderson, *From Irving to Olivier: A Social History of the Acting Profession* (London: Athlone Press, 1984); Tracy C. Davis, *Actresses as Working Women: Their Social Identity in Victorian Culture* (London: Routledge, 1991). See also Michael Baker, *The Rise of the Victorian Actor* (London: Croom Helm, 1978).

32 Denise McKenna, 'The photoplay or the pickaxe: Extras, gender, and labour in early Hollywood', *Film History*, 23/1 (2011), 5–19; Heidi Kenaga, 'Making the "studio girl": The Hollywood Studio Club and industry regulation of female labour', *Film History*, 18/2 (2006), 129–39; Charlie Keil, 'Leo Rosencrans, movie-struck boy: A (half-)year in the life of a Hollywood extra', *Film History*, 26/2 (2014), 31–51; Hilary A. Hallett, *Go West, Young Woman! The Rise of Early Hollywood* (Berkeley: University of California Press, 2013); Anthony Slide, *Hollywood Unknowns: A History of Extras, Bit Players, and Stand-Ins* (Jackson: University of Mississippi Press, 2012).

33 Herbert Morgan, *Careers for Boys and Girls* (London: Methuen, 1926), p. 166; Kristin Thompson, *Exporting Entertainment: America in the World Film Market 1907–34* (London: British Film Institute, 1985), p. 125.

34 Valentia Steer, *The Secrets of the Cinema: Your Favourite Amusement from Within* (London: Pearson, 1920), p. 25.

35 For instance, see Andrew Higson (ed.), *Young and Innocent? The Cinema in Britain 1896–1930* (Exeter: University of Exeter Press, 2002); Burrows, *Legitimate Cinema*; Christine Gledhill, *Reframing British Cinema, 1918–1928: Between Passion and Restraint* (London: British Film Institute, 2003); Lawrence Napper, *British Cinema and Middlebrow Culture in the Interwar Years* (Exeter: University of Exeter Press, 2009).

36 Anne Morey, *Hollywood Outsiders: The Adaptation of the Film Industry, 1913–1934* (Minneapolis: University of Minnesota Press, 2003), p. 1.

37 Kathryn Hegelson Fuller, 'The boundaries of participation: The problem of spectatorship and American film audiences, 1905–1930', *Film & History*, 20/4 (1990), 75–86; Marsha Orgeron, '"You are invited to participate": Interactive fandom in the age of the movie magazine', *Journal of Film and Video*, 61/3 (2009), 3–23.

38 Stephen Constantine, *Social Conditions in Britain 1918–1939* (London: Methuen, 1983), pp. 3–4; Miriam Glucksmann, *Women Assemble: Women Workers and the New Industries in Inter-War Britain* (London: Routledge, 1990).

39 Elizabeth Roberts, *Women's Work 1840–1940* (Basingstoke: Macmillan, 1988), pp. 37–8; Gregory Anderson (ed.), *The White-Blouse Revolution: Female Office Workers since 1870* (Manchester: Manchester University Press, 1988).

40 Ray Strachey, 'Changes in employment', in Ray Strachey (ed.), *Our Freedom and Its Results, by Five Women* (London: Hogarth Press, 1936), p. 136.

41 Dudley Baines and Paul Johnson, 'In search of the "traditional" working class: Social mobility and occupational continuity in interwar London', *Economic History Review*, 52/4 (1999), 692–713.
42 Selina Todd, *Young Women, Work, and Family in England 1918–1950* (Oxford: Oxford University Press, 2005), p. 91.
43 Jon Lawrence, 'The British sense of class', *Journal of Contemporary History*, 35/2 (2000), 307–18; James Hinton, '"The 'class' complex": Mass-Observation and cultural distinction in pre-war Britain', *Past & Present*, 199 (2008), 207–36.
44 McKibbin, *Classes and Cultures*, p. 527.
45 Peter Bailey, 'White collars, gray lives? The lower middle class revisited', *Journal of British Studies*, 30/3 (1999): 286–7; Mark Glancy, *Hollywood and the Americanization of Britain: From the 1920s to the Present* (London: I.B.Tauris, 2014), pp. 51–2.
46 Bailey, 'White collars, gray lives?', 287.
47 'Mary Pickford as a popular idol', *The Times*, 23 June 1920, p. 13. See also Leo Lowenthal, 'The triumph of the mass idols', in his *Literature, Popular Culture, and Society* (Englewood Cliffs: Prentice-Hall, 1961).
48 D.L. LeMahieu, *A Culture for Democracy: Mass Communication and the Cultivated Mind in Britain between the Wars* (Oxford: Clarendon, 1988), p. 48.
49 Warren I. Susman, *Culture as History: The Transformation of American Society in the Twentieth Century* (New York: Pantheon, 1984), pp. 80–2; Mike Featherstone, 'The body in consumer culture', *Theory, Culture & Society*, 1/2 (1983): 27–8.
50 Featherstone, 'The body in consumer culture', 28.
51 J.B. Priestley, *English Journey* (London: Heinemann, 1934; repr. London: Folio Society, 1997), pp. 325–6.
52 David Fowler, *The First Teenagers: The Lifestyle of Young Wage-earners in Interwar Britain* (London: Routledge, 1996), pp. 100, 116–37; Annette Kuhn, *An Everyday Magic: Cinema and Cultural Memory* (London: I.B.Tauris, 2002).
53 Glancy, *Hollywood and the Americanization of Britain*, pp. 42–77; Jane Bryan, '"The cinema looking glass": The British film fan magazine, 1911–1918', unpublished PhD thesis (Norwich: University of East Anglia, 2006); Lisa Rose Stead, '"So oft to the movies they've been": British fan writing and female audiences in the silent era', *Transformative Works and Cultures*, 6 (2011). Available at http://journal.transformativeworks.org/index.php/twc/article/view/224/210 (accessed 29 January 2016).
54 Adrian Bingham, *Gender, Modernity, and the Popular Press in Inter-War Britain* (Oxford: Clarendon, 2004), pp. 224–5; Martin Conboy, *The Press and Popular Culture* (London: SAGE, 2002), p. 114.
55 Marsha Orgeron, 'Making "It" in Hollywood: Clara Bow, fandom, and consumer culture', *Cinema Journal*, 42/4 (2003): 77–8.
56 Su Holmes, 'Dreaming a dream: Susan Boyle and celebrity culture', *Velvet Light Trap*, 65 (2010): 74–5.

57 Laura E. Nym Mayhall, 'The Prince of Wales *versus* Clark Gable: Anglophone celebrity and citizenship between the wars', *Cultural and Social History*, 4/4 (2007), 529-43.

1. In and out of the studio: The silent film actor in Britain

1 'If I win!', *Pictures and the Picturegoer*, 21 September 1918, p. 299.
2 Paul McDonald, 'Reconceptualising stardom', in Richard Dyer, *Stars*, new edition with a supplementary chapter by Paul McDonald (London: British Film Institute, 1998), p. 195.
3 'Risking life for pictures', *The Pictures*, 17 February 1912, p. 8.
4 Jennifer M. Bean, 'Technologies of early stardom and the extraordinary body', *Camera Obscura*, 16/3 (2001), 9-57.
5 Richard deCordova, *Picture Personalities: The Emergence of the Star System in America* (Chicago: University of Illinois Press, 1990), p. 108
6 For actors in the early modern period, see Andrew Gurr, *The Shakespearean Stage 1574-1642*, fourth edition (Cambridge: Cambridge University Press, 2009), pp. 100-39; and Shearer West, *The Image of the Actor: Verbal and Visual Representation in the Age of Garrick and Kemble* (London: Pinter, 1991).
7 Tracy C. Davis, *Actresses as Working Women: Their Social Identity in Victorian Culture* (London: Routledge, 1991), p. 3.
8 Ibid.
9 Michael Baker, *The Rise of the Victorian Actor* (London: Croom Helm, 1978), p. 29.
10 Ibid., pp. 44-52.
11 Ibid., pp. 102-3; Davis, *Actresses as Working Women*, p. 3.
12 Baker, *Rise of the Victorian Actor*, pp. 62-4.
13 Ibid., pp. 86-8.
14 Kate Phillips, quoted in Christopher Kent, 'Image and reality: The actress and society', in Martha Vicinus (ed.), *A Widening Sphere: Changing Roles of Victorian Women* (Bloomington: Indiana University Press, 1977), p. 111.
15 Baker, *Rise of the Victorian Actor*, p. 107.
16 Tracy C. Davis, *The Economics of the British Stage 1800-1914* (Cambridge: Cambridge University Press, 2000), p. 316; Baker, *Rise of the Victorian Actor*, p. 91.
17 See Harold Perkin, *The Rise of Professional Society: England since 1880* (London: Routledge, 1989).
18 Baker, *Rise of the Victorian Actor*, p. 152.
19 Michael Sanderson, *From Irving to Olivier: A Social History of the Acting Profession in England 1880-1983* (London: Athlone, 1984), pp. 39-50.

20 Ibid., pp. 96–7; Joseph Macleod, *The Actor's Right to Act* (London: Lawrence and Wishart, 1981), pp. 68–74.
21 Baker, *Rise of the Victorian Actor*, p. 14; Sanderson, *From Irving to Olivier*, p. 1.
22 Sanderson, *From Irving to Olivier*, p. 133.
23 Ibid., pp. 79–81.
24 Davis, *Actresses as Working Women*, p. 4.
25 Jan McDonald, 'Lesser ladies of the Victorian stage', *Theatre Research International*, 13/3 (1998), 234–49; Christine Woodworth, 'Luggage, lodgings, and landladies: The practicalities for actresses on the British provincial circuits in the late nineteenth and early twentieth centuries', *Theatre Symposium*, 22 (2014), 22–32.
26 H.C. Shuttleworth (ed.), *The Diary of an Actress; or, Realities of Stage Life* (London: Griffith, 1885), p. 38, quoted in Viv Gardner, 'The three nobodies: Autobiographical strategies in the work of Alma Ellerslie, Kitty Marion and Ina Rozant', in Maggie B. Gale and Viv Gardner (eds), *Auto/biography and Identity: Women, Theatre and Performance* (Manchester: Manchester University Press, 2004), p. 19.
27 Margot Peter, *Mrs. Pat: The Life of Mrs. Patrick Campbell* (London: Bodley Head, 1984); Nina Auerbach, *Ellen Terry: Player in Her Time* (London: Phoenix House, 1987).
28 Davis, *Actresses as Working Women*, pp. 78, 86–97; Woodworth, 'Luggage, lodgings, and landladies', 26.
29 Sanderson, *From Irving to Olivier*, p. 12.
30 Davis, *Actresses as Working Women*, p. 12; Carol Dyhouse, *Girls Growing Up in Late Victorian and Edwardian England* (London: Routledge and Kegan Paul, 1981), pp. 40–4.
31 Sanderson, *From Irving to Olivier*, pp. 189–97, 223; Macleod, *Actor's Right to Act*, pp. 169–86.
32 Clive Barker, 'Theatre and society: The Edwardian legacy, the First World War and the inter-war years', in Clive Barker and Maggie B. Gale (eds), *British Theatre between the Wars, 1918–1939* (Cambridge: Cambridge University Press, 2000), pp. 4–37; Sanderson, *From Irving to Olivier*, pp. 182–5.
33 Sanderson, *From Irving to Olivier*, pp. 188–9.
34 For radio, see Val Gielgud, *British Radio Drama, 1922–1956: A Survey* (London: Harrap, 1957).
35 Sanderson, *From Irving to Olivier*, p. 331.
36 Ibid., pp. 180–1.
37 Peter Bailey, '"Naughty but nice": Musical comedy and the rhetoric of the girl', in Michael R. Booth and Joel Kaplan (eds), *The Edwardian Theatre: Essays on Performance and the Stage* (Cambridge: Cambridge University Press, 1996), p. 39; Jon Burrows, 'Girls on film: The musical matrices of film stardom in early British cinema', *Screen*, 44/4 (2003), 314–25.

38 James Ross Moore, 'Girl crazy: Musicals and revues between the wars', in Barker and Gale (eds), *British Theatre between the Wars*, pp. 88–112.
39 Charles Musser, 'The changing status of the actor', in Charles Musser and Jay Leyda (eds), *Before Hollywood: Turn-of-the-Century Film from American Archives* (New York: American Federation of Arts, 1986), p. 57.
40 Richard Brown and Barry Anthony, *A Victorian Film Enterprise: The History of the British Mutoscope and Biograph Company, 1897–1915* (Trowbridge: Flicks Books, 1999), p. 228.
41 Ibid., p. 229.
42 Musser, 'Changing status of the actor', p. 57.
43 Cecil Hepworth, *Came the Dawn: Memoirs of a Film Pioneer* (London: Phoenix House, 1951), p. 63.
44 Ibid., p. 67.
45 Interview with Lewin Fitzhamon (n.d.), Dennis Gifford Audio Collection, British Film Institute (BFI) Reuben Library.
46 Richard Abel, *The Ciné Goes to Town: French Cinema 1896–1914* (Berkeley: University of California Press, 1994), p. 22.
47 Musser, 'Changing status of the actor', p. 58.
48 Roberta Pearson, *Eloquent Gestures: The Transformation of Performance Style in the Griffith Biograph Films* (Berkeley: University of California Press, 1992), pp. 82–4.
49 Interview with Chrissie White (1968), Dennis Gifford Audio Collection, BFI Reuben Library.
50 Interview with Dorothy Bellew (n.d.), Dennis Gifford Audio Collection, BFI Reuben Library.
51 Rachael Low, *The History of the British Film, 1906–1914* (London: Allen & Unwin, 1950), p. 97.
52 Dave Aylott, 'Reminiscences of a showman', *Cinema Studies*, 2/1 (1965): 5.
53 R.W. Paul, C.M. Hepworth and W.G. Barker, 'Before 1910: Kinematograph experiences', *Proceedings of the Kinematograph Society*, 38 (1936): 14.
54 'Artists wanted', *The Era*, 10 August 1912, p. 26; 'Artists wanted', *The Era*, 24 August 1912, p. 27.
55 'Bioscope model', in George Edgars (ed.), *Careers for Men, Women, and Children*, 16 vols (London: Newnes, 1911–12), vol. 2, pp. 4–5.
56 Jill Liddington and Elizabeth Crawford, '"Women do not count, neither shall they be counted": Suffrage, citizenship and the battle for the 1911 census', *History Workshop Journal*, 71/1 (2011): 98–9.
57 1911 census of England and Wales, London, Kingsgate Mansions, Red Lion Square, Sylvani household schedule.
58 1911 census of England and Wales, Middlesex, Shepperton, Rosewell household schedule.
59 1911 census of England and Wales, London, 36 Buckingham Gate, Foster household schedule.

60 1911 census of England and Wales, London, 97 Turners Road, Bow, Brett household schedule.
61 deCordova, *Picture Personalities*, p. 64.
62 Andrew Shail, 'Max Linder and the emergence of film stardom', *Early Popular Visual Culture*, 14/1 (2016), 55–86.
63 Janet Staiger, 'Seeing stars', in Christine Gledhill (ed.), *Stardom: Industry of Desire* (London: Routledge, 1991), pp. 3–16.
64 Jon Burrows, *Legitimate Cinema: Theatre Stars in Silent British Films, 1908–1918* (Exeter: University of Exeter Press, 2003), pp. 44–62.
65 deCordova, *Picture Personalities*, p. 98; Ian Christie, 'From screen personalities to stars: Analysing early film fame in Europe', in Martin Loiperdinger and Uli Jung (eds), *Importing Asta Nielsen: The International Film Star in the Making* (New Barnet: Libbey, 2013), pp. 353–63.
66 *The Film Life of Mary Pickford* ([London: J.D. Walker, 1915]).
67 Ibid., p. 4.
68 'Items of interest', *The Bioscope*, 2 May 1912, p. 321.
69 'A picture palace star', *The Bystander*, 3 April 1912, p. 31; 'Items of interest', *The Bioscope*, 23 May 1912, p. 543; 'Film gossip', *The Era*, 2 March 1912, p. 26.
70 'Items of interest', *The Bioscope*, 27 June 1912, p. 923; 'Items of interest', *The Bioscope*, 26 December 1912, p. 963.
71 'Result of our greatest British film players contest', *Pictures and the Picturegoer*, 3 July 1915, p. 246.
72 Patrick Glynn, 'Miss Dorothy Foster', *The Pictures*, 25 May 1912, p. 19; 'Interview with Lieut. Daring, R.N.', *The Bioscope*, 28 March 1912, p. 929.
73 *The Picture Players' Gallery* (Cardiff: Crayle, 1913); 'The girl on the film. No. 1: Miss Dorothy Bellew', *Picturegoer*, 8 November 1913, pp. 130–1.
74 Jane Bryan, '"The cinema looking glass": The British film fan magazine, 1911–1918', unpublished PhD thesis (Norwich: University of East Anglia, 2006), pp. 121–89.
75 Gerben Bakker, *Entertainment Industrialised: The Emergence of the International Film Industry, 1890–1940* (Cambridge: Cambridge University Press, 2008), p. 291.
76 Rachael Low, *The History of the British Film, 1918–1929* (London: Allen & Unwin, 1971), p. 275.
77 'Gossip and opinion', *Kinematograph and Lantern Weekly*, 27 March 1919, p. 5.
78 Sanderson, *From Irving to Olivier*, p. 80.
79 'New film star', *Daily Mirror*, 31 July 1920, p. 7.
80 Contract between Chili Bouchier and the British and Dominions Film Corporation Limited, 11 May 1931, Papers of Chili Bouchier, Women's Library, London School of Economics, 7/CHB/1/2/1.
81 Draft contract, Atlantic Union Films Limited, 9 September 1924, Papers of Sir Patrick Joseph Henry Hannon MP, Parliamentary Archives, HNN/12/7. Thanks to Polly Goodwin for bringing this source to my attention.

82 Sanderson, *From Irving to Olivier*, pp. 59–60.
83 *Film-Land: How to Get There. By a Cinema Actor* (London: Reeder and Walsh, n.d. [c. 1921]), p. 6.
84 Letter from the Samuelson Film Manufacturing Company, 20 May 1918, Teddy Baird Collection, BFI Special Collections, Item 43. According to the information in Baird's diary, the film was *Tinker, Tailor, Soldier, Sailor* (Rex Wilson, 1918).
85 'The picture playwright', *The Bioscope*, 20 March 1913, p. 887.
86 'A screen-struck public', *The Era*, 24 September 1919, p. 22; Sanderson, *From Irving to Olivier*, p. 180.
87 Arnold Kohler, 'Some aspects of conditions of employment in the film industry', *International Labour Review*, 23/6 (1931): 782.
88 Low, *History of the British Film, 1918–1929*, p. 275.
89 For 'supers' in the theatre, see Jean Chothia, 'The triumph of the supers: Hauptmann's *The Weavers* as theatrical event', *Nineteenth Century Theatre and Film*, 34/1 (2007), 45–68.
90 Iris N. Carpenter, 'A day as a film super', *Picturegoer*, June 1927, p. 32.
91 Charles Berry, quoted in Kohler, 'Some aspects', 782.
92 Arthur Applin, *The Beautiful Miss Barry* (London: Long, 1925), p. 92.
93 Fred Dangerfield and Norman Howard, *How to Become a Film Artiste: The Art of Photo-Play Acting* (London: Odhams, 1921), p. 32; Lilian Bamburg, *Film Acting as a Career* (London: Foulsham, 1929), p. 11.
94 Diary of engagements, 1917–21, Teddy Baird Collection, BFI Special Collections, Item 43.
95 Michael J. Childs, *Labour's Apprentice: Working-Class Lads in Late Victorian and Edwardian England* (London: Hambledon Press, 1992), pp. 54–7; Jerry White, *The Worst Street in North London: Campbell Bunk, Islington, between the Wars* (London: Routledge, 1986), pp. 162–3.
96 Handwritten note, Teddy Baird Collection, BFI Special Collections, Item 43; 'Edward Baird', in Brian McFarlane (ed.), *The Encyclopedia of British Film*, third edition (London: Methuen, 2008), pp. 41–2.
97 Jack Cardiff, *Magic Hour* (London: Faber & Faber, 1996).
98 Low, *History of the British Film, 1918–1929*, p. 107.
99 Stella Wolfe Murray, 'The film', in *Lloyd's A.B.C. of Careers for Girls* (London: United Press, n.d. [c. 1922]), p. 168.
100 Hepworth, *Came the Dawn*, p. 51.
101 Low, *History of the British Film, 1918–1929*, p. 218.
102 Ibid., pp. 218–19.
103 Thomas Burke, *The London Spy: A Book of Town Travels* (London: Butterworth, 1922), pp. 74–5.
104 Joan Morgan, *Camera!* (London: Chapman and Hall, n.d. [c. 1940]), p. 23.

105 Tony Fletcher and Ronald Grant, 'A lowland Cinderella: Joan Morgan's silent career, 1912–1929', *Griffithiana*, 65 (1999): 77.
106 Cardiff, *Magic Hour*, p. 10.
107 Jonathan Croall, *Forgotten Stars: My Father and the British Silent Film World* (London: Fantom, 2013), p. 79.
108 Burke, *London Spy*, p. 78.
109 Davis, *Actresses as Working Women*, p. 17; Miriam Glucksmann, *Women Assemble: Women Workers and the New Industries in Inter-War Britain* (London: Routledge, 1990), p. 36.
110 'Film stars' romance', *Daily Mirror*, 14 November 1922, p. 1.
111 'A factory of art', *Motion Picture Studio*, 15 October 1921, p. 13.
112 Stanley Bruce, 'Film actors' grievances', *The Bioscope*, 5 June 1919, p. 51.
113 Basil Karslake, 'A worm's eye view', *Films and Filming* (August 1984): 17.
114 *Film-Land: How to Get There*, p. 12; Cardiff, *Magic Hour*, p. 10.
115 Willy Clarkson, 'The art of screen make-up', *The Bioscope*, 24 October 1918, p. 95; Leslie Eveleigh, 'Panchromatic make-up', *The Bioscope*, 11 July 1928, supplement, pp. vii–viii.
116 Helena Chalmers, *The Art of Make-Up: For the Stage, the Screen, and Social Use* (London: Appleton, 1930), p. 160.
117 Burke, *London Spy*, p. 76.
118 L.C. MacBean, *Kinematograph Studio Technique* (London: Pitman, 1922), p. 14.
119 Ibid., pp. 14–15.
120 Cardiff, *Magic Hour*, p. 11.
121 Michael Balcon, *Michael Balcon Presents... A Lifetime of Films* (London: Hutchinson, 1969), p. 15.
122 Chili Bouchier, *Shooting Star: The Last of the Silent Film Stars* (London: Atlantis, 1996), p. 54.
123 Stanley Bruce, 'Film actors' grievances', *The Bioscope*, 5 June 1919, p. 51; 'Why there are no British stars (by one of them)', *Kinematograph Weekly*, 6 January 1921, p. 169.
124 Jon Burrows, 'Big studio production in the pre-quota years', in Robert Murphy (ed.), *The British Cinema Book*, third edition (London: British Film Institute, 2009), p. 160.
125 Dangerfield and Howard, *How to Become a Film Artiste*, p. 8.
126 Low, *History of the British Film, 1918–1929*, p. 225.
127 Gladys Cooper, *Gladys Cooper* (London: Hutchinson, 1931), p. 147.
128 Fay Compton, *Rosemary: Some Remembrances* (London: Alston Rivers, 1926), p. 239.
129 See Bean, 'Technologies of early stardom'.
130 Dangerfield and Howard, *How to Become a Film Artiste*, p. 2. See also deCordova, *Picture Personalities*, p. 103.

131 Barker in Paul, et al., 'Before 1910', 14.
132 Low, *History of the British Film, 1918-1929*, p. 221; Balcon, *Michael Balcon Presents*, p. 16.
133 Karslake, 'A worm's eye view', 17.
134 Diary of engagements, 1917-21, Teddy Baird Collection, BFI Special Collections, Item 43.
135 Cardiff, *Magic Hour*, p. 11.
136 Geoff Brown, '"Sister of the stage": British film and British theatre', in Charles Barr (ed.), *All Our Yesterdays: 90 Years of British Cinema* (London: British Film Institute, 1986), pp.143-67.
137 Brown, 'Sister of the stage', p. 145; Burrows, *Legitimate Cinema*.
138 Clive Brook, 'The eighty four ages of Clive Brook: His life and times', unpublished typescript, n.d. (c. 1971), Clive Brook Collection, BFI Special Collections, Item 83, p. 22.
139 Ibid., pp. 61-71.
140 Ibid., p. 72.
141 Ibid., p. 76.
142 Ibid., p. 89.
143 Brian Aherne, *A Proper Job* (Boston: Houghton Mifflin, 1969), pp. 64-5.
144 Aherne may have appeared in another film before this for the Gaumont Company, *The Eleventh Commandment* (George A. Cooper, 1924).
145 Aherne, *A Proper Job*, p. 91.
146 Ibid., p. 92.
147 Ibid., pp. 90-2.
148 'Making stars', *The Bioscope*, 4 July 1928, p. 28.
149 Aherne, *A Proper Job*, p. 217. For the early British presence in Hollywood, see Ian Scott, *From Pinewood to Hollywood: British Filmmakers in American Cinema, 1910-1969* (Basingstoke: Palgrave Macmillan, 2010).
150 Sanderson, *From Irving to Olivier*, p. 208.
151 Ann-Marie Cook, 'The adventures of the "Vitagraph Girl" in England', in Alan Burton and Laraine Porter (eds), *Pimple, Pranks and Pratfalls: British Film Comedy Before 1930* (Trowbridge: Flicks Books, 2000), pp. 33-41; Compton, *Rosemary*; Cooper, *Gladys Cooper*.
152 Mabel Poulton, 'Tessa and I', unpublished typescript, Mabel Poulton Collection, BFI Special Collections, Item 2, p. 1.
153 Jerry White, *Worst Street in North London*, p. 188; Poulton, 'Tessa and I', p. 2.
154 For the increasing opportunities for women in clerical work, see Elizabeth Roberts, *Women's Work 1840-1940* (Basingstoke: Macmillan, 1988), pp. 37-8; and Gregory Anderson (ed.), *The White-Blouse Revolution: Female Office Workers since 1870* (Manchester: Manchester University Press, 1988).
155 Poulton, 'Tessa and I', p. 4.

156 Poulton, 'Tessa and I'; George Pearson, *Flashback: The Autobiography of a British Film-maker* (London: Allen & Unwin, 1957), p. 86.
157 Mabel Poulton, 'Cockles and caviare: A story of theatre and film studios', unpublished typescript, Mabel Poulton Collection, BFI Special Collections, Item 3, p. 11. This is a fictionalised account of a silent film actress named Jenny Lynton, but handwritten notes indicate that it is largely autobiographical.
158 G.A. Atkinson, 'Seen on the screen', *Sunday Express*, 24 October 1920, p. 4; Poulton, 'Tessa and I', p. 11. See also Poulton, 'Cockles and caviare', p. 10.
159 Bouchier, *Shooting Star*, pp. 41, 53.
160 For instance, see 'An Anglo-French beauty', *Illustrated Sporting and Dramatic News*, 2 March 1928, and the front page of *The Bystander*, 7 August 1929, where she is pictured as the 'beautiful Anglo-French film star', newspaper clippings, Press Cuttings Book, 1927–30, Papers of Chili Bouchier, Women's Library, London School of Economics, 7/CHB/5/1.
161 Bouchier, *Shooting Stars*, p. 32.
162 Ibid., pp. 34–5.
163 Ibid., pp. 38–49.
164 Contract between Chili Bouchier and the British and Dominions Film Corporation Limited, 11 May 1931, Papers of Chili Bouchier, Women's Library, London School of Economics, 7/CHB/1/2/1.
165 For instance, see 'Mannequin to film star', *Illustrated Sporting and Dramatic News*, 29 December 1928, and 'First be a mannequin', *Manchester Evening Chronicle*, 2 January 1929, newspaper clippings, Press Cuttings Book, 1927–30, Papers of Chili Bouchier, Women's Library, London School of Economics, 7/CHB/5/1.
166 Joyce Castle, 'Factory work for women: Courtaulds and GEC between the wars', in Bill Lancaster and Tony Mason (eds), *Life and Labour in a Twentieth Century City: The Experience of Coventry* (Coventry: Cryfield Press, 1987), pp. 133–71; Selina Todd, 'Poverty and aspiration: Young women's entry to employment in inter-war England', *Twentieth Century British History*, 15/2 (2004), 119–42.
167 Poulton, 'Tessa and I', p. 2.
168 Bouchier, *Shooting Star*, p. 54.
169 Ibid., p. 53.
170 Ibid., p. 52.

2. Learn to act for the cinema in your own home: Instructional guides to film acting

1 John Galsworthy, 'A family man' (1921), in *The Plays of John Galsworthy* (London: Duckworth, 1929), pp. 598–600.

2 'Learn to act for the cinema in your own home', *Pictures and the Picturegoer*, 1 November 1919, p. 525.
3 Janet Staiger, 'The eyes are really the focus: Photoplay acting and film form and style', *Wide Angle*, 6/4 (1985), 14–23; Roberta E. Pearson, *Eloquent Gestures: The Transformation of Performance Style in the Griffith Biograph Films* (Berkeley: University of California Press, 1992), pp. 89–94; Amy Sargeant, 'Manuals and mantras: Advice to British screen actors', in Laura Vichi (ed.), *L'Uomo visibile: l'attore dale origini del cinema alle soglie del cinema moderno/The Visible Man: Film Actor from Early Cinema to the Eve of Modern Cinema* (Udine: Forum, 2002), pp. 311–20; Mattia Lento, ' "Basta la mossa!" or not? Silent film, theatre and the pedagogy of actors in Italy', in Katharina Klung, Susie Trenka and Geesa Tuch (eds), *Dokumentation des 24: Film- und Fernsehwissenschaftliches Kolloquiums* (Marburg: Schüren, 2013), pp. 394–404. For the survival rate of silent films, see Paolo Cherchi Usai, 'The early years: Origins and survival', in Geoffrey Nowell-Smith (ed.), *The Oxford History of World Cinema* (Oxford: Oxford University Press, 1996), p. 12.
4 David Mayer, 'Acting in silent film: Which legacy of the theatre?', in Peter Krämer and Alan Lovell (eds), *Screen Acting* (London: Routledge, 1999), p. 17.
5 Sargeant, 'Manuals and mantras', p. 318.
6 For criticisms of the cinema as a passive form of recreation in the silent period, see Claire Langhamer, *Women's Leisure in England 1920–60* (Manchester: Manchester University Press, 2000), pp. 58–70; Brad Beavan, *Leisure, Citizenship and Working-Class Men in Britain, 1850–1945* (Manchester: Manchester University Press, 2005), pp. 187–90.
7 Jackie Stacey, *Star Gazing: Hollywood Cinema and Female Spectatorship* (London: Routledge, 1994); Annette Kuhn, *An Everyday Magic: Cinema and Cultural Memory* (London: I.B.Tauris, 2002).
8 Marsha Orgeron, ' "You are invited to participate": Interactive fandom in the age of the movie magazine', *Journal of Film and Video*, 61/3 (2009): 4.
9 Anthony Slide, *Inside the Hollywood Fan Magazine: A History of Star Makers, Fabricators, and Gossip Mongers* (Jackson: University Press of Mississippi, 2010), pp. 11–32.
10 Kathryn H. Fuller, *At the Picture Show: Small-Town Audiences and the Creation of Movie Fan Culture* (Charlottesville: University of Virginia Press, 2001), p. 137.
11 Ibid., pp. 145, 152.
12 Orgeron, 'You are invited to participate', 5.
13 Ibid.
14 Jane Bryan, 'From film stories to film stars: The beginnings of the fan magazine in Britain, 1911–16', in Alan Burton and Laraine Porter (eds), *Scene Stealing: Sources for British Cinema before 1930* (Trowbridge: Flicks Books, 2003), p. 69.

15 Jane Bryan, '"The cinema looking glass": The British film fan magazine, 1911–1918', unpublished PhD thesis (Norwich: University of East Anglia, 2006), p. 22.
16 Bryan, 'The cinema looking glass', p. 216; Cynthia L. White, *Women's Magazines 1693–1968* (London: Joseph, 1970), pp. 96–8.
17 'Editorial', *Film Flashes*, 13 November 1915, p. 10.
18 'Little chats with film favourites: No. 1. Alma Taylor', *Pictures and the Picturegoer*, 25 January 1919, p. 103; 'Fay Filmer's film chat', *Girls' Cinema*, 16 October 1920, p. 14; Mark Glancy, 'Temporary American citizens? British audiences, Hollywood films and the threat of Americanization in the 1920s', *Historical Journal of Film, Radio and Television*, 26/4 (2006): 476.
19 Glancy, 'Temporary American citizens?', 477; *Picturegoer*, August 1928, p. 56, quoted in Lisa Stead, 'Audiences from the archive: Women's writing and silent cinema', in Nandana Bose and Lee Grieveson (eds), *Using Moving Image Archives* (Nottingham: Scope e-Book, 2010), p. 36. Available at http://www.nottingham.ac.uk/scope/issues/2010/june-issue-17.aspx (accessed 29 January 2016).
20 Kathryn Hegelsen Fuller, 'The boundaries of participation: The problem of spectatorship and American film audiences, 1905–1930', *Film & History*, 20/4 (1990): 80.
21 Ibid.
22 Ibid., 81.
23 Ibid., 80.
24 Ibid., 81.
25 C.E. Graham, *How to Write Picture Plays* (London: Cinema Playwriting School, n.d. [*c.* 1913]); Harold Weston, *The Art of Photo-Play Writing* (London: McBride, Nast, 1916).
26 Rachael Low, *The History of the British Film, 1914–1918* (London: Allen & Unwin, 1950), p. 92; '£200 for a new cinema play', *Sunday Express*, 30 March 1919, p. 7; '£1,000 for a film plot', *Weekly Dispatch*, 4 March 1928, p. 1.
27 Daniel John Gritten, 'The profession and practice of screenwriting in British cinema: The 1920s and 1930s', unpublished PhD thesis (Bristol: University of Bristol, 2007), pp. 30–1.
28 Ibid., p. 26.
29 The earliest British instructional guide to film acting may be Cavendish Morton's book, *Cinema Acting: A Handbook for Amateurs*, published in London by A&C Black, advertised in *Pictures and the Picturegoer*, 14 November 1914, p. 216. The book is presumed lost.
30 For instance, Inez Klumph and Helen Klumph's book, *Screen Acting: Its Requirements and Rewards* (New York: Falk, 1922), was sold in Britain by S. Rentelle and Co., 93 Long Acre, London, along with other technical guides to filmmaking: see 'S. Rentelle & Co., Ltd.', *Kinematograph Weekly*, 8 March 1928, p. 113.

31 *Film-Land: How to Get There. By a Cinema Actor* (London: Reeder and Walsh, n.d. [c. 1921]); Lilian Bamburg, *Film Acting as a Career* (London: Foulsham, 1929).
32 William J. Elliott, *How to Become a Film Actor* (London: Picture Palace News, n.d. [c. 1916]). The original articles were published in *Picture Palace News* between 13 December 1915 and 17 January 1916. Elliott also contributed a short-lived column to the same magazine on film acting called 'The picture player', beginning in *Picture Palace News*, 7 February 1916, p. 331.
33 Fred Dangerfield and Norman Howard, *How to Become a Film Artiste: The Art of Photo-Play Acting* (London: Odhams, 1921).
34 'Kinema handbooks', *Picturegoer*, March 1924, p. 55; 'Bibliography', *International Review of Educational Cinematography*, 4/6 (1932), 491–2.
35 Dangerfield and Howard, *How to Become a Film Artiste*, p. v.
36 H. Simonis, *The Street of Ink: An Intimate History of Journalism* (London: Cassell, 1917), p. 274.
37 'Replies', *Pictures and the Picturegoer*, 21 August 1915, p. 404. For the job of the film fiction writer, see Julia Thorogood, *Margery Allingham: A Biography* (London: Heinemann, 1991), pp. 87–8. Allingham wrote short story versions of film plots for the magazine *Picture Show* in the 1920s.
38 Dangerfield and Howard, *How to Become a Film Artiste*, p. 1.
39 Ibid., pp. 1–2.
40 *Cinema Acting as a Profession* (London: Charrisse, 1915), p. 37. The author, credited as the writer of other guides to elocution and stage acting, was most likely Leopold Wagner.
41 Dangerfield and Howard, *How to Become a Film Artiste*, p. 35.
42 Ibid., p. 2.
43 Ibid., p. 4.
44 For early attempts to differentiate the cinema from other media, see André Gaudreault and Philippe Marion, 'A medium is always born twice...', *Early Popular Visual Culture*, 3/1 (2005), 3–15.
45 Dangerfield and Howard, *How to Become a Film Artiste*, p. 2.
46 Agnes Platt, *Practical Hints on Acting for the Cinema* (London: Paul, 1920), p. 28. For Platt's work as a theatrical producer and agent, see 'The theatres', *The Times*, 31 July 1919, p. 10, and the minutes of the London County Council Public Control Committee, meeting of 20 February 1920, London Metropolitan Archives, LCC/MIN/9599.
47 Platt, *Practical Hints on Acting for the Cinema*, p. 29.
48 Mayer, 'Acting in silent film', p. 24.
49 Dangerfield and Howard, *How to Become a Film Artiste*, p. 39.
50 Ibid., pp. 39–40; Eileen Bowser, *The Transformation of Cinema, 1907–1915* (New York: Scribner, 1990), p. 89.
51 Dangerfield and Howard, *How to Become a Film Artiste*, pp. 39–40.
52 Platt, *Practical Hints on Acting for the Cinema*, p. 38.

53 Elliott, *How to Become a Film Actor*, p. 56.
54 A series of film caricatures from *Punch* were collected in Dudley Clark's spoof travelogue *Bateman and I in Filmland* (London: Fisher Unwin, 1926). For trade journal parodies, see, for instance, 'Film types', *The Bioscope*, 16 March 1916, p. 1129.
55 For a discussion of *So This Is Jollygood* and Brunel's other 'burlesque' films, see Jamie Sexton, *Alternative Film Culture in Inter-War Britain* (Exeter: University of Exeter Press, 2008), pp. 58–9.
56 Dangerfield and Howard, *How to Become a Film Artiste*, p. 22. For the 'lines of business' tradition in the theatre, see Michael R. Booth, *Theatre in the Victorian Age* (Cambridge: Cambridge University Press, 1991), pp. 125–6.
57 Stewart Rome, 'The value of specialisation', in *Cinema Acting as a Profession: A Splendid Course in 10 Lessons* (London: Standard Art Book, n.d. [*c.* 1919]), Lesson 9.
58 Rome, 'The value of specialisation', p. 12.
59 Mary Pickford, 'How to act for the screen', in *Cinema Acting as a Profession: A Splendid Course*, Lesson 1, pp. 28–9.
60 Dangerfield and Howard, *How to Become a Film Artiste*, p. 22.
61 Ibid.
62 Harry Furniss, *Our Lady Cinema: How and Why I Went into the Photo-Play World and What I Found There* (Bristol: Arrowsmith, 1914), p. 56.
63 Constance Talmadge and Richard Barthelmess played Chinese characters in *East Is West* (Sidney Franklin, 1922) and *Broken Blossoms* (D.W. Griffith, 1919), respectively. For Matheson Lang and Moore Marriott, see Christine Gledhill, *Reframing British Cinema 1918–1928: Between Passion and Restraint* (London: British Film Institute, 2003), pp. 68–71, 74–5.
64 Lilian Bamburg, *Film Acting as a Career* (London: Foulsham, 1929), p. 104.
65 V.I. Pudovkin, *On Film Technique: Three Essays and an Address*, trans. Ivor Montagu (London: Gollancz, 1929), pp. 131–2.
66 Iris Barry, *Let's Go to the Pictures* (London: Chatto and Windus, 1926), p. 111.
67 Dangerfield and Howard, *How to Become a Film Artiste*, p. 23.
68 Russell Hallen, *The Way to the Studio* (London: Wardour, n.d. [*c.* 1926]), p. 8.
69 Harold Dickinson, *How to Write a Picture Play* (Hythe: New Kinema Publishing, n.d. [*c.* 1916]), p. 7.
70 Dangerfield and Howard, *How to Become a Film Artiste*, p. 46. For actors' use of spoken dialogue in silent-era French cinema, see Isabelle Raynauld, 'Dialogues in early silent screenplays: What actors really said', in Richard Abel and Rick Altman (eds), *The Sounds of Early Cinema* (Bloomington: Indiana University Press, 2001), pp. 69–78.
71 Dangerfield and Howard, *How to Become a Film Artiste*, pp. 45, 40.
72 Platt, *Practical Hints on Acting for the Cinema*, p. 61.
73 Elliott, *How to Become a Film Actor*, pp. 47–8.

74 E. Camiller, *How to Get Film Work* (London: Film Bureau, n.d. [c. 1922]), p. 10.
75 Dangerfield and Howard, *How to Become a Film Artiste*, p. 85.
76 'Film-picture actors', *The Bioscope*, 2 October 1908, p. 18; Henry Morrell, 'On acting before the kinematograph', in Colin N. Bennett (ed.), *The Handbook of Kinematography* (London: Kinematograph Weekly, 1911), p. 218.
77 Platt, *Practical Hints on Acting for the Cinema*, p. 108.
78 Ibid., p. 109.
79 Hallen, *Way to the Studio*, p. 11.
80 Dangerfield and Howard, *How to Become a Film Artiste*, p. 45.
81 Jon Burrows, *Legitimate Cinema: Theatre Stars in British Films, 1908–1918* (Exeter: University of Exeter Press, 2003), pp. 29–34.
82 Gledhill, *Reframing British Cinema*, pp. 62–7.
83 Platt, *Practical Hints on Acting for the Cinema*, pp. 87–90.
84 Bamburg, *Film Acting as a Career*, p. 20.
85 Richard Koszarksi, *An Evening's Entertainment: The Age of the Silent Feature Picture 1915–1928* (New York: Scribner, 1990), p. 124.
86 Dangerfield and Howard, *How to Become a Film Artiste*, p. 43.
87 Ibid.
88 Austin C. Lescarboura, *The Cinema Handbook* (London: Low, Marston, n.d. [c. 1922]), p. 27.
89 Aurèle Sydney, 'General advice', in *Cinema Acting as a Profession: A Splendid Course*, Lesson 4, p. 22.
90 Platt, *Practical Hints on Acting for the Cinema*, p. 45.
91 A. Morrison, 'Familiar faces on the screen', *Pictures and the Picturegoer*, 1 June 1918, p. 534.
92 Robert Donat, 'Film acting', in Charles Davy (ed.), *Footnotes to the Film* (London: Dickson, 1937), pp. 21–2.
93 Dangerfield and Howard, *How to Become a Film Artiste*, p. 43.
94 For instance, see 'Norma Talmadge's many faces in "Poppy"', *Kinematograph and Lantern Weekly*, 14 March 1918, pp. 10–11; and 'Nazimova: The star of a thousand moods', *Kinematograph and Lantern Weekly*, 18 September 1919, supplement, p. xx.
95 For instance, see 'The expressions of Geraldine Farrar', *Picture Show*, 16 April 1921, p. 9.
96 'The world's best girl', *Evening News*, 13 February 1919, p. 4.
97 'The world's best girl', *Evening News*, 15 February 1919, p. 4; E. Allingham, 'The fellow who loved Violet Hopson', *Picture Show*, 6 December 1919, supplement, p. 102. The rest of the novel was serialised in the magazine *Cheerio!*, 3 January–6 March 1920.
98 Elizabeth Bowen, 'Dead Mabelle', in *Joining Charles and Other Stories* (London: Constable, 1929), p. 100.

99 *A Guide to Cinema Acting, & Course of Training* ([London: Foyle, 1920]), pp. 17–21.
100 Elliott, *How to Become a Film Actor*, p. 56.
101 Platt, *Practical Hints on Acting for the Cinema*, p. 73.
102 Bamburg, *Film Acting as a Career*, p. 96.
103 *Guide to Cinema Acting, & Course of Training*, p. 17.
104 Dangerfield and Howard, *How to Become a Film Artiste*, pp. 42–3.
105 *Guide to Cinema Acting, & Course of Training*, p. 20.
106 Violet Hopson, 'Hints for the cinema actress', in *Cinema Acting as a Profession: A Splendid Course*, Lesson 9, p. 22. See also Amy Sargeant, 'On receiving letters from despised lovers', in Vanessa Toulmin and Simon Popple (eds), *Visual Delights: Essays on the Popular and Projected Image in the Nineteenth* (Trowbridge: Flicks Books, 2000), pp. 84–92.
107 Hallen, *Way to the Studio*, p. 12.
108 Hopson, 'Hints for the cinema actress', p. 19.
109 Stella Wolfe Murray, 'The film', in *Lloyd's A.B.C. of Careers for Girls* (London: United Press, n.d. [c. 1922]), p. 169.
110 Mabel Poulton, 'Tessa and I', unpublished typescript, Mabel Poulton Collection, British Film Institute Special Collections, Item 2, p. 7.
111 Kuhn, *An Everyday Magic*, p. 101; Stacey, *Star Gazing*, pp. 162–7.
112 Elliott, *How to Become a Film Actor*, p. 55.
113 *Guide to Cinema Acting, & Course of Training*, p. 21.
114 Hopson, 'Hints for the cinema actress', pp. 17–18.
115 Kuhn, *An Everyday Magic*, pp. 103, 110–16; Stacey, *Star Gazing*, pp. 160–1.
116 J.P. Mayer, *Sociology of Film: Studies and Documents* (London: Faber & Faber, 1946), p. 205.
117 Ibid., p. 251.
118 'Fifteen articles of kinema faith', *Kinematograph Weekly*, 25 September 1919, p. 87.
119 Amelie Hastie, *Cupboards of Curiosity: Women, Recollection, and Film History* (Durham: Duke University Press, 2007), p. 157.
120 'Famous film stars will teach you to act for the cinema in your own home', *Pictures and the Picturegoer*, 11 October 1919, p. 455.
121 Hastie, *Cupboards of Curiosity*, p. 193.
122 Warren I. Susman, *Culture as History: The Transformation of American Society in the Twentieth Century* (New York: Pantheon, 1984), p. 282; Samantha Barbas, *Movie Crazy: Fans, Stars and the Cult of Celebrity* (Basingstoke: Palgrave, 2001), p. 51.
123 Mae Marsh, *Screen Acting* (Los Angeles: Photo-Star, n.d. [c. 1920]); Pickford, 'How to act for the screen'; Rome, 'The value of specialisation'; Hopson, 'Hints for the cinema actress'; Sydney, 'General advice'; José Collins, 'Advanced study', in *Cinema Acting as a Profession: A Splendid Course*, Lesson 8; Gladys

Brockwell, 'Things to remember', in *Cinema Acting as a Profession: A Splendid Course*, Lesson 10.
124 For advice from stage actors, see R.C. Buchanan, *How to Become an Actor* (London: French, 1896); J.A. Hammerton (ed.), *The Actor's Art: Theatrical Reminiscences, Methods of Study and Advice to Aspirants* (London: Redway, 1897).
125 Dangerfield and Howard, *How to Become a Film Artiste*, pp. 86, 84.
126 Ibid., p. 91.
127 Ibid., p. 98.
128 Ibid., p. 65.
129 Ibid., pp. 68–81.
130 Elliott, *How to Become a Film Actor*, p. 19.

3. The common round: Finding film work in interwar London

1 Katherine Mansfield, 'Pictures', in *Bliss, and Other Stories* (London: Constable, 1920), pp. 157–71. The story first appeared as 'The pictures', *Arts and Letters*, 2/4 (1919), 153–62.
2 Katherine Mansfield, 'The common round', *New Age*, 21/5 (1917), 113–15. For a possible source, see Lena Ashwell, 'Acting as a profession', in Edith J. Morley (ed.), *Women Workers in Seven Professions: A Survey of their Economic Conditions and Prospects* (London: Routledge, 1914), pp. 298–313.
3 J. Middleton Murry (ed.), *Journal of Katherine Mansfield* (New York: Knopf, 1928), p. 24; Anthony Alpers, *The Life of Katherine Mansfield* (London: Cape, 1980), p. 233.
4 G.A. Atkinson, 'The hard road to film fame', *Daily Express*, 6 June 1922, p. 6.
5 For the Hollywood 'extra girl', see Shelley Stamp, '"It's a long way to filmland": Starlets, screen hopefuls, and extras in early Hollywood', in Charlie Keil and Shelley Stamp (eds), *American Cinema's Transitional Era: Audiences, Institutions, Practices* (Berkeley: University of California, 2004), pp. 332–51; Denise McKenna, 'The photoplay or the pickaxe: Extras, gender, and labour in early Hollywood', *Film History*, 23/1 (2011), 5–19; Heidi Kenaga, 'Making the "studio girl": The Hollywood Studio Club and industry regulation of female labor', *Film History*, 18/2 (2006), 129–39; and 'Promoting *Hollywood Extra Girl* (1935)', *Screen*, 51/2 (2011), 82–8.
6 Rachael Low, *The History of the British Film, 1918–1929* (London: Allen & Unwin, 1971), pp. 218–20; Patricia Warren, *British Film Studios: An Illustrated History*, second edition (London: Batsford, 2001). See also Chapter 1.
7 For instance, see James A. Jones's characterisation of Wardour Street as 'the street of films' in 'Village streets of London', *Evening News*, 4 March 1932, p. 9.

8 *Film-Land: How to Get There. By a Cinema Actor* (London: Reeder and Walsh, n.d. [*c.* 1921]), p. 6.
9 Walter West, quoted in Valentia Steer, *The Secrets of the Cinema: Your Favourite Amusement From Within* (London: Pearson, 1920), p. 26.
10 'May earn £3 per annum', *Evening Telegraph* (Dundee), 29 June 1921, p. 9.
11 See Ernest G. Allighan, 'Low and high', *Motion Picture Studio*, 26 August 1922, pp. 12–13; Harry Furniss, *Our Lady Cinema: How and Why I Went into the Photo-Play World and What I Found There* (Bristol: Arrowsmith, 1914), pp. 76–87.
12 William J. Elliott, *How to Become a Film Actor* (London: Picture Palace News, n.d. [*c.* 1916]), p. 22.
13 Ibid., p. 24. A 'shop' was film and theatre terminology for a job.
14 William J. Elliott, *Shadow Show: A Romance of Studio Life in the Days of the Silent Movie* (London: Swan, n.d. [*c.* 1942]), p. 173.
15 James De Felice, 'The London theatrical agent', *Theatre Notebook*, 23/3 (1969), 87–94.
16 Tracy C. Davis, *The Economics of the British Stage 1800–1914* (Cambridge: Cambridge University Press, 2000), p. 316.
17 Minutes of the London County Council (LCC) Public Control Committee, meeting of 2 December 1910, London Metropolitan Archives (LMA), LCC/MIN/9591; and meeting of 3 December 1920, LMA, LCC/MIN/9599.
18 Minutes of the LCC Public Control Committee, meetings of 28 November and 12 December 1930, LMA, LCC/MIN/9619.
19 Davis, *Economics of the British Stage*, p. 316; 'The finding of employment for artistes', *International Labour Review*, 18/4–5 (1928): 622. For fraudulent agencies, see E. Camiller, *How to Get Film Work* (London: Film Bureau, n.d. [*c.* 1922]), p. 7.
20 'Cinema agency clue', *Dundee Evening Telegraph*, 16 July 1920, p. 4. See also Introduction.
21 Charles Bennett, 'Import from England', in Ronald L. Davis (ed.), *Words into Images: Screenwriters on the Studio System* (Jackson: University Press of Mississippi, 2007), p. 4.
22 Jessie Matthews, *Over My Shoulder: An Autobiography* (London: Allen, 1974), p. 43.
23 Minutes of the LCC Public Control Committee, meetings of 5 December 1919 and 3 December 1920, LMA, LCC/MIN/9599. For 'Agency-land', see Michael Sanderson, *From Irving to Olivier: A Social History of the Acting Profession in England 1880–1983* (London: Athlone Press, 1984), p. 185.
24 'Sidney Jay, cinema artistes' agency', *Kinematograph Weekly*, 6 January 1921, p. 175.
25 Leslie Goodwin, 'Film advantages in England', *Motion Picture News*, 14 August 1920, p. 1377.

26 'Sidney Jay returns to England', *Exhibitor's Trade Review*, 15 July 1922, p. 523; Low, *History of the British Film, 1918-1929*, p. 133.
27 Allighan, 'Low and high', p. 12; 'Training for the films', *The Times*, 28 January 1928, p. 9. In comparison, there were 17,614 extras registered with the Central Casting Agency in Los Angeles in 1929, suggesting that Jay's claim of 20,000-30,000 clients was somewhat exaggerated: see Arnold Kohler, 'Some aspects of conditions of employment in the film industry', *International Labour Review*, 23/6 (1931): 780.
28 Minutes of the LCC Public Control Committee, meeting of 14 May 1920, LMA, LCC/MIN/9599.
29 Adrian Brunel, *Nice Work: The Story of Thirty Years in British Film Production* (London: Robertson, 1949), p. 53.
30 Ibid., p. 54.
31 'British studios', *Kinematograph Weekly*, 6 January 1921, p. 164.
32 Brunel, *Nice Work*, p. 55; Tony Fletcher and Ronald Grant, 'A lowland Cinderella: Joan Morgan's silent career, 1912-1929', *Griffithiana*, 65 (1999): 53.
33 Brunel, *Nice Work*, p. 55.
34 Basil Karslake, 'A worm's eye view', *Films and Filming* (August 1984): 16.
35 'Kinema Club launched', *Motion Picture Studio*, 22 October 1921, p. 6.
36 'Enthusiasm reigns at Kinema Club opening', *The Bioscope*, 26 January 1922, p. 21.
37 'Kinema Club launched'.
38 For instance, the Kinema Club chairman wrote to the LCC about a bogus film school in 1923: see 'A "film school" licence refused', *Motion Picture Studio*, 12 May 1923, p. 11.
39 'A new professional club', *The Era*, 22 August 1928, p. 4. For Central Casting, see Kenaga, 'Making the "studio girl"'; and Anthony Slide, *Hollywood Unknowns: A History of Extras, Bit Players, and Stand-Ins* (Jackson: University of Mississippi Press, 2012), pp. 62-81.
40 Minutes of the LCC Public Control Committee, meeting of 27 April 1928, LMA, LCC/MIN/9614.
41 Brian Aherne, *A Proper Job* (Boston: Houghton Mifflin, 1969), pp. 150-1.
42 Joseph Macleod, *The Actor's Right to Act* (London: Lawrence and Wishart, 1981), pp. 123, 169-86; 'Film players' union', *The Times*, 13 September 1920, p. 7.
43 Macleod, *Actor's Right to Act*, pp. 168-88; 'Proposed new association for actors', *The Times*, 3 November 1929, p. 17.
44 Geoff Brown, '"Sister of the stage": British film and British theatre', in Charles Barr (ed.), *All Our Yesterdays: 90 Years of British Cinema* (London: British Film Institute, 1986), p. 145.
45 'The "extra" player's 10 per cent', *Kinematograph Weekly*, 28 November 1929, p. 35; 'Private employment agencies', *The Times*, 19 February 1930, p. 9.
46 'The finding of employment agencies for artistes', 622.

47 'Schools for picture acting', *Film Censor*, 17 July 1912, pp. 1–2.
48 'Cinema acting school – lessons', *Manchester Evening News*, 19 January 1914, p. 1 (Miss Nesta Young's school, Manchester); 'Beginners wanted for cinema acting', *Midland Daily Telegraph*, 20 December 1917, p. 4 (A1 Cinema College, Birmingham); *Kinematograph Year Book 1920* (London: Kinematograph Weekly, 1920), p. 313 (A1 Cinema School, Glasgow and Premier Cinema School, Southsea); 'Success Films', *Pictures and the Picturegoer*, 27 July 1919, p. 63 (Success Films, Liverpool); 'The Mutley Dancing and Cinema Academy', *Western Morning News*, 1 September 1922, p. 1 (Mutley Dancing and Cinema Academy, Plymouth); 'Film star as witness', *Daily Mail* (Hull), 18 December 1919, p. 8 (Joseph Doyle Hammill's school, Hull). See also, 'Cinema actors – beginners', *Western Times*, 31 October 1913, p. 4 (Cinema Studio, Leicester); 'Cinema acting taught by film actress by post', *Daily Mirror*, 24 December 1919, p. 8 (Star Cinema College, Cambridge); 'Gossip', *The Bioscope*, 9 September 1920, p. 7 (Alhambra Film College, Oldham); 'Wanted', *Burnley Express*, 18 August 1915, p. 1 (Trafalgar Cinema Bureau, Burnley); 'Cinema acting', *Hastings and St Leonard's Observer*, 17 March 1928, p. 14 (unnamed cinema school, Hastings); 'Met at film school', *Yorkshire Evening Post*, 31 October 1923, p. 7 (unnamed cinema school, Southampton).
49 'Cinema acting', *Pictures and the Picturegoer*, 2 June 1917, p. 213.
50 'New Oxford Cinema School', *Pictures and the Picturegoer*, 24 October 1914, p. 174.
51 'British studios', *Kinematograph Weekly*, 26 February 1920, p. 107.
52 'Can acting be taught?', *The Bioscope*, 1 January 1920, p. 37.
53 'Topics of the week', *The Bioscope*, 5 February 1920, p. 4. See also 'Film star as witness', *Daily Mail* (Hull), 18 December 1919, p. 8.
54 *Kinematograph Year Book 1921* (London: Kinematograph Weekly, 1921), p. 538; 'Cinema acting, the new profession for ladies', *Pictures and the Picturegoer*, 10 April 1915, p. 35.
55 Minutes of the LCC Public Control Committee, meeting of 21 January 1916, LMA, LCC/MIN/9597; *Post Office London Directory 1915* (London: Kelly's Directories, 1915), p. 569.
56 'Weekly notes', *Kinematograph and Lantern Weekly*, 25 November 1915, p. 5; 'The founder of a successful business', *Picture Palace News*, 10 June 1916, p. 104.
57 *Victoria Cinema College & Studios: Guide to Cinema Acting* (London: Victoria Cinema College, [c.1917]).
58 'A cinema college and studio', *The Era*, 14 February 1917, p. 20.
59 *Victoria Cinema College & Studios*, p. 28.
60 Lee Holcombe, *Victorian Ladies at Work: Middle-Class Working Women in England and Wales, 1850–1914* (Newton Abbot: David & Charles, 1973), pp. 145–6.

61 *Victoria Cinema College & Studios*, p. 28.
62 Ibid.
63 'Cinema Artists' Association, Ltd', *The Bioscope*, 13 January 1921, p. 26.
64 *Victoria Cinema College & Studios*, p. 8.
65 *Kinematograph Year Book 1921* (London: Kinematograph Weekly, 1921), p. 538; Nicholas Hiley, 'British and Colonial Kinematograph Company', in Richard Abel (ed.), *Encyclopedia of Early Cinema* (London: Routledge, 2005), pp. 84–5.
66 'British studios', *Kinematograph and Lantern Weekly*, 3 July 1919, p. 86.
67 'London letter', *Devon and Exeter Gazette*, 20 November 1920, p. 6.
68 Mabel Poulton, 'Tessa and I', unpublished typescript, Mabel Poulton Collection, British Film Institute (BFI) Special Collections, Item 2.
69 Ibid.
70 Mabel Poulton, 'Cockles and caviare: A story of theatre and film studios', unpublished typescript, Mabel Poulton Collection, BFI Special Collections, Item 3.
71 Ibid.
72 Edward Godal, 'American stars' invasion', *Kinematograph Weekly*, 31 August 1922, p. 54; Low, *History of the British Film, 1918–1929*, p. 137.
73 Poulton, 'Cockles and caviare'.
74 Poulton, 'Tessa and I'.
75 Chili Bouchier, *Shooting Star: The Last of the Silent Film Stars* (London: Atlantis, 1996), p. 48.
76 Ibid.
77 Ibid., pp. 48–9.
78 For instance, see 'A screen-struck public', *The Era*, 24 September 1919, p. 22; 'Long shots and close-ups', *Kinematograph Weekly*, 1 September 1921, p. 33.
79 Sydney A. Moseley, *The Night Haunts of London* (London: Paul, 1920), p. 104.
80 'Cinema stage morals', *The Bioscope*, 16 December 1920, p. 7.
81 G.A. Atkinson, 'The hard road to film fame', *Daily Express*, 6 June 1922, p. 6.
82 Ibid.
83 Ibid.
84 Stephen Constantine, *Unemployment in Britain between the Wars* (London: Longman, 1980), p. 3.
85 Ibid., p. 41; Matt Perry, *Bread and Work: Social Policy and the Experience of Unemployment, 1918–39* (London: Pluto Press, 2000), p. 59.
86 Constantine, *Unemployment in Britain between the Wars*, p. 18
87 Elizabeth Roberts, *Women's Work 1840–1940* (Basingstoke: Macmillan, 1988), pp. 67–8; Gail Braybon, *Women Workers in the First World War: The British Experience* (London: Croom Helm, 1981), pp. 185–204.
88 Sally Alexander, 'Men's fears and women's work: Responses to unemployment in London between the wars', *Gender & History*, 12/2 (2000): 401.
89 Judith R. Walkowitz, *City of Dreadful Delight: Narratives of Sexual Danger in Late-Victorian London* (London: Virago, 1992).

90 Richard deCordova, *Picture Personalities: The Emergence of the Star System in America* (Chicago: University of Illinois Press, 1990), p. 139. For Rappe, see also Hilary A. Hallett, *Go West, Young Woman!: The Rise of Early Hollywood* (Berkeley: University of California Press, 2013), pp. 180–212.
91 'Gomorrah of the golden West', *Daily Express*, 21 September 1921, p. 4.
92 'Miss Carleton's death. "Doping" parties in flats', *The Times*, 13 December 1918, p. 3; Marek Kohn, *Dope Girls: The Birth of the British Drug Underground* (London: Lawrence and Wishart, 1992), pp. 78–9.
93 '"Fatty" accused of killing a girl', *News of the World*, 18 September 1921, p. 4.
94 Hallett, *Go West, Young Woman!*, p. 210.
95 For the evolution of the 'flapper' figure, see Billie Melman, *Women and the Popular Imagination in the Twenties: Flappers and Nymphs* (Basingstoke: Macmillan, 1988), pp. 27–9.
96 *Manchester Evening News*, 6 February 1920, p. 7, quoted in Claire Langhamer, *Women's Leisure in England, 1920–1960* (Manchester: Manchester University Press, 2000), p. 54.
97 Adrian Bingham, *Gender, Modernity, and the Popular Press in Inter-War Britain* (Oxford: Clarendon, 2004), pp. 60–3.
98 Bree Narran [pseud.], *The Kinema Girl* (London: Anglo-Eastern, n.d. [c. 1920]), p. 38. The authorship of the Bree Narran novels is uncertain, but research by John Arnold and James Doig suggests that the most likely candidate is Catherine Mercy Marion Simmons, also known as Mercy Lehane Willis: see John Arnold and James Doig, 'William Nicholas Willis, père, fils and family and the Anglo-Eastern Publishing Company', *Script & Print*, 39/4 (2015), 197–220. Thanks to John Arnold for sharing an early version of this article with me.
99 For Limehouse, see Jon Burrows, '"A vague Chinese quarter elsewhere": Limehouse in the cinema 1914–36', *Journal of British Cinema and Television*, 6/2 (2009), 282–301; Kohn, *Dope Girls*, pp. 78–9.
100 Adolphus Raymond, *Film-Struck; or, A Peep Behind the Curtain* (London: Paul, 1923).
101 Ibid., p. 27.
102 For instance, see 'Schools and their pupils', *Motion Picture Studio*, 25 March 1922, p. 15.
103 Raymond, *Film-Struck*, p. 213.
104 'Stanley Paul's latest novels', *The Times*, 7 September 1923, p. 6.
105 Draft report on employment agencies, presented papers of the LCC Public Control Committee, meeting of 28 November 1919, LMA, LCC/MIN/9752, Item 3.
106 Susan D. Pennybacker, *A Vision for London 1889–1914: Labour, Everyday Life and the LCC Experiment* (London: Routledge, 1995), p. 182.
107 Gwilym Gibbon and Reginald W. Bell, *History of the London County Council, 1889–1939* (London: Macmillan, 1939), p. 564.

108 Minutes of the LCC Public Control Committee, meeting of 3 December 1920, LMA, LCC/MIN/9599.
109 'Gossip', *The Bioscope*, 9 December 1920, p. 6.
110 Information about Quigley's aliases and possible biography comes from the newspaper reports and court documents cited below.
111 'Lessons for film stage', *Pall Mall Gazette*, 27 January 1920, p. 2.
112 'Art of film acting', *The Times*, 17 March 1920, p. 13.
113 'Daughter of a peer', *Pall Mall Gazette*, 23 March 1920, p. 4; 'Film fraud sentence', *Daily Mail*, 25 March 1920, p. 5.
114 'Peer's daughter or barmaid', *Empire News*, 28 March 1920, p. 8.
115 'Lessons in film acting', *The Times*, 25 March 1920, p. 13.
116 'Frauds on film aspirants', *The Times*, 15 February 1922, p. 7. For evidence of Welding's track record as a cinema school operator and confidence trickster, see the report of an earlier case involving a man known as Glenville, Watson or Wilson (pseudonyms similar to those used by Welding in the 1920s): 'Candidates for the cinema', *The Times*, 18 November 1915, p. 4.
117 'Lessons in film acting', *The Times*, 3 March 1921, p. 5; 'In the courts', *Kinematograph Weekly*, 31 March 1921, p. 71.
118 'Film "academy" fined', *The Times*, 17 August 1921, p. 5.
119 Minutes of the LCC Public Control Committee, meeting of 3 December 1920, LMA, LCC/MIN/9599.
120 'Film "academy" fined', *The Times*, 17 August 1921, p. 5; 'Wriggly Quigley's diddled damsels', *John Bull*, 8 September 1923, p. 8.
121 'Cinema school prosecution', *The Times*, 18 December 1921, p. 8; 'Wriggly Quigley's diddled damsels', *John Bull*, 8 September 1923, p. 8.
122 'Alleged cinema school frauds', *The Times*, 21 January 1922, p. 7.
123 After-trial calendars for London, including Central Criminal Court, 1922, The National Archives (TNA), HO 140/373, Entries 46–7.
124 'Frauds on film aspirants', *The Times*, 15 February 1922, p. 7.
125 'Lessons in film acting', *The Times*, 25 March 1920, p. 13.
126 'Training for the films', *The Times*, 4 August 1923, p. 5; 'Marion Quigley again!', *Motion Picture Studio*, 28 July 1923, p. 11; Deposition of Emily Elinor Gertrude Wells, 19 December 1923, TNA, CRIM 1/265, 'Defendant: Wilding, Jessie. Charge: False pretences, Session: January 1924'.
127 Deposition of Emily Elinor Gertrude Wells, 19 December 1923, TNA, CRIM 1/265; 'Swindler unmasked', *News of the World*, 13 January 1924, p. 6.
128 Deposition of Thomas Clarke Reeve, 19 December 1923, TNA, CRIM 1/265.
129 Deposition of David Lannon, 5 December 1923, TNA, CRIM 1/265.
130 Deposition of Lawrence Sidney Poole, Metropolitan Police 'C' Division, 23 November 1923, TNA, CRIM 1/265; *Daily Mirror*, 24 November 1923, p. 2; 'Swindler unmasked', *News of the World*, 13 January 1924, p. 6.
131 'Baby in prison', *Daily Mirror*, 24 November 1923, p. 2.

132 After-trial calendars for London, including Central Criminal Court, 1924, TNA, HO 140/385, Entry 47; 'Swindler unmasked', *News of the World*, 13 January 1924, p. 6.
133 Matt Houlbrook, 'Commodifying the self within: Ghosts, libels, and the crook life story in interwar Britain', *Journal of Modern History*, 85/2 (2013), 321–63; Angus McLaren, 'Smoke and mirrors: Willy Clarkson and the role of disguise in inter-war England', *Journal of Social History*, 40/3 (2007), 597–618. See also April Miller, 'Bloody blondes and bobbed-hair bandits: The execution of justice and the construction of the celebrity criminal in the 1920s popular press', in Su Holmes and Diane Negra (eds), *In the Limelight and Under the Microscope: Forms and Functions of Female Celebrity* (London: Continuum, 2011), pp. 61–81; and Matt Houlbrook, *Prince of Tricksters: The Incredible True Story of Netley Lucas, Gentleman Crook* (Chicago: University of Chicago Press, 2016).
134 Houlbrook, 'Commodifying the self within', 332.
135 Ibid., 351.
136 'Wriggly Quigley's diddled damsels', *John Bull*, 8 September 1923, p. 8.
137 'Swindler unmasked', *News of the World*, 13 January 1924, p. 6; Houlbrook, 'Commodifying the self within', 349–50; Elizabeth Carolyn Miller, *Framed: The New Woman Criminal in British Culture at the Fin de Siècle* (Ann Arbor: University of Michigan Press, 2008), pp. 70–100.
138 'Swindler unmasked', *News of the World*, 13 January 1924, p. 6.
139 'Film acting', *Pall Mall Gazette*, 9 March 1921, p. 2; 'Lessons in film acting', *The Times*, 10 March 1921, p. 5.
140 'Lessons in art of film acting', *Daily Mirror*, 14 February 1920, p. 2.
141 'Acting the part', *Pall Mall Gazette*, 17 March 1920, p. 4.
142 'Film aspirants' lessons', *The Times*, 19 March 1920, p. 13.
143 For instance, see 'In the courts', *Kinematograph Weekly*, 31 March 1921, p. 71; 'Marion Quigley again!', *Motion Picture Studio*, 28 July 1923, p. 11; 'The "Empire School of Kinematography"', *Motion Picture Studio*, 11 August 1923, p. 9; 'Baker Street bogus "school"', *Motion Picture Studio*, 1 September 1923, p. 11; and 'Jessie Quigley goes to prison', *Motion Picture Studio*, 19 January 1924, pp. 8–9.
144 Raymond, *Film-Struck*, p. 31; Narran, *Kinema Girl*, p. 39.
145 Bouchier, *Shooting Star*, p. 48.
146 'Lessons for film stage', *Pall Mall Gazette*, 27 January 1920, p. 2; 'Girl with a film face', *The Times*, 18 March 1920, p. 13.
147 'Sad plight of Scots girl', *Glasgow Sunday Post*, 25 December 1921, p. 2; '"Star" parts for film pupils', *The Times*, 27 December 1921, p. 14.
148 'Film acting', *Pall Mall Gazette*, 9 March 1921, p. 2; 'Lessons in film acting', *The Times*, 10 March 1921, p. 5; 'In the courts', *Kinematograph Weekly*, 31 March 1921, p. 71.
149 '"Star" parts for film pupils', *The Times*, 27 December 1921, p. 14.

150 'The "Empire School of Kinematography"', *Motion Picture Studio*, 11 August 1923, p. 9; 'Training for the films', *The Times*, 4 August 1923, p. 5.
151 'Film acting', *Pall Mall Gazette*, 9 March 1921, p. 2; 'Lessons in film acting', *The Times*, 10 March 1921, p. 5.
152 'Film "academy" fined', *The Times*, 17 August 1921, p. 5.
153 Depositions of Violetta Derry and Dora White, 19 December 1923, TNA, CRIM 1/265.
154 Selina Todd, *Young Women, Work, and Family in England 1918-1950* (Oxford: Oxford University Press, 2005), pp. 96-7.
155 'Lessons in film acting', *Daily Mail* (Hull), 14 February 1922, p. 5.
156 Deposition of Matilda Mary Sutherland, 19 December 1923, TNA, CRIM 1/265.
157 'Schools from within', *Motion Picture Studio*, 19 August 1922, p. 6.
158 '"Star" parts for film pupils', *The Times*, 27 December 1921, p. 14.
159 'Film aspirants' lessons', *The Times*, 19 March 1920, p. 13.
160 'Acting the part', *Pall Mall Gazette*, 17 March 1920, p. 4; 'Art of film acting', *The Times*, 17 March 1920, p. 13.
161 Bennett, 'Import from England', p. 4.
162 'Ex-Gordon's ambition', *Aberdeen Journal*, 13 February 1920, p. 4. See also Martin Petter, '"Temporary gentlemen" in the aftermath of the Great War: Rank, status and the ex-officer problem', *Historical Journal*, 37/1 (1994), 127-52.
163 '"Star" parts for film pupils', *The Times*, 27 December 1921, p. 14.
164 'Cinema school prosecution', *The Times*, 9 January 1922, p. 8.
165 Deposition of William Burghett Moss, 19 December 1923, TNA, CRIM 1/265.
166 *Hansard*, HC Deb, 3 March 1927, vol. 203 col. 531. For a record of Day's agency, see the minutes of the LCC Public Control Committee, meeting of 28 November 1930, LMA, LCC/MIN/9619, p. 1173.
167 *Hansard*, HC Deb, 14 April 1927, vol. 205 col. 526, and 14 November 1927, vol. 210 col. 690.
168 Evelyn Waugh, *Vile Bodies* (1929), ed. by Richard Jacobs (London: Penguin, 1996), p. 125.
169 Letter from P.L. Mannock, 15 December 1927, presented papers of the LCC Public Control Committee, meeting of 27 January 1928, LMA, LCC/MIN/9998.
170 'A "film school" licence refused', *Motion Picture Studio*, 12 May 1923, p. 11.
171 Minutes of the LCC Public Control Committee, meeting of 28 January 1928, LMA, LCC/MIN/9614.
172 'Victoria Cinema College', *Kinematograph Weekly*, 2 February 1928, p. 41.
173 Minutes of the LCC Public Control Committee, meeting of 30 November 1928, LMA, LCC/MIN/9615.

174 The company's last financial statement was filed at the end of 1928, and the company was dissolved by notice in the *London Gazette* in 1931: see 'Victoria Cinema College and Studios, Limited', TNA, BT 31/27423/184759.
175 Victor Hilton, 'That film school', *Picturegoer*, May 1928, p. 50.

4. Stand forth, Mary Pickford the second! Searching for British stars

1 Edgar Wallace, *The Avenger* (London: Long, 1926), p. 30. The novel was originally serialised as 'The extra girl' in *Picture Show*, 10 November 1923–16 February 1924.
2 Ibid.
3 John Parris Springer, *Hollywood Fictions: The Dream Factory in American Popular Literature* (Norman: University of Oklahoma Press, 2000).
4 'Once they lined up for pay!', *Picture Show*, 14 February 1925, pp. 14–15, 23.
5 For existing scholarship on British star searches, see Jenny Hammerton, 'Screen-struck: The lure of Hollywood for British women in the 1920s', in Alan Burton and Laraine Porter (eds), *Crossing the Pond: Anglo-American Film Relations Before 1930* (Trowbridge: Flicks Books, 2002), pp. 100–5; Jane Bryan, '"The cinema looking glass": The British film fan magazine, 1911–1918', unpublished PhD thesis (Norwich: University of East Anglia, 2006), pp. 240–6; and Luke McKernan, 'Just a Brixton shop girl', *The Keaton Chronicle*, 19/3 (2011), published in an earlier version as 'Just a shop girl from Brixton' on the International Buster Keaton Society website. Available at http://www.busterkeaton.com/Margaret/shop1.htm (accessed 29 January 2016). Marsha Orgeron briefly discusses American star searches in '"You are invited to participate": Interactive fandom in the age of the movie magazine', *Journal of Film and Video*, 61/3 (2009): 15–16. More space is given to early 'movie talent contests' in local American newspapers in Richard Abel, *Menus for Movieland: Newspapers and the Emergence of American Film Culture, 1913–1916* (California: University of California Press, 2015), pp. 135–8. Thanks to Mara Arts for pointing out this last source to me.
6 Marjorie Hume and Miss June, best known for her performance in *The Lodger* (Alfred Hitchcock, 1926), were both finalists in the 1919 star search run by the *Sunday Express*: see 'Winners of the £500 cinema star competition', *Sunday Express*, 6 July 1919, p. 2. Mabel Poulton was a semi-finalist in the Pathé Screen Beauty Contest the following year: see 'Romance of grace and beauty', *Sunday Express*, 28 March 1920, p. 7. Chili Bouchier also entered a national beauty contest later in the decade: see 'Our prizes for –', *Daily Mirror*, 24 July 1926, p. 8.
7 'The picture theatre', *The Bioscope*, 31 July 1913, p. 375; Low Warren, *The Showman's Advertising Book: Containing Hundreds of Money-Making Tips and Wrinkles* (London: Kinematograph Weekly, 1914), p. 121.

8 'Contest for film actors', *The Era*, 5 April 1913, p. 28; 'Items of interest', *The Bioscope*, 3 April 1913, p. 10.
9 'The exhibition', *The Bioscope*, 19 February 1914, p. 772.
10 Bryan, 'The cinema looking glass', pp. 240–6.
11 'From the editor's chair', *Picture Palace News*, 2 September 1916, p. 331; 'Do you want to act for the pictures?', *Picture News*, 23 September 1916, p. 45.
12 'Our great popularity contest', *Picture News*, 27 January 1917, p. 396.
13 'An English "Mary Pickford"', *Pictures and the Picturegoer*, 18 July 1918, p. 67.
14 'Who will be the "Pictures" girl?', *Pictures and the Picturegoer*, 24 August 1918, p. 198.
15 'Finding the girl of girls', *Pictures and the Picturegoer*, 7 December 1918, p. 588.
16 'The "Pictures girl"', *Pictures and the Picturegoer*, 8 March 1919, p. 247.
17 'Round the studios', *The Bioscope*, 1 May 1919, p. 76; 'Cinema screen coiffure', *Pictures and the Picturegoer*, 26 July 1919, p. 112.
18 Walter West, 'Where are our stars?', *Kinematograph and Lantern Weekly*, 19 June 1919, p. 77.
19 'Britain's million pound film producing co.', *The Bioscope*, 20 October 1919, p. 8.
20 'Your chance to act for the pictures!', *Picture Plays*, 15 November 1919, pp. 12–13.
21 Edith Nepean, 'Gossip about British players', *Picture Show*, 4 July 1925, p. 19. For details of Nepean, see 'A Welsh novelist', *Stoll's Editorial News*, 11 August 1921, p. 11. Available at https://womenandsilentbritishcinema.wordpress.com/the-women/edith-nepean (accessed 29 January 2016).
22 Edith Nepean, 'Round the British studios', *Picture Show*, 10 October 1925, p. 10; Geoffrey Macnab, 'What was it like to be in a Hitchcock film? I can't remember', *The Guardian*, 20 January 2004. Available at http://www.theguardian.com/film/2004/jan/20/1 (accessed 29 January 2016).
23 Edith Nepean, 'Round the British studios', *Picture Show*, 10 October 1925, p. 10.
24 *Picture Show*, 10 October 1925, front cover.
25 Adrian Bingham, *Family Newspapers? Sex, Private Life, and the British Popular Press 1918–1978* (Oxford: Oxford University Press, 2009), p. 16.
26 Aled Jones, 'The British press, 1919–1945', in Dennis Griffiths (ed.), *The Encyclopedia of the British Press, 1422–1992* (Basingstoke: Macmillan, 1992), pp. 47–55.
27 Harold Herd, *The Making of Modern Journalism* (London: Allen & Unwin, 1927), p. 100.
28 Adrian Bingham, *Gender, Modernity, and the Popular Press in Inter-War Britain* (Oxford: Clarendon, 2004), p. 30.
29 Ibid., pp. 34–6.
30 'Who is the loveliest woman in the world?', *Daily Mirror*, 2 August 1907, p. 7.
31 'Mr. Geo. Edwardes' novel proposal', *Daily Mirror*, 6 November 1908, p. 3; 'Contest for stage prizes', *Daily Mirror*, 12 November 1908, p. 4.

32 '£1,000 for war work belles', *Daily Mirror*, 4 November 1918, p. 2; '£2,000 for the most beautiful sports girl', *Daily Mirror*, 7 April 1924, p. 2; '£1,000 in prizes for beauties', *Daily Mirror*, 9 July 1926, p. 2.
33 Rebecca Conway, 'Making the mill girl modern? Beauty, industry, and the popular newspaper in 1930s' England', *Twentieth Century British History*, 24/4 (2013), 518–41; Bingham, *Gender, Modernity, and the Popular Press*, p. 146.
34 Memo from Lord Northcliffe to Thomas Marlowe, 6 July 1919, quoted in Bingham, *Gender, Modernity, and the Popular Press*, p. 224.
35 'From bank clerk to film star', *Daily Mirror*, 10 April 1919, p. 15. Miriam Sabbage acted in the British film *The Bridal Chair* (G.B. Samuelson, 1919).
36 Martin Conboy, *The Press and Popular Culture* (London: SAGE, 2002), p. 114.
37 Robert Allen, *Voice of Britain: The Inside Story of the Daily Express* (Cambridge: Stephens, 1983), pp. 28, 34.
38 Anne Chisholm and Michael Davie, *Beaverbrook: A Life* (London: Hutchinson, 1992), pp. 207–8.
39 Letter from A.W. Rider to Lord Beaverbrook, 24 January 1919, Beaverbrook Papers, Parliamentary Archives, BBK/H/44.
40 Report from Reeves (Circulation Manager) to Lord Beaverbrook, undated, *c.* 24 January 1919, Beaverbrook Papers, Parliamentary Archives, BBK/H/44.
41 Chisholm and Davie, *Beaverbrook*, p. 227.
42 '£200 for a new cinema play', *Sunday Express*, 30 March 1919, p. 7.
43 Letter from Hugh Muir to Lord Beaverbrook, 2 April 1919, Beaverbrook Papers, Parliamentary Archives, BBK/H/44.
44 'Opportunity for a new film star', *Sunday Express*, 6 April 1919, p. 7.
45 '£500 cinema star competition', *Sunday Express*, 13 April 1919, p. 2.
46 Nathalie Morris, 'An eminent British studio: The Stoll film companies and British cinema 1918-1928', unpublished PhD thesis (Norwich: University of East Anglia, 2009), pp. 45–6.
47 Ibid., p. 177; Jon Burrows, 'Big studio production in the pre-quota years', in Robert Murphy (ed.), *The British Cinema Book*, third edition (London: British Film Institute, 2009), p. 156.
48 'Opportunity for a new film star', *Sunday Express*, 6 April 1919, p. 7.
49 Ibid.
50 Sydney A. Moseley, *The Truth about a Journalist* (London: Pitman, 1935), p. 330.
51 'On the first rung of the ladder of fame', *Sunday Express*, 29 June 1919, p. 2; 'Peace celebrations as seen by the camera', *Sunday Express*, 29 June 1919, p. 5.
52 Conway, 'Making the mill girl modern?', 539.
53 'Winners of the £500 cinema star competition', *Sunday Express*, 6 July 1919, p. 2; Tommy Sinclair, 'My first step toward success', *Sunday Express*, 13 July 1919, p. 3.

54 'Film fame lure', *Daily Mirror*, 19 July 1920, p. 2; 'What our readers have to say', *Daily Mirror*, 27 May 1929, p. 11.
55 'Acting for the "movies"', *Evening News*, 22 April 1919, p. 6; 'How can I get my girl on the film?', *Sunday Express*, 20 March 1921, p. 3; Betty Balfour, 'How to become a film star', *Daily Mirror*, 20 May 1927, p. 4.
56 Sydney A. Moseley, *The Night Haunts of London* (London: Paul, 1920), p. 104; Moseley, *Truth about a Journalist*, pp. 330–1. For Moseley's attack on 'cinema stage morals', see Chapter 3.
57 Bingham, *Gender, Modernity, and the Popular Press*, p. 52.
58 Luke McKernan, *Topical Budget: The Great British News Film* (London: British Film Institute, 1992), p. 4.
59 Jenny Hammerton, 'Everything that constitutes life: Pathé cinemagazines 1918–1969', in Luke McKernan (ed.), *Yesterday's News: The British Cinema Newsreel Reader* (London: British Universities Film & Video Council, 2002), pp. 268–80; Emily Crosby, 'The "colour supplement" of the cinema: The British cinemagazine, 1918–38', *Journal of British Cinema and Television*, 5/1 (2008), 1–18.
60 Bingham, *Family Newspapers?*, p. 22.
61 Rachael Low, *The History of the British Film 1918–1929* (London: Allen & Unwin, 1971), p. 44; 'Lord Beaverbrook buys', *Variety*, 5 March 1920, p. 66.
62 Richard Abel, *French Cinema: The First Wave, 1915–1929* (Princeton: Princeton University Press, 1984), pp. 12–13; 'International combine', *Wid's Daily*, 10 March 1920, p. 3.
63 'Pathé Pictorial', in Emily Crosby and Linda Kaye (eds), *Projecting Britain: The Guide to British Cinemagazines* (London: British Universities Film & Video Council, 2008), pp. 172–3.
64 Letter from Frank Smith to Lord Beaverbrook, 4 February 1920, Beaverbrook Papers, Parliamentary Archives, BBK/H/274.
65 Ibid.
66 Ibid. For sales of the *Pathé Gazette*, see the letter from Frank Smith to Lord Beaverbrook, 2 February 1920, Beaverbrook Papers, Parliamentary Archives, BBK/H/274.
67 Letter from Frank Smith to Lord Beaverbrook, 4 February 1920, Beaverbrook Papers, Parliamentary Archives, BBK/H/274. The French scheme referred to was most likely the contest organised by the daily newspaper *Le Journal* to find 'La plus belle femme de France' won by Agnès Souret: see 'Prize French beauty', *Daily Express*, 12 May 1920, p. 1.
68 Letter from Frank Smith to Lord Beaverbrook, 4 February 1920, Beaverbrook Papers, Parliamentary Archives, BBK/H/274.
69 '£1,000 in prizes!', *Daily Mirror*, 12 March 1920, p. 13.
70 'Search for a film beauty', *Sunday Express*, 21 March 1920, p. 7.
71 'British beauty for the films', *Daily Express*, 4 March 1920, p. 7.

72 'British Pearl White', *Daily Express*, 5 March 1920, p. 7.
73 'Search for a film beauty', *Sunday Express*, 21 March 1920, p. 7.
74 'Romance of grace and beauty', *Sunday Express*, 28 March 1920, p. 7.
75 'Miss K. Coulson of Cambridge', *Sunday Express*, 13 June 1920, p. 7.
76 'Grace and beauty election', *Daily Express*, 25 March 1920, p. 6.
77 'Who will be the film queen?', *Sunday Express*, 11 July 1920, p. 5; Chisholm and Davie, *Beaverbrook*, p. 92.
78 'Six pretty Pathé girls', *Sunday Express*, 10 October 1920, p. 4.
79 'Scotland wins Pathé's great screen beauty contest', *Sunday Express*, 12 December 1920, p. 4.
80 For surviving screen tests, see *Pathé's Beauty Contest 3* (1920) and *Beauty Competition* (1920), British Pathé Archive. Available at http://www.british-pathe.com/video/pathes-beauty-contest-3 and http://www.britishpathe.com/video/beauty-competition (accessed 29 January 2016).
81 'Miss Phyllis Nadell', *Sunday Express*, 6 February 1921, p. 1; 'Mannerisms from the screen', *Dundee Evening Telegraph*, 8 February 1921, p. 9.
82 Letter from Major Holt to Lord Beaverbook, 19 October 1920, Beaverbrook Papers, Parliamentary Archives, BBK/H/275.
83 'New stage and film stars', *Daily Mail*, 10 March 1920, pp. 7–8. The name was a reference to the classical myth of the Judgement of Paris.
84 'Britain's beauty on the screen', *The Bioscope*, 11 March 1920, supplement, p. iii.
85 '*Around the Town*', in Crosby and Kaye, *Projecting Britain*, pp. 172–3.
86 Crosby, 'The "colour supplement" of the cinema', 3.
87 Letter from Frank Smith to Lord Beaverbrook, 4 February 1920, Beaverbrook Papers, Parliamentary Archives, BBK/H/274.
88 Crosby, 'The "colour supplement" of the cinema', 3.
89 'New stage and film stars', *Daily Mail*, 10 March 1920, pp. 7–8; '"Golden Apple" result', *Daily Mail*, 22 December 1920, p. 5.
90 'New stage and film stars', *Daily Mail*, 10 March 1920, p. 8.
91 'Girls chance to be "international"', *Daily Mail*, 16 March 1920, p. 5.
92 '"Stars" of the future', *Weekly Dispatch*, 14 March 1920, p. 3.
93 'Stage and film "stars"', *Daily Mail*, 12 May 1920, p. 4.
94 '"Golden Apple" result', *Daily Mail*, 22 December 1920, p. 5.
95 'Short stuff', *Kinematograph Weekly*, 6 January 1921, p. 179.
96 'Scotland wins Pathé's great screen beauty contest', *Sunday Express*, 12 December 1920, p. 4.
97 'Another quest for a film star', *Kinematograph and Lantern Weekly*, 10 April 1919, p. 64e; 'Gaumont enterprise', *The Bioscope*, 6 January 1921, p. 28.
98 '*Daily Sketch*', in Griffiths (ed.), *Encyclopedia of the British Press*, p. 186; Bingham, *Gender, Modernity, and the Popular Press*, p. 13.
99 McKernan, *Topical Budget*, pp. 72–4; Low, *History of the British Film, 1918–1928*, p. 72.

100 S. Charles Einfield, 'History of First National', *Variety*, 25 June 1930, p. 28.
101 'First National in special coast session', *Motion Picture News*, 18 January 1929, p. 367; 'Talmadge signed', *Wid's Daily*, 29 April 1919, p. 1.
102 'Buster Keaton signs with First National', *Exhibitors Herald*, 21 May 1921, p. 35.
103 'Your opportunity for film fame', *Daily Sketch*, 11 September 1922, p. 7.
104 'Norma Talmadge protegees', *Motion Picture Studio*, 14 October 1922, pp. 6–7; 'Wonderful London yesterday', *Daily Graphic*, 16 October 1922, p. 4.
105 'British First National plans', *Exhibitors Trade Review*, 22 April 1922, p. 1472; 'The film and its exploitation', *The Bioscope*, 6 July 1922, p. 48.
106 Ralph J. Pugh, 'Replying for Joseph M. Schenck', *Kinematograph Weekly*, 14 September 1922, p. 44; 'First National plans', *Kinematograph Weekly*, 4 January 1923, p. 30.
107 'Long shots and close-ups', *Kinematograph Weekly*, 7 September 1922, p. 40; '"Big" pictures and the exhibitor', *Kinematograph Weekly*, 14 September 1922, p. 45. For tensions over the distribution of American films in Britain during the 1920s, see Ian Jarvie, *Hollywood's Overseas Campaign: The North Atlantic Movie Trade, 1920–1950* (Cambridge: Cambridge University Press, 1992), pp. 103–34.
108 'First National's Talmadge boom', *Kinematograph Weekly*, 14 September 1922, p. 52; 'Service for the showmen', *The Bioscope*, 28 September 1922, pp. 48–9.
109 'The film and its exploitation', *The Bioscope*, 6 July 1922, p. 48. Pontefract's role as publicity manager at Pathé is mentioned in Amy Sargeant, '"Everybody's doing the Riviera" because "it's so much nicer in Nice"', in Laraine Porter and Bryony Dixon (eds), *Picture Perfect: Landscape, Place and Travel in British Cinema before 1930* (Exeter: Exeter Press, 2007), p. 92.
110 'Talmadges sail Sept. 3', *Film Daily*, 25 July 1922, p. 1.
111 'Smiling Through', *The Times*, 12 September 1922, p. 7; 'No more trade shows', *Kinematograph Weekly*, 21 September 1922, p. 52.
112 'The Talmadge stunt exposed', *Motion Picture Studio*, 21 October 1922, p. 9.
113 Ibid. Newsreel footage of the publicity stunt survives in the item 'Will one of these be new British film star?', *Topical Budget 582-1* (1922), British Film Institute (BFI) National Archive.
114 'Daily Sketch beauties', *Topical Budget 586-1* (1922), BFI National Archive; 'Stage and film "stars"', *Daily Mail*, 12 May 1920, p. 4.
115 'Your opportunity for film fame', *Daily Sketch*, 11 September 1922, p. 7.
116 'Film fame may be yours', *Daily Sketch*, 12 September 1922, p. 2.
117 For instance, see Norma Talmadge, 'All about myself', *Cinema Chat*, 1 December 1919, p. 32.
118 Christine Gledhill, *Reframing British Cinema, 1918–1928: Between Passion and Restraint* (London: British Film Institute, 2003), p. 79.
119 'Film fame may be theirs', *Daily Sketch*, 14 September 1922, p. 2.

120 Ibid.
121 'Daily Sketch girl is chosen', *Daily Sketch*, 14 November 1922, p. 2.
122 'Trade notes', *The Bioscope*, 14 June 1923, p. 33; 'Margaret comes home to-day', *Daily Sketch*, 11 June 1923, p. 15.
123 'Norma Talmadge protegees', *Motion Picture Studio*, 14 October 1922, p. 6.
124 'Film section', *The Encore*, 5 October 1922, p. 10.
125 Jarvie, *Hollywood's Overseas Campaign*, p. 130.
126 'Miss Talmadge's letter', *Motion Picture Studio*, 21 October 1922, p. 5.
127 Chris Waters, 'Beyond "Americanization": Rethinking Anglo-American cultural exchange between the wars', *Cultural and Social History*, 4/4 (2007): 453.
128 'Reviews of the week', *Kinematograph Weekly*, 28 June 1923, p. 44; 'Criticisms of the films', *The Bioscope*, 5 July 1923, p. 43.
129 'New film girl', *Daily Sketch*, 4 June 1923, p. 2.
130 'Margaret Leahy's return', *Motion Picture Studio*, 9 June 1923, p. 6.
131 Lisa Stead, 'Audiences from the film archive: Women's writing and silent cinema', in Nandana Bose and Lee Grieveson (eds), *Using Moving Image Archives* (Nottingham: Scope e-Book, 2010), pp. 40–2. Available at http://www.nottingham.ac.uk/scope/issues/2010/june-issue-17.aspx (accessed 29 January 2016)
132 '£100 for a film face', *Weekly Dispatch*, 26 February 1928, p. 3.
133 Low, *History of British Films, 1918–1928*, pp. 182–3.
134 'Can you write a screen story?', *Weekly Dispatch*, 4 March 1928, p. 1.
135 'Job in prize picture', *Weekly Dispatch*, 11 March 1928, p. 3.
136 'Which face will capture fame and fortune?', *Sunday Dispatch*, 22 July 1928, p. 15.
137 Ibid.
138 'Film plot winner', *Sunday Dispatch*, 19 August 1928, p. 13. Although the winning film plot was not picked up, one of the runners-up, Herbert C. Price's *A Cottage on Dartmoor*, was produced by BIF the following year (Anthony Asquith, 1929).
139 'Amami film star quest', *Daily Express*, 30 March 1928, p. 6.
140 Low, *History of British Films, 1918–1928*, p. 186; 'Hollywood for England', *Daily Express*, 31 December 1927, p. 1.
141 'The Amami beauty book', *Daily Mirror*, 2 March 1928, p. 14. For BIP's internationalism, see Andrew Higson, 'Polyglot films for an international market: E.A. Dupont, the British film industry, and the idea of a European cinema, 1926–1930', in Andrew Higson and Richard Maltby (eds), *'Film Europe' and 'Film America': Cinema, Commerce and Cultural Exchange, 1920–1939* (Exeter: University of Exeter Press, 1999), pp. 274–301.
142 'We are re-opening the Amami film star quest', *Daily Mirror*, 28 November 1928, p. 12; 'Amami film star quest result', *Daily Mirror*, 23 November 1928, p. 23.

143 G.A. Atkinson, 'What's wrong with the talkies?', *Daily Express*, 30 September 1929, p. 16. *The Lady from the Sea* was also known as *The Goodwin Sands*.
144 Claire Langhamer, *Women's Leisure in England, 1920-1960* (Manchester: Manchester University Press, 2000), pp. 95-6; Alan Yardley (ed.), *Sunrise to Sunset: An Autobiography by Mary Bertenshaw* (Bury: Printwise, 1991), p. 110; L.C.B. Seaman, *Life in Britain between the Wars* (London: Batsford, 1970), p. 130.
145 'Selling an "expensive luxury" to the mass market', *Advertiser's Weekly*, 22 March 1929, p. 481.
146 Ibid.
147 Ibid.
148 T.R. Nevett, *Advertising in Britain: A History* (London: Heineman, 1982), p. 146.
149 'Selling an "expensive luxury"', p. 481.
150 Marlis Schweitzer, '"The mad search for beauty": Actresses' testimonials, the cosmetics industry, and the democratization of beauty', *Journal of the Gilded Age and Progressive Era*, 4/3 (2005): 259.
151 Gerben Bakker, *Entertainment Industrialised: The Emergence of the International Film Industry, 1890-1940* (Cambridge: Cambridge University Press, 2008), p. 284.
152 Geoffrey Macnab, *Searching for Stars: Stardom and Screen Acting in British Cinema* (London: Cassell, 2000), p. 55.
153 Jonathan Croall, *Forgotten Stars: My Father and the British Silent Film World* (London: Fantom, 2013), p. 123.
154 'Picturegoer beautiful hair competition', *Pictures and the Picturegoer*, June 1925, p. 52; 'Clara Bow uses it', *Daily Mirror*, 22 April 1927, p. 15.
155 'Selling an "expensive luxury"', p. 481.
156 'Post this coupon to-day', *Daily Express*, 4 May 1928, p. 12.
157 'To some lucky Amami girl', *Weekly Dispatch*, 11 March 1928, p. 9.
158 'Wanted a girl', *Daily Mirror*, 13 April 1928, p. 10.
159 Mike Featherstone, 'The body in consumer culture', *Theory, Culture & Society*, 1/2 (1983), 18-33; Kathy Peiss, 'Making up, making over: Cosmetics, consumer culture, and women's identity', in Victoria de Grazia with Ellen Furlough (eds), *The Sex of Things: Gender and Consumption in Historical Perspective* (Berkeley: University of California Press, 1996), pp. 311-36.
160 'Have you seen the "Amami" girl?', *Pictures and the Picturegoer*, February 1924, p. 65; 'Amami film star quest result', *Daily Mirror*, 23 November 1928, p. 23.
161 'Amami girls!', *Daily Mirror*, 8 February 1929, p. 12; 'Choose the ideal film hero for Miss Eugenie Amami', *Daily Express*, 1 March 1929, p. 6.
162 'Selling an "expensive luxury"', Supplement, p. iv.
163 Ibid.

164 Samantha Barbas, *Movie Crazy: Fans, Stars and the Cult of Celebrity* (Basingstoke: Palgrave, 2001), p. 82.
165 '3 Amami girls off to Hollywood and fame!', *Daily Mirror*, 6 October 1933, p. 8.
166 Sarah Banet-Weiser, *The Most Beautiful Girl in the World: Beauty Pageants and National Identity* (Berkeley: University of California Press, 1999), pp. 6–7; Conway, 'Making the mill girl modern?', 524; Sarah Street, *British National Cinema* (London: Routledge, 1997), pp. 145–6.
167 1911 census of England and Wales, London, 178 Guinness Trust Buildings, Bermondsey, Leahy household schedule.
168 Margaret Leahy, 'Before I was found by the "Daily Sketch"', *Daily Sketch*, 14 November 1922, p. 7.
169 'Your opportunity for film fame', *Daily Sketch*, 11 September 1922, p. 7.
170 Olive Wadsley, 'Romance of new Cinderella', *Daily Sketch*, 17 November 1922, p. 9.
171 'She is coming soon!', *Daily Sketch*, 2 June 1923, p. 6; 'America meets Margaret', *Daily Sketch*, 3 December 1922, p. 6.
172 Bernard Rolt, *Cinderella of the Cinema* (London: Heinemann, 1927); Olive Wadsley, 'Romance of new Cinderella', *Daily Sketch*, 17 November 1922, p. 9.
173 Rolt, *Cinderella of the Cinema*, p. 145.
174 Ibid., p. 312.
175 'Daily Sketch girl on tour', *Daily Sketch*, 15 November 1922, p. 2.
176 'Bubbles' first-night ovation', *Daily Sketch*, 17 November 1922, p. 9; 'Triumphal tour of "Bubbles"', *Daily Sketch*, 18 November 1922, p. 2.
177 '"Our girl's" big tour', *Daily Sketch*, 16 November 1922, p. 7; 'The film and its exploitation', *The Bioscope*, 6 July 1922, p. 48.
178 For instance, see 'Amazing triumph of the new British film star', *Topical Budget 587-2* (1922), BFI National Archive.
179 McKernan, *Topical Budget*, p. 116.
180 'Our girl's week end letter', *Daily Sketch*, 9 December 1922, p. 6.
181 Mark Glancy, *Hollywood and the Americanization of Britain: From the 1920s to the Present* (London: I.B.Tauris, 2014), p. 59.
182 'Margaret's Christmas diary', *Daily Sketch*, 30 December 1922, p. 4.
183 Laura E. Nym Mayhall, 'The Prince of Wales *versus* Clark Gable: Anglophone celebrity and citizenship between the wars', *Cultural and Social History*, 4/4 (2007): 540.
184 Rudi Blesh, *Keaton* (London: Secker and Warburg, 1967), pp. 217–18; Marion Meade, *Buster Keaton: Cut to the Chase* (London: Bloomsbury, 1996), p. 135.
185 'Greenroom jottings', *Motion Picture Magazine*, April 1923, p. 119.
186 'Margaret gets a great surprise', *Daily Sketch*, 6 January 1923, p. 6.
187 'New film girl', *Daily Sketch*, 4 June 1923, p. 2.
188 'News of Margaret', *Daily Sketch*, 1 June 1923, p. 2; 'Margaret's day', *Daily Sketch*, 13 June 1923, p. 2.

189 'Margaret's home-coming plans', *Daily Sketch*, 2 June 1923, p. 4.
190 'Margaret comes home to-day', *Daily Sketch*, 11 June 1923, p. 15.
191 'Margaret comes home to-day', *Daily Sketch*, 22 June 1923, p. 2.
192 'Have you the hair of a film star?', *Daily Sketch*, 25 June 1923, p. 8.
193 'Margaret comes home to-day', *Daily Sketch*, 22 June 1923, p. 2; 'Long shots and close-ups', *Kinematograph Weekly*, 28 June 1923, pp. 34–5.
194 'Normarose', *Daily Sketch*, 14 June 1923, p. 2; 'Margaret's day', *Daily Sketch*, 25 June 1923, p. 2.
195 'Margaret's triumphant and tumultuous West End welcome', *Daily Sketch*, 26 June 1923, p. 2; 'Margaret feted', *Daily Sketch*, 26 June 1923, p. 19.
196 'Margaret's pluck', *Daily Sketch*, 2 July 1923, p. 2.
197 Meade, *Buster Keaton*, p. 136.
198 Edwin Schallert and Eliza Schallert, 'Hollywood high lights', *Picture-Play Magazine*, July 1923, p. 66.
199 'Margaret Leahy claims for damages', *Motion Picture Studio*, 29 December 1923, p. 8.
200 'Let George do it!', *Pictures and the Picturegoer*, August 1924, p. 65; 'Let George do it!', *Pictures and the Picturegoer*, May 1925, p. 73.
201 'A clipping for a Valentine cools heart of actress wife', *Brooklyn Daily Eagle*, 13 March 1935, p. 3; ' "Miss England" awarded divorce', press photograph, dated 14 March 1935, author's collection.
202 Meade, *Buster Keaton*, p. 396.
203 Author interview with Gary Piele, 20 March 2015.
204 Meade, *Buster Keaton*, p. 396.
205 Springer, *Hollywood Fictions*, p. 116.
206 The items were left by Margaret Leahy to her cousin's family in South London, and have since been donated to the British Universities Film & Video Council (BUFVC): author interview with Gary Piele, 20 March 2015.
207 Photograph album, Margaret Leahy Collection, BUFVC Special Collections; Blesh, *Keaton*, p. 218; Meade, *Buster Keaton*, p. 136.
208 Newspaper clippings book, Margaret Leahy Collection, BUFVC Special Collections.
209 Bakker, *Entertainment Industrialised*, pp. 312–13.

Epilogue: From silence to sound

1 Billie Melman, *Women and the Popular Imagination in the Twenties: Flappers and Nymphs* (Basingstoke: Macmillan, 1988).
2 Kim Allen, 'Girls imagining careers in the limelight: Social class, gender and fantasies of "success"', in Su Holmes and Diane Negra (eds), *In the Limelight and Under the Microscope: Forms and Functions of Female Celebrity* (London: Continuum, 2011), pp. 147–73.

3 Tom Ryall, 'A British studio system: The Associated British Picture Corporation and the Gaumont-British Picture Corporation in the 1930s', in Robert Murphy (ed.), *The British Cinema Book*, third edition (London: British Film Institute, 2009), pp. 202–10.
4 Hepworth, in R.W. Paul, C.M. Hepworth and W.G. Barker, 'Before 1910: Kinematograph experiences', *Proceedings of the British Kinematograph Society*, 38 (1936), 14.
5 Rachael Low, *The History of the British Film, 1918–1929* (London: Allen & Unwin, 1971), p. 203. For the exhibition of *The Jazz Singer* in America, see Donald Crafton, *The Talkies: America's Transition to Sound, 1926–1931* (New York: Scribner, 1997), pp. 516–31.
6 Low, *History of the British Film, 1918–1929*, p. 203.
7 Mark Glancy, *Hollywood and the Americanization of Britain: From the 1920s to the Present* (London: I.B.Tauris, 2014), p. 82; Mark Jancovich and Lucy Faire with Sarah Stubbings, *The Place of the Audience: Cultural Geographies of Film Consumption* (London: British Film Institute, 2003), pp. 92–4.
8 Robert Murphy, 'The coming of sound to the cinema in Britain', *Historical Journal of Film, Radio and Television*, 4/2 (1984), 143–60.
9 Lionel Collier, 'The silent future', *Picturegoer*, August 1929, pp. 20–1.
10 R.J. Whiteley, 'The film world reviewed', *Daily Mirror*, 1 April 1929, p. 19; G.A. Atkinson, 'Have the talkies come to stay?', *Daily Express*, 10 April 1929, p. 10.
11 Lilian Bamburg, *Film Acting as a Career* (London: Foulsham, 1929).
12 Murphy, 'Coming of sound', 153.
13 L.C. Moen, 'B.I.P. sound studios', *Kinematograph Weekly*, 28 March 1929, p. 25; W.H.M., 'B.I.P.'s new sound studio', *The Bioscope*, 10 April 1929, p. 25.
14 'Gaumont studio', *Kinematograph Weekly*, 6 June 1929, p. 30; 'Gainsborough studio converted', *Kinematograph Weekly*, 27 June 1929, p. 25.
15 'The film world', *The Times*, 11 December 1929, p. 12.
16 L.C. Moen, 'B.I.P. sound studios', *Kinematograph Weekly*, 28 March 1929, p. 25.
17 Murphy, 'Coming of sound', 156.
18 'At Twickenham', *Kinematograph Weekly*, 10 October 1929, p. 25. The French-language version was known as *Le mystère de la villa rose*.
19 Bamburg, *Film Acting as a Career*, p. 30.
20 Ginette Vincendeau, 'Hollywood Babel: The coming of sound and the multiple-language version', *Screen*, 29/2 (1988), 24–39.
21 For instance, see Scott Eyman, *The Speed of Sound: Hollywood and the Talkie Revolution, 1926–1930* (New York: Simon & Schuster, 1997), pp. 181–6.
22 Glancy, *Hollywood and the Americanization of Britain*, pp. 81–8.
23 'Piccadilly Theatre', *The Times*, 26 October 1928, p. 14. The reviewer was commenting on the Warner Brothers film *The Terror*.
24 Bamburg, *Film Acting as a Career*, p. 29.
25 Brian Aherne, *A Proper Job* (Boston: Houghton Mifflin, 1969), p. 160.

26 Ibid., p. 161.
27 Chili Bouchier, *Shooting Star: The Last of the Silent Film Stars* (London: Atlantis, 1996), pp. 52, 62–4.
28 Mabel Poulton interviewed in the BBC documentary *The Talkies Come to Britain* (Stephen Peet, 1971).
29 Bouchier, *Shooting Star*, p. 52.
30 Vicky Lowe, '"The best speaking voices in the world": Robert Donat, stardom and the voice in British cinema', *Journal of British Cinema and Television*, 1/2 (2004), 181–96.
31 Alberto Cavalcanti, 'Sound in films' (1939), in Elisabeth Weis and John Belton (eds), *Film Sound: Theory and Practice* (New York: Columbia University Press, 1985), p. 102.
32 Murphy, 'Coming of sound', 153.
33 Linda Wood, 'Low-budget British films in the 1930s', in Murphy (ed.), *British Cinema Book*, pp. 211–19.
34 Lawrence Napper, 'A despicable tradition? Quota quickies in the 1930s', in Murphy (ed.), *British Cinema Book*, pp. 199–200; Stephen Guy, 'Calling all stars: Musical films in a musical decade', in Jeffrey Richards (ed.), *The Unknown 1930s: An Alternative History of the British Cinema, 1929–1939* (London: I.B.Tauris, 2000), pp. 99–120.
35 Mabel Poulton, 'Tessa and I', unpublished typescript, Mabel Poulton Collection, British Film Institute (BFI) Special Collections, Item 2.
36 J.P. Mayer, *British Cinemas and their Audiences* (London: Dobson, 1948), p. 31.
37 Basil Tozer, *Confidence Crooks and Blackmailers: Their Ways and Methods* (London: Werner Laurie, 1929), p. 16. Thanks to Matt Houlbrook for directing me to this source.
38 Ibid., p. 21.
39 'The film world', *The Times*, 22 May 1929, p. 14. For the training of actors for radio, see Michael Sanderson, *From Irving to Olivier: A Social History of the Acting Profession in England 1880–1983* (London: Athlone Press, 1984), p. 222.
40 Samantha Barbas, *Movie Crazy: Fans, Stars and the Cult of Celebrity* (Basingstoke: Palgrave, 2001), pp. 60, 80. See also Charles Eckert, 'The Carole Lombard in Macy's window', in John Belton (ed.), *Movies and Mass Culture* (London: Athlone, 1996), pp. 95–118.
41 Marsha Orgeron, '"You are invited to participate": Interactive fandom in the age of the movie magazine', *Journal of Film and Video*, 61/3 (2009), 16, 19.
42 Sue Bowden, 'The new consumerism', in Paul Johnson (ed.), *Twentieth-Century Britain: Economic, Social and Cultural Change* (London: Longman, 1994), pp. 242–62; David Fowler, *The First Teenagers: The Lifestyle of Young Wage-Earners in Interwar Britain* (London: Woburn Press, 1995), pp. 93–115.
43 For instance, see Sally Alexander, 'Becoming a woman in London in the 1920s and 1930s', in David Feldman and Gareth Stedman Jones (eds),

Metropolis – London: Histories and Representations since 1800 (London and New York: Routledge, 1989), p. 264.

44 Annette Kuhn, 'Cinema culture and femininity in the 1930s', in Christine Gledhill and Gillian Swanson (eds), *Nationalising Femininity: Culture, Sexuality and British Cinema in the Second World War* (Manchester: Manchester University Press, 1996), pp. 185–6.

45 For instance, see the tips for the 'screen-struck' in R.J. Whitley, 'Spending £80,000 a year in-', *Daily Mirror*, 20 April 1934, p. 20.

Select filmography

Ella Cinders (Dir. Alfred E. Green, USA, 1926)
The Extra Girl (Dir. F. Richard Jones, USA, 1923)
Shooting Stars (Dir. A.V. Bramble and Anthony Asquith, UK, 1928)
Smilin' Through (Dir. Sidney Franklin, USA, 1922)
So This Is Jollygood (Dir. Adrian Brunel, UK, 1925)
Starlings of the Screen (Dir. T.C. Elder, UK, 1925)
The Three Ages (Dir. Buster Keaton and Edward F. Cline, USA, 1923)
Within the Law (Dir. Frank Lloyd, USA, 1923)

Select bibliography

Archives

- Bill Douglas Cinema Museum, University of Exeter
- British Film Institute (BFI) National Archive
- British Film Institute (BFI) Reuben Library
- British Film Institute (BFI) Special Collections
- British Pathé Archives
- British Universities Film & Video Council Special Collections
- London Metropolitan Archives
- The National Archives
- Parliamentary Archives
- Women's Library, London School of Economics

Unpublished material

Brook, Clive, 'The eighty four ages of Clive Brook: His life and times', unpublished typescript, n.d. (*c.* 1971), Clive Brook Collection, British Film Institute Special Collections, Item 83.

Bryan, Jane, ' "The cinema looking glass": The British film fan magazine, 1911–1918', unpublished PhD thesis (Norwich: University of East Anglia, 2006).

Gritten, Daniel John, 'The profession and practice of screenwriting in British cinema: The 1920s and 1930s', unpublished PhD thesis (Bristol: University of Bristol, 2007).

Poulton, Mabel, 'Tessa and I', unpublished typescript, Mabel Poulton Collection, British Film Institute Special Collections, Item 2.

___ 'Cockles and caviare: A story of theatre and film studios', unpublished typescript, Mabel Poulton Collection, British Film Institute Special Collections, Item 3.

Chapters and journal articles

Alexander, Sally, 'Becoming a woman in London in the 1920s and 1930s', in David Feldman and Gareth Stedman Jones (eds), *Metropolis – London: Histories*

Select bibliography

and *Representations since 1800* (London and New York: Routledge, 1989), pp. 245–71.

—— 'Men's fears and women's work: Responses to unemployment in London between the wars', *Gender & History*, 12/2 (2000), 401–25.

Allen, Kim, 'Girls imagining careers in the limelight: Social class, gender and fantasies of "success"', in Holmes and Negra (eds), *In the Limelight and Under the Microscope*, pp. 147–73.

Anon., 'The finding of employment for artistes', *International Labour Review*, 18/4–5 (1928), 610–31.

Ashwell, Lena, 'Acting as a profession', in Edith J. Morley (ed.), *Women Workers in Seven Professions: A Survey of their Economic Conditions and Prospects* (London: Routledge, 1914), pp. 292–313.

Aylott, Dave, 'Reminiscences of a showman', *Cinema Studies*, 2/1 (1965), 3–6.

Bailey, Peter, '"Naughty but nice": Musical comedy and the rhetoric of the girl', in Michael R. Booth and Joel Kaplan (eds), *The Edwardian Theatre: Essays on Performance and the Stage* (Cambridge: Cambridge University Press, 1996), pp. 36–60.

—— 'White collars, gray lives? The lower middle class revisited', *Journal of British Studies*, 30/3 (1999), 273–90.

Baines, Dudley and Paul Johnson, 'In search of the "traditional" working class: Social mobility and occupational continuity in interwar London', *Economic History Review*, 52/4 (1999), 692–713.

Barker, Clive, 'Theatre and society: The Edwardian legacy, the First World War and the inter-war years', in Barker and Gale (eds), *British Theatre between the Wars*, pp. 4–37.

Bean, Jennifer M., 'Technologies of early stardom and the extraordinary body', *Camera Obscura*, 48 (2001), 9–56.

Bennett, Charles, 'Import from England', in Ronald L. Davis (ed.), *Words into Images: Screenwriters on the Studio System* (Jackson: University Press of Mississippi, 2007), pp. 4–19.

Bowden, Sue, 'The new consumerism', in Paul Johnson (ed.), *Twentieth-Century Britain: Economic, Social and Cultural Change* (London: Longman, 1994), pp. 242–62.

Brown, Geoff, '"Sister of the stage": British film and British theatre', in Charles Barr (ed.), *All our Yesterdays: 90 Years of British Cinema* (London: British Film Institute, 1986), pp. 143–67.

Bryan, Jane, 'From film stories to film stars: The beginnings of the fan magazine in Britain, 1911–16', in Alan Burton and Laraine Porter (eds), *Scene Stealing: Sources for British Cinema before 1930* (Trowbridge: Flicks Books, 2003), pp. 65–70.

Burrows, Jon, '"Our English Mary Pickford": Alma Taylor and ambivalent British stardom in the 1910s', in Bruce Babington (ed.), *British Stars and Stardom: From Alma Taylor to Sean Connery* (Manchester: Manchester University Press, 2001), pp. 29–41.

Select bibliography

___ 'Girls on film: The musical matrices of film stardom in early British cinema', *Screen*, 44/4 (2003), 314–25.
___ 'Big studio production in the pre-quota years', in Murphy (ed.), *British Cinema Book*, pp. 155–62.
Cavalcanti, Alberto, 'Sound in films' (1939), in Elisabeth Weis and John Belton (ed.), *Film Sound: Theory and Practice* (New York: Columbia University Press, 1985), pp. 98–111.
Conway, Rebecca, 'Making the mill girl modern? Beauty, industry, and the popular newspaper in 1930s' England', *Twentieth Century British History*, 24/4 (2013), 518–41.
Crosby, Emily, 'The "colour supplement" of the cinema: The British cinemagazine, 1918–38', *Journal of British Cinema and Television*, 5/1 (2008), 1–18.
De Felice, James, 'The London theatrical agent', *Theatre Notebook*, 23/3 (1969), 87–94.
Donat, Robert, 'Film acting', in Charles Davy (ed.), *Footnotes to the Film* (London: Dickson, 1937), pp. 16–36.
Featherstone, Mike, 'The body in consumer culture', *Theory, Culture & Society*, 1/2 (1983), 18–33.
Fletcher, Tony and Ronald Grant, 'A lowland Cinderella: Joan Morgan's silent career, 1912–1929', *Griffithiana*, 65 (1999), 48–86.
Fuller, Kathryn Hegelson, 'The boundaries of participation: The problem of spectatorship and American film audiences, 1905–1930', *Film & History*, 20/4 (1990), 75–86.
Gardner, Viv, 'The three nobodies: Autobiographical strategies in the work of Alma Ellerslie, Kitty Marion and Ina Rozant', in Maggie B. Gale and Viv Gardner (eds), *Auto/biography and Identity: Women, Theatre and Performance* (Manchester: Manchester University Press, 2004), pp. 10–38.
Glancy, Mark, 'Temporary American citizens? British audiences, Hollywood films and the threat of Americanization in the 1920s', *Historical Journal of Film, Radio and Television*, 26/4 (2006), 461–84.
Haller, Andrea, 'Diagnosis: "flimmeritis": Female cinemagoing in Imperial Germany, 1911–18', in Daniel Biltereyst, Richard Maltby and Philippe Meers (eds), *Cinema, Audiences and Modernity: New Perspectives on European Cinema History* (London: Routledge, 2012), pp. 130–41.
Hammerton, Jenny, 'Everything that constitutes life: Pathé cinemagazines 1918–1969', in Luke McKernan (ed.), *Yesterday's News: The British Cinema Newsreel Reader* (London: British Universities Film & Video Council, 2002), pp. 268–80.
___ 'Screen-struck: The lure of Hollywood for British women in the 1920s', in Alan Burton and Laraine Porter (eds), *Crossing the Pond: Anglo-American Film Relations Before 1930* (Trowbridge: Flicks Books, 2002), pp. 100–5.
Higson, Andrew, 'Polyglot films for an international market: E.A. Dupont, the British film industry, and the idea of a European cinema, 1926–1930', in Andrew Higson and Richard Maltby (eds), *'Film Europe' and 'Film America': Cinema,*

Select bibliography

Commerce and Cultural Exchange, 1920–1939 (Exeter: University of Exeter Press, 1999), pp. 274–301.

Hiley, Nicholas, 'The British cinema auditorium', in Karel Dibbets and Bert Hogenkamp (eds), *Film and the First World War* (Amsterdam: Amsterdam University Press, 1995), pp. 160–70.

Hinton, James, '"The 'class' complex": Mass-Observation and cultural distinction in pre-war Britain', *Past & Present*, 199 (2008), 207–36.

Houlbrook, Matt, 'Commodifying the self within: Ghosts, libels, and the crook life story in interwar Britain', *Journal of Modern History*, 85/2 (2013), 321–63.

Jones, Aled, 'The British press, 1919–1945', in Griffiths (ed.), *Encyclopedia of the British Press, 1422–1992*, pp. 47–55.

Karslake, Basil, 'A worm's eye view', *Films and Filming* (August 1984), 16–18.

Keil, Charlie, 'Leo Rosencrans, movie-struck boy: A (half-)year in the life of a Hollywood extra', *Film History*, 26/2 (2014), 31–51.

Kenaga, Heidi, 'Making the "studio girl": The Hollywood Studio Club and industry regulation of female labour', *Film History*, 18/2 (2006), 129–39.

____ 'Promoting *Hollywood Extra Girl* (1935)', *Screen*, 51/2 (2011), 82–8.

Kent, Christopher, 'Image and reality: The actress and society', in Martha Vicinus (ed.), *A Widening Sphere: Changing Roles of Victorian Women* (Bloomington: Indiana University Press, 1977), pp. 94–116.

Kohler, Arnold, 'Some aspects of conditions of employment in the film industry', *International Labour Review*, 23/6 (1931), 773–804.

Kuhn, Annette, 'Cinema culture and femininity in the 1930s', in Christine Gledhill and Gillian Swanson (eds), *Nationalising Femininity: Culture, Sexuality and British Cinema in the Second World War* (Manchester: Manchester University Press, 1996), pp. 177–92.

Lawrence, Jon, 'The British sense of class', *Journal of Contemporary History*, 35/2 (2000), 307–18.

Lento, Mattia, '"Basta la mossa!" or not? Silent film, theatre and the pedagogy of actors in Italy', in Katharina Klung, Susie Trenka and Geesa Tuch (eds), *Dokumentation des 24: Film- und Fernsehwissenschaftliches Kolloquiums* (Marburg: Schüren, 2013), pp. 394–404.

Lowe, Vicky, '"The best speaking voices in the world": Robert Donat, stardom and the voice in British cinema', *Journal of British Cinema and Television*, 1/2 (2004), 181–96.

McDonald, Jan, 'Lesser ladies of the Victorian stage', *Theatre Research International*, 13/3 (1998), 234–49.

McDonald, Paul, 'Reconceptualising stardom', in Richard Dyer, *Stars*, new edition with a supplementary chapter by Paul McDonald (London: British Film Institute, 1998), pp. 177–211.

McKenna, Denise, 'The photoplay or the pickaxe: Extras, gender, and labour in early Hollywood', *Film History*, 23/1 (2011), 5–19.

Select bibliography

McLaren, Angus, 'Smoke and mirrors: Willy Clarkson and the role of disguise in inter-war England', *Journal of Social History*, 40/3 (2007), 597–618.

Mayer, David, 'Acting in silent film: Which legacy of the theatre?', in Peter Krämer and Alan Lovell (eds), *Screen Acting* (London: Routledge, 1999), pp. 10–30.

Mayhall, Laura E. Nym, 'The Prince of Wales *versus* Clark Gable: Anglophone celebrity and citizenship between the wars', *Cultural and Social History*, 4/4 (2007), 529–43.

Moore, James Ross, 'Girl crazy: Musicals and revues between the wars', in Barker and Gale (eds), *British Theatre between the Wars*, pp. 88–112.

Morrell, Henry, 'On acting before the kinematograph', in Colin N. Bennett (ed.), *The Handbook of Kinematography* (London: Kinematograph Weekly, 1911), pp. 215–19.

Murphy, Robert, 'The coming of sound to the cinema in Britain', *Historical Journal of Film, Radio and Television*, 4/2 (1984), 143–60.

Musser, Charles, 'The changing status of the actor', in Charles Musser and Jay Leyda (eds), *Before Hollywood: Turn-of-the-Century Film from American Archives* (New York: American Federation of Arts, 1986), pp. 57–62.

Napper, Lawrence, 'A despicable tradition? Quota quickies in the 1930s', in Murphy (ed.), *British Cinema Book*, pp. 192–201.

Orgeron, Marsha, 'Making "It" in Hollywood: Clara Bow, fandom, and consumer culture', *Cinema Journal*, 42/4 (2003), 76–97.

___ '"You are invited to participate": Interactive fandom in the age of the movie magazine', *Journal of Film and Video*, 61/3 (2009), 3–23.

O'Rourke, Chris, 'How to become a bioscope model: Transition, mediation and the language of film performance', *Early Popular Visual Culture*, 9/3 (2011), 191–201.

___ '"On the first rung of the ladder of fame": Would-be film actors in silent-era Britain', *Film History*, 26/3 (2014), 84–105.

Paul, R.W., C.M. Hepworth and W.G. Barker, 'Before 1910: Kinematograph experiences', *Proceedings of the Kinematograph Society*, 38 (1936).

Peiss, Kathy, 'Making up, making over: Cosmetics, consumer culture, and women's identity', in Victoria de Grazia with Ellen Furlough (eds), *The Sex of Things: Gender and Consumption in Historical Perspective* (Berkeley: University of California Press, 1996), pp. 311–36.

Raynauld, Isabelle, 'Dialogues in early silent screenplays: What actors really said', in Richard Abel and Rick Altman (eds), *The Sounds of Early Cinema*, (Bloomington: Indiana University Press, 2001), pp. 69–78.

Ryall, Tom, 'A British studio system: The Associated British Picture Corporation and the Gaumont-British Picture Corporation in the 1930s', in Murphy (ed.), *British Cinema Book*, pp. 202–10.

Select bibliography

Sargeant, Amy, 'On receiving letters from despised lovers', in Vanessa Toulmin and Simon Popple (eds.), *Visual Delights: Essays on the Popular and Projected Image in the Nineteenth* (Trowbridge: Flicks Books, 2000), pp. 84–92.

―― 'Manuals and mantras: Advice to British screen actors', in Laura Vichi (ed.), *L'Uomo visibile: l'attore dale origini del cinema alle soglie del cinema moderno/ The Visible Man: Film Actor from Early Cinema to the Eve of Modern Cinema* (Udine: Forum, 2002), pp. 311–20.

Schweitzer, Marlis, '"The mad search for beauty": Actresses' testimonials, the cosmetics industry, and the democratization of beauty', *Journal of the Gilded Age and Progressive Era*, 4/3 (2005), 255–92.

Shail, Andrew, 'Max Linder and the emergence of film stardom', *Early Popular Visual Culture*, 14/1 (2016), 55–86.

Staiger, Janet, 'The eyes are really the focus: Photoplay acting and film form and style', *Wide Angle*, 6/4 (1985), 14–23

―― 'Seeing stars', in Christine Gledhill (ed.), *Stardom: Industry of Desire* (London: Routledge, 1991), pp. 3–16.

Stamp, Shelley, '"It's a long way to filmland": Starlets, screen hopefuls, and extras in early Hollywood', in Charlie Keil and Shelley Stamp (eds), *American Cinema's Transitional Era: Audiences, Institutions, Practices* (Berkeley: University of California, 2004), pp. 332–51.

Stead, Lisa, 'Audiences from the archive: Women's writing and silent cinema', in Nandana Bose and Lee Grieveson (eds), *Using Moving Image Archives* (Nottingham: Scope e-Book, 2010), pp. 32–47. Available at http://www.nottingham.ac.uk/scope/issues/2010/june-issue-17.aspx (accessed 29 January 2016).

―― '"So oft to the movies they've been": British fan writing and female audiences in the silent era', *Transformative Works and Cultures*, 6 (2011). Available at http://journal.transformativeworks.org/index.php/twc/article/view/224/210 (accessed 29 January 2016).

Strachey, Ray, 'Changes in employment', in Ray Strachey (ed.), *Our Freedom and its Results, by Five Women* (London: Hogarth Press, 1936), pp. 117–72.

Todd, Selina, 'Poverty and aspiration: Young women's entry to employment in inter-war England', *Twentieth Century British History*, 15/2 (2004), 119–42.

Waters, Chris, 'Beyond "Americanization": Rethinking Anglo-American cultural exchange between the wars', *Cultural and Social History*, 4/4 (2007), 451–9.

Wood, Linda, 'Low-budget British films in the 1930s', in Murphy (ed.), *British Cinema Book*, pp. 211–19.

Woodworth, Christine, 'Luggage, lodgings, and landladies: The practicalities for actresses on the British provincial circuits in the late nineteenth and early twentieth centuries', *Theatre Symposium*, 22 (2014), 22–32.

Vincendeau, Ginette, 'Hollywood Babel: The coming of sound and the multiple-language version', *Screen*, 29/2 (1988), 24–39.

Select bibliography

Books

Abel, Richard, *Menus for Movieland: Newspapers and the Emergence of American Film Culture, 1913–1916* (California: University of California Press, 2015).
Aherne, Brian, *A Proper Job* (Boston: Houghton Mifflin, 1969).
Anderson, Gregory (ed.), *The White-Blouse Revolution: Female Office Workers since 1870* (Manchester: Manchester University Press, 1988).
Anon., *The Picture Players' Gallery* (Cardiff: Crayle, 1913).
___ *Cinema Acting as a Profession* (London: Charrisse, 1915).
___ *The Film Life of Mary Pickford* ([London: Walker, 1915]).
___ *Victoria Cinema College & Studios: Guide to Cinema Acting* (London: Victoria Cinema College, n.d. [c.1917]).
___ *Cinema Acting as a Profession: A Splendid Course in 10 Lessons* (London: Standard Art Book, n.d. [c. 1919]).
___ *A Guide to Cinema Acting, & Course of Training* (London: Foyle, n.d. [c. 1920]).
___ *Film-Land: How to Get There. By a Cinema Actor* (London: Reeder and Walsh, n.d. [c. 1921]).
___ *Lloyd's A.B.C. of Careers for Girls* (London: United Press, 1922).
Applin, Arthur, *The Beautiful Miss Barry* (London: Long, 1925).
Baker, Michael, *The Rise of the Victorian Actor* (London: Croom Helm, 1978).
Bakker, Gerben, *Entertainment Industrialised: The Emergence of the International Film Industry, 1890–1940* (Cambridge: Cambridge University Press, 2008).
Balcon, Michael, *Michael Balcon Presents… A Lifetime of Films* (London: Hutchinson, 1969).
Bamburg, Lilian, *Film Acting as a Career* (London: Foulsham, 1929).
Bamford, Kenton, *Distorted Images: British National Identity and Film in the 1920s* (London: I.B.Tauris, 1999).
Banet-Weiser, Sarah, *The Most Beautiful Girl in the World: Beauty Pageants and National Identity* (Berkeley: University of California Press, 1999).
Barker, Clive and Maggie B. Gale (eds), *British Theatre between the Wars, 1918–1939* (Cambridge: Cambridge University Press, 2000).
Baron, Cynthia and Sharon Marie Carnicke, *Reframing Screen Performance* (Ann Arbor: University of Michigan Press, 2008).
Barry, Iris, *Let's Go to the Pictures* (London: Chatto and Windus, 1926).
Bingham, Adrian, *Gender, Modernity, and the Popular Press in Inter-War Britain* (Oxford: Clarendon, 2004).
___ *Family Newspapers? Sex, Private Life, and the British Popular Press 1918–1978* (Oxford: Oxford University Press, 2009).
Bouchier, Chili, *Shooting Star: The Last of the Silent Film Stars* (London: Atlantis, 1996).
Bowen, Elizabeth, *Joining Charles and Other Stories* (London: Constable, 1929).

Select bibliography

Braybon, Gail, *Women Workers in the First World War: The British Experience* (London: Croom Helm, 1981).

Brunel, Adrian, *Nice Work: The Story of Thirty Years in British Film Production* (London: Robertson, 1949).

Buchanan, R.C., *How to Become an Actor* (London: French, 1896).

Burke, Thomas, *The London Spy: A Book of Town Travels* (London: Butterworth, 1922).

Burrows, Jon, *Legitimate Cinema: Theatre Stars in Silent British Films, 1908–1918* (Exeter: University of Exeter Press, 2003).

Camiller, E., *How to Get Film Work* (London: Film Bureau, n.d. [c. 1922]).

Cardiff, Jack, *Magic Hour* (London: Faber & Faber, 1996).

Chalmers, Helena, *The Art of Make-Up: For the Stage, the Screen, and Social Use* (London: Appleton, 1930).

Chisholm, Anne and Michael Davie, *Beaverbrook: A Life* (London: Hutchinson, 1992).

Compton, Fay, *Rosemary: Some Remembrances* (London: Alston Rivers, 1926).

Conboy, Martin, *The Press and Popular Culture* (London: SAGE, 2002).

Constantine, Stephen, *Unemployment in Britain between the Wars* (London: Longman, 1980).

___ *Social Conditions in Britain 1918–1939* (London: Methuen, 1983).

Cooper, Gladys, *Gladys Cooper* (London: Hutchinson, 1931).

Croall, Jonathan, *Forgotten Stars: My Father and the British Silent Film World* (London: Fantom, 2013).

Crosby, Emily and Linda Kaye (eds), *Projecting Britain: The Guide to British Cinemagazines* (London: British Universities Film & Video Council, 2008).

Dangerfield, Fred and Norman Howard, *How to Become a Film Artiste: The Art of Photo-Play Acting* (London: Odhams, 1921).

Davis, Tracy C., *Actresses as Working Women: Their Social Identity in Victorian Culture* (London: Routledge, 1991).

___ *The Economics of the British Stage 1800–1914* (Cambridge: Cambridge University Press, 2000).

deCordova, Richard, *Picture Personalities: The Emergence of the Star System in America* (Chicago: University of Illinois Press, 1990).

Dickinson, Harold, *How to Write a Picture Play* (Hythe: New Kinema Publishing, n.d. [c. 1916]).

Edgars, George (ed.), *Careers for Men, Women, and Children*, 16 vols (London: Newnes, 1911–1912).

Elliott, William J., *How to Become a Film Actor* (London: Picture Palace News, n.d. [c. 1916]).

___ *Shadow Show: A Romance of Studio Life in the Days of the Silent Movie* (London: Swan, n.d. [c. 1942]).

Fowler, David, *The First Teenagers: The Lifestyle of Young Wage-Earners in Interwar Britain* (London: Routledge, 1996).

Select bibliography

Fuller, Kathryn H., *At the Picture Show: Small-Town Audiences and the Creation of Movie Fan Culture* (Charlottesville: University of Virginia Press, 2001).

Furniss, Harry, *Our Lady Cinema: How and Why I Went into the Photo-Play World and What I Found There* (Bristol: Arrowsmith, 1914).

Glancy, Mark, *Hollywood and the Americanization of Britain: From the 1920s to the Present* (London: I.B.Tauris, 2014).

Gledhill, Christine, *Reframing British Cinema, 1918–1928: Between Passion and Restraint* (London: British Film Institute, 2003).

Glucksmann, Miriam, *Women Assemble: Women Workers and the New Industries in Inter-War Britain* (London: Routledge, 1990).

Graham, C.E., *How to Write Picture Plays* (London: Cinema Playwriting School, n.d. [*c.* 1913]).

Graves, Robert and Alan Hodge, *The Long Weekend: A Social History of Great Britain, 1918–1939* (London: Faber & Faber, 1940).

Griffiths, Dennis (ed.), *The Encyclopedia of the British Press, 1422–1992* (Basingstoke: Macmillan, 1992).

Hallen, Russell, *The Way to the Studio* (London: Wardour, n.d. [*c.* 1926]).

Hallett, Hilary A., *Go West, Young Woman! The Rise of Early Hollywood* (Berkeley: University of California Press, 2013).

Hammerton, J.A., (ed.), *The Actor's Art: Theatrical Reminiscences, Methods of Study and Advice to Aspirants* (London: Redway, 1897).

Hastie, Amelie, *Cupboards of Curiosity: Women, Recollection, and Film History* (Durham: Duke University Press, 2007).

Hepworth, Cecil, *Came the Dawn: Memoirs of a Film Pioneer* (London: Phoenix House, 1951).

Herd, Harold, *The Making of Modern Journalism* (London: Allen & Unwin, 1927).

Higson, Andrew (ed.), *Young and Innocent? The Cinema in Britain 1896–1930* (Exeter: University of Exeter Press, 2002).

Holmes, Su and Diane Negra (eds), *In the Limelight and Under the Microscope: Forms and Functions of Female Celebrity* (London: Continuum, 2011).

Horrall, Andrew, *Popular Culture in London, c. 1890–1918: The Transformation of Entertainment* (Manchester: Manchester University Press, 2001).

Houlbrook, Matt, *Prince of Tricksters: The Incredible True Story of Netley Lucas, Gentleman Crook* (Chicago: University of Chicago Press, 2016).

Jarvie, Ian, *Hollywood's Overseas Campaign: The North Atlantic Movie Trade, 1920–1950* (Cambridge: Cambridge University Press, 1992).

Klevan, Andrew, *Film Performance: From Achievement to Appreciation* (London: Wallflower, 2005).

Klumph, Inez and Helen Klumph, *Screen Acting: Its Requirements and Rewards* (New York: Falk, 1922).

Select bibliography

Kuhn, Annette, *An Everyday Magic: Cinema and Cultural Memory* (London: I.B.Tauris, 2002).
Langhamer, Claire, *Women's Leisure in England 1920-60* (Manchester: Manchester University Press, 2000).
LeMahieu, D.L., *A Culture for Democracy: Mass Communication and the Cultivated Mind in Britain between the Wars* (Oxford: Clarendon, 1988).
Lescarboura, Austin C., *The Cinema Handbook* (London: Low, Marston, n.d. [c.1922]).
Low, Rachael, *The History of the British Film, 1906-1914* (London: Allen & Unwin, 1950).
___ *The History of the British Film, 1914-1918* (London: Allen & Unwin, 1950).
___ *The History of the British Film, 1918-1929* (London: Allen & Unwin, 1971).
MacBean, L.C., *Kinematograph Studio Technique* (London: Pitman, 1922).
McFarlane, Brian (ed.), *The Encyclopedia of British Film*, third edition (London: Methuen, 2008).
McKernan, Luke, *Topical Budget: The Great British News Film* (London: British Film Institute, 1992).
McKibbin, Ross, *Classes and Cultures: England 1918-1951* (Oxford: Oxford University Press, 1998).
Macleod, Joseph, *The Actor's Right to Act* (London: Lawrence and Wishart, 1981).
Macnab, Geoffrey, *Searching for Stars: Stardom and Acting in the British Cinema* (London: Cassell, 2000).
Marsh, Mae, *Screen Acting* (Los Angeles: Photo-Star, n.d. [c. 1920]).
Matthews, Jessie, *Over My Shoulder: An Autobiography* (London: Allen, 1974).
Mayer, J.P., *Sociology of Film: Studies and Documents* (London: Faber & Faber, 1946).
___ *British Cinemas and their Audiences* (London: Dobson, 1948).
Melman, Billie, *Women and the Popular Imagination in the Twenties: Flappers and Nymphs* (Basingstoke: Macmillan, 1988).
Morey, Anne, *Hollywood Outsiders: The Adaptation of the Film Industry, 1913-1934* (Minneapolis: University of Minnesota Press, 2003).
Morgan, Herbert, *Careers for Boys and Girls* (London: Methuen, 1926).
Morgan, Joan, *Camera!* (London: Chapman and Hall, n.d [c. 1940]).
Moseley, Sydney A., *The Night Haunts of London* (London: Paul, 1920).
___ *The Truth about a Journalist* (London: Pitman, 1935).
Murphy, Robert (ed.), *The British Cinema Book*, third edition (London: British Film Institute, 2009).
Napper, Lawrence, *British Cinema and Middlebrow Culture in the Interwar Years* (Exeter: University of Exeter Press, 2009).
Naremore, James, *Acting in the Cinema* (Berkeley: University of California Press, 1992).
Narran, Bree [pseud.], *The Kinema Girl* (London: Anglo-Eastern, n.d. [c. 1920]).

Select bibliography

Pearson, George, *Flashback: The Autobiography of a British Film-Maker* (London: Allen & Unwin, 1957).

Pearson, Roberta E., *Eloquent Gestures: The Transformation of Performance Style in the Griffith Biograph Films* (Berkeley: University of California Press, 1992).

Platt, Agnes, *Practical Hints on Acting for the Cinema* (London: Paul, 1920).

Priestley, J.B., *English Journey* (London: Heinemann, 1934; repr. London: Folio Society, 1997).

Pudovkin, V.I., *On Film Technique: Three Essays and an Address*, trans. Ivor Montagu (London: Gollancz, 1929).

Raymond, Adolphus, *Film-Struck; or, A Peep Behind the Curtain* (London: Paul, 1923).

Roberts, Elizabeth, *Women's Work 1840–1940* (Basingstoke: Macmillan, 1988).

Rolt, Bernard, *Cinderella of the Cinema* (London: Heinemann, 1927).

Sanderson, Michael, *From Irving to Olivier: A Social History of the Acting Profession* (London: Athlone Press, 1984).

Scott, Ian, *From Pinewood to Hollywood: British Filmmakers in American Cinema, 1910–1969* (Basingstoke: Palgrave Macmillan, 2010).

Seaman, L.C.B., *Life in Britain between the Wars* (London: Batsford, 1970).

Sexton, Jamie, *Alternative Film Culture in Inter-War Britain* (Exeter: University of Exeter Press, 2008).

Simonis, H., *The Street of Ink: An Intimate History of Journalism* (London: Cassell, 1917).

Slide, Anthony, *Inside the Hollywood Fan Magazine: A History of Star Makers, Fabricators, and Gossip Mongers* (Jackson: University Press of Mississipi, 2010).

___ *Hollywood Unknowns: A History of Extras, Bit Players, and Stand-Ins* (Jackson: University of Mississippi Press, 2012).

Springer, John Parris, *Hollywood Fictions: The Dream Factory in American Popular Literature* (Norman: University of Oklahoma Press, 2000).

Stacey, Jackie, *Star Gazing: Hollywood Cinema and Female Spectatorship* (London: Routledge, 1994).

Stamp, Shelley, *Movie-Struck Girls: Women and Motion Picture Culture after the Nickelodeon* (Princeton: Princeton University Press, 2000).

Steer, Valentia, *The Secrets of the Cinema: Your Favourite Amusement from within* (London: Pearson, 1920).

Street, Sarah, *British National Cinema* (London: Routledge, 1997).

Susman, Warren I., *Culture as History: The Transformation of American Society in the Twentieth Century* (New York: Pantheon, 1984).

Sweet, Matthew, *Shepperton Babylon: The Lost Worlds of British Cinema* (London: Faber & Faber, 2006).

Thompson, Kristin, *Exporting Entertainment: America in the World Film Market 1907–34* (London: British Film Institute, 1985).

Select bibliography

Todd, Selina, *Young Women, Work, and Family in England 1918–1950* (Oxford: Oxford University Press, 2005).

Wallace, Edgar, *The Avenger* (London: Long, 1926).

Warren, Low, *The Showman's Advertising Book: Containing Hundreds of Money-Making Tips and Wrinkles* (London: Kinematograph Weekly, 1914).

Warren, Patricia, *British Film Studios: An Illustrated History*, second edition (London: Batsford, 2001).

Weston, Harold, *The Art of Photo-Play Writing* (London: McBride, Nast, 1916).

White, Cynthia L., *Women's Magazines 1693–1968* (London: Joseph, 1970).

White, Jerry, *The Worst Street in North London: Campbell Bunk, Islington, between the Wars* (London: Routledge, 1986).

Williams, Michael, *Ivor Novello: Screen Idol* (London: British Film Institute, 2003).

Yardley, Alan, (ed.), *Sunrise to Sunset: An Autobiography by Mary Bertenshaw* (Bury: Printwise, 1991).

Ziegler, Philip, *Diana Cooper: The Biography of Lady Diana Cooper* (Harmondsworth: Penguin, 1981).

Index

All italicised titles refer to films unless otherwise indicated. Italicised page references refer to illustrations.

Academy of Dramatic Art, *see* Royal Academy of Dramatic Art
acting styles 52, 57–58
actors
   early cinema and 19–20
   publicity and 24, 121, 132
   social status of 15–19, 41
   sound cinema and 135–38
   theatre and 15–19, 23, 34, 37, 50, 52–53, 55, 138
   training of 17, 76, 78, 80, 139
   wages of 17, 20–21, 24–25, 27
   working conditions of 18, 29–33, 136
   see also extras; stock companies
Actors' Association 17, 75
Aherne, Brian 34, *35*, 36–37, 41, 71, 75, 137
Alexander, Sally 82
Alhambra Theatre (London) 38, 79
Alice in Wonderland (1903) 20
Alliance Film Corporation 102
Amami shampoo 120–22, *123*, 124, 128, 140
Ames, Gerald 76
Applin, Arthur 27
Arbuckle, Roscoe ('Fatty') 83
Around the Town (cinemagazine) 112–13
Asquith, Anthony 28, 120
Associated First National Pictures, *see* First National

Astra Films 27
At the Villa Rose (1930) 136
Atkinson, G.A. 81–83, 135
Atlantic (1929) 136
Atlantic Union Films 25
Aylott, Dave 21

B&C, *see* British and Colonial Kinematograph Company
Bailey, Peter 10
Baird, Edward ('Teddy') *26*, 27–28, 33
Baker, Michael 16
Balcon, Michael 32–33
Balfour, Betty 25, 40, 121
Barbas, Samantha 139
Barker, Will 21–23
Barry, Iris 56
Barthelmess, Richard 55
Beautiful Miss Barry, The (book) 27
Beaverbrook, Lord 106, 109–12
Beerbohm Tree, Herbert 20, 23
Belcher, Lionel 83
Bellew, Dorothy 21, 24
Bennett, Charles 95
Bentley, Thomas 40
Bernhardt, Sarah 23
Bingham, Adrian 84
Blackmail (1929) 95
Blackton, J. Stuart 74
Blythe, Betty 27, 36

Index

Bouchier, Chili 38, *39*, 40–41, 80, 93, 137–38
Bow, Clara 12, 121
Bowen, Elizabeth 62
Bramlins (employment agency) 73–74, 80
Breed of the Treshams, The (1920) 27
Brisson, Carl 120
British Actors' Equity Association 19, 75
British Broadcasting Company (BBC) 129, 138
British and Colonial Kinematograph Company (B&C) 21–22, 24, 48, 79
British and Dominions Film Corporation 41, 138
British Instructional Films (BIF) 28, 48, 120
British International Pictures (BIP) 120, 122, 135–36
British Mutoscope and Biograph Company 20
Broadwest Film Company 32, 34, 36, 71, 76, 102
Brockwell, Gladys 67
Broken Blossoms (1919) 38
Brook, Clive 34, *35*, 36–37, 40, 74, 124
Brown, Geoff 34, 75
Brunel, Adrian 54, 73–74
Bryan, Jane 46
Bunny, John 67
Burke, Thomas 29–31
Burrows, Jon 23, 58
Butt, Alfred 112

Campbell, Mrs Patrick 18
Cardiff, Jack 28, 30, 32
Carleton, Billie 83–84
Carnival (1921) 28
Castles in Spain (1920) 28
Cavalcanti, Alberto 138
Central School of Speech and Drama 17

Chaney, Lon 55
Chaplin, Charlie 5, 7, 24, 130
Charlot, André 122
Cinderella of the Cinema (book) 126
cinemagazines 109–10, 112
  see also *Around the Town*; *Pathé Pictorial*
Cinematograph Films Act (1927) 48, 119–20, 134, 136
City of Play, The (1929) 137
Clarendon Film Company 21, 24, 76
Clark, Marguerite 67
Clarkson, Willy 74
Close, Ivy 24, 106
close-ups 59, 62
Collins, José 67
Colman, Ronald 37, 124
Compson, Betty 32
Compton, Fay 33, 38
Constant Nymph, The (1928) 40
consumer culture 121, 132, 139–40
Cooper, Gladys 32–33, 38
Cooper, Lady Diana 3
cosmetics, see make-up
Cottage on Dartmoor, A (1929) 175n.138
Cricks and Martin 21, 101
crowd players, see extras

Dangerfield, Fred 49
Davis, Tracy 7, 15
Day, Harry 96
demobilised soldiers 73, 95
Diana of the Crossways (1922) 33
Doro, Marie 79
Downhill (1927) 103
Dupont, E.A. 120

Edwards, Henry 31
Elder, T.C. 103
Ella Cinders (1926) 43–44
Elvey, Maurice 88, 107

Index

employment agencies 19, 69, 70, 72–75, 85
   see also Bramlins; Film Artistes' Guild; Motley Club
Extra Girl, The (1923) 43
extras 27–28, 31, 33, 75, 79, 96

facial expressions 59–60, *61*, 63, *64*, 65
Fairbanks, Douglas 5, 50, 66
Family Man, A (stage play) 43
Famous Players-Lasky British 29, *30*
fan magazines 49, 60, 76, 99, 132
   participatory culture and 45–47, 139–40
   star searches and 101–3
   see also Film Flashes; *Picture Palace News*; *Picture Show*; *Picturegoer*; *Pictures and the Picturegoer*
Farrar, Geraldine *61*
Fields, Gracie 138
Film Artistes' Guild 75
Film Booking Offices (FBO) 114, 117, 128
Film Flashes (magazine) 47
Film-Struck (book) 84, 93
First National 114–18, 127–28
Fitzhamon, Lewin 20, 22
Foster, Dorothy 22, 24
Fuller, Kathryn 46–48

Gaiety Theatre (London) 19, 105
Gainsborough Pictures 135
Galsworthy, John 43
Gaumont Company 23, 25, 77, 112, 135
Gilmer, A. Coulson 75
Gish, Dorothy 67
Gish, Lillian 7, 38
Glancy, Mark 127, 136
Gledhill, Christine 58, 117
Godal, Edward 76–77, 79–80
Griffith, D.W. 7, 21, 127

Grossmith, George 113
Grossman, Joseph 36, 88

Hall-Davis, Lilian 73, 120
Hallett, Hilary 83
Hamlet (1910) 21
Haselden, W.K. 3, *4*
Hastie, Amelie 67
Hawtrey, Charles 36
Hearts Adrift (1914) 23
Henry VIII (1911) 23
Hepworth, Cecil 8, 20–22, 24, 29, 32, 101, 134
Hitchcock, Alfred 95, 120
Hopcroft, Winifred 1, *2*, 73
Hopson, Violet 32, 62–63, 65–67, 76
Houlbrook, Matt 90
Howard, Lionelle 73, 76
Howard, Norman 49
'how-to' books, *see* instructional guides
Hulcup, Jack 21–22
Hulton, Edward 114, 117, 126, 128–29
Hume, Marjorie 100

Ideal Film Company 48, 72
Ince, Thomas 36
instructional guides 8–9, 78
   authorship of 44, 49, 52
   celebrity culture and 67
   as evidence of acting practice 44
   national stereotypes and 57–58
   scenario writing and 48
   training exercises suggested in 62–63, *64*, 65
Irving, Henry 17

James, Benedict 73, 77
Jay, Sidney 1–2, 73, 95, 97
Jazz Singer, The (1927) 134

Karslake, Basil 31, 33
Keaton, Buster 114, 117, 127–30, *131*

Kinema Club 74, 118
Kinema Girl, The (book) 84, 93
King John (1899) 20
'Klieg eye' 29, 37
Kuhn, Annette 10, 140

Lady from the Sea, The (1929) 120
Lang, Matheson 55
Laurillard, Edward 112
Leahy, Margaret 117–18, 124, *125*, 126–30, *131*, 132
LeMahieu, D.L. 10
Life Story of David Lloyd George, The (1918) 33
Linder, Max 23
Lloyd, Frank 128
location, filming on 25, 32–33
Lohr, Marie 3
London County Council (LCC) 72, 85–86, 88–89, 93, 96–97
Loos, Anita 120
Lorraine, Harry 76
Lupino, Stanley 138

MacBean, L.C. 32
McDowell, J.B. 79
McKernan, Luke 127
McKibbin, Ross 9
make-up 30–31, 55, 74, 80, 121–22, 124
Mannock, Patrick 96
Mansfield, Katherine 69
Marble Arch Pavilion (London) 126, 129
Marriot, Moore 55
Marsh, Mae 67, 73, 87
Martin-Harvey, John 27
Matthews, Jessie 73, 138
Mayer, David 44
Miss June 100
mood music 32, 137
Moore, Colleen 43
Moran, Percy 24

Morey, Anne 8
Morgan, Joan 29, 74
Moseley, Sydney 81, 109
Motley Club 75
Mr. Wu (1919) 55
Musser, Charles 20

Nazimova, Alla 60
Nepean, Edith 103
newspapers
  'craze' for film acting and 3–5
  moral panic and 81–83
  star searches and 103, 105–9, 114
newsreels 109, 112
  see also Pathé Gazette; Topical Budget
Nielsen, Asta 23, 57
Normand, Mabel 43
Northcliffe, Lord 105, 112, 119
Northcote, P.G. 24
Nothing Else Matters (1920) 38
Novello, Ivor 7

Orgeron, Marsha 45–46, 139–40
Owd Bob (1924) 25

Paddy the Next Best Thing (1923) 73
Pathé Frères 36, 109, 116
Pathé Gazette (newsreel) 110
Pathé Pictorial (cinemagazine) 110–12
Payne, John 73–74, 80
Pearson, George 38, 65, 68, 77
Phillipson, Percy 127
Piccadilly (1929) 31, 33
Pickford, Mary 1, 5, 10, 23–24, 50, 54, 67, 119, 121
Picture Palace News (magazine) 49, 101
picture personalities, *see* star system
Picture Show (magazine) 47, 60, *61*, 103, *104*
Picturegoer (magazine) 27, 47, 96–97, *98*, 119, 135

Index

Pictures and the Picturegoer (magazine) 47–48, 50, 60, 102
Plumb, Hay 21–22
Pontefract, Harold 116
Poulton, Mabel 38, *39*, 40–41, 65, 79–80, 100, 137–38
Pridelle, Claire 21–22
Priestley, J.B. 10
Pudovkin, V.I. 56
Pugh, Ralph 115
Purviance, Edna 121

Quigley, Marion 86–90, *91*, 92–95

radio 19, 129, 132, 139
Rappe, Virginia 83
Raymond, Adolphus 84
registering, *see* facial expressions
Réjane, Gabrielle 23
Remembrance (1927) 27
Rescued by Rover (1905) 20
Risdon, Elisabeth 24
Rolt, Bernard 126
Romance of a Movie Star, The (1920) 6
Romance of Seville, A (1929) 120
Rome, Stewart 24, 30, 54, 67
Romeo and Juliet (1908) 23
Rosher, Max 80, 97
Royal Academy of Dramatic Art (RADA) 17, 139
Royds, George S. 121–22

Sahara Love (1925) 103
Samuelson, G.B. 27
Samuelson Film Manufacturing Company 25, *26*
Sanderson, Michael 7, 19, 37
Sargeant, Amy 44
Schenck, Joseph 114, 128–29
screen tests 65, 102–3, 107, 110–13, 120

screen types 53–56
self-improvement 9
Shaftesbury Pavilion (London) 116
She (1925) 27
Shooting Stars (1928) 37, 41
Singin' in the Rain (1953) 136
Sinless Sinner, A (1919) 79
Smilin' Through (1922) 115–16
So This Is Jollygood (1925) 54
Sorrows of Satan, The (1917) 32
Squire of Long Hadley, The (1925) 36
Stamp, Shelley 5
star searches 100
    Amami Film Star Quest 120–22, *123*
    American examples of 12, 169n.5
    beauty contests and 105, 107
    Cinema Star Competition (*Sunday Express*) 103, 106–7, *108*
    cinemas and 101, 116
    Daily Sketch contest 114–19, 126–29
    Golden Apple Challenge 112–13
    Pathé Screen Beauty Contest 109–12
    Picture Palace News contest 101
    Picture Plays contest 102
    Picture Show contest 103, *104*
    Pictures and the Picturegoer contest 102
    Weekly Dispatch Film Face contest 119–20
    see also fan magazines; newspapers; women
star system 23–24, 56, 102, 133
Starlings of the Screen (1925) 103
Stead, Lisa 119
stock companies 21, 23, 54
Stoll Film Company (Stoll Picture Productions) 31–32, 36, 71, 88, 103, 107
Stuart, John 30, 121

Index

studios 29–32, 135
   Cricklewood, 29, 31–32, 36, 71, 103
   Elstree 29, 31, 120, 135–37
   Isleworth 30
   Islington 29, *30*, 135
   Twickenham 30, 136
   Walton-on-Thames 29
   Welwyn 29
Swanson, Gloria 99
Sydney, Aurèle 25, 59, 67
Sylvani, Gladys 21–22

'talkies' 134–39
Talmadge, Constance 55, 114, 119, 129
Talmadge, Natalie 114
Talmadge, Norma 60, 114–19, 125–27, 129
Taylor, Alma 7, 21, 24
Taylor, William Desmond 83
Tearle, Godfrey 23
Terror, The (1928) 134
Terry, Ellen 18
Tesha (1928) 31
Tessibel of the Storm Country (1914) 23
Thanhouser Film Company 47
Three Ages, The (1923) 117–18, 127–30, *131*
Three Musketeers, The (1898) 20
Tilly the Tomboy (film series) 21
Tinker, Tailor, Soldier, Sailor (1918) 150n.84
Topical Budget (newsreel) 114, 116, 126–27
Trent's Last Case (1920) 34
Turner, Florence 38

Ultus (film series) 25
unemployment 9, 27, 40, 82

Valentino, Rudolph 66, 99
Variety Artistes' Federation 75
Victoria Cinema College 76, *77*, *78*, 79–80, 84, 93, 96–97, 101
Vile Bodies (book) 96

W Plan, The (1930) 137
Wadsley, Olive 126–27
Wallace, Edgar 99
Waller, Lewis 20
Ward, Warwick 73
Wardour Street 71, 73–74, 84, 110, 118
Waugh, Evelyn 96
Welding, Oxford 87–90, 92
Welsh-Pearson 25, 38, 40
West, Walter 32, 71, 102
White, Chrissie 21, 31
White Cargo (stage play) 37
Whoso Is Without Sin (1916) 48
Wilcox, Herbert 73, 138
Within the Law (1923) 117, 127
Woman Redeemed, A (1927) 37
Woman to Woman (1922) 32
women
   as 'cinema-struck' 3, 5, 81, 97, *98*, 108, 140
   cinema schools and 85–86, 93–94
   labour market and 9, 30, 41, 82
   media attitudes towards 83–84, 105, 133
   star searches and 106, 110–11, 122, 124
Wyndham, Charles 17

Ziegler, Philip 3

www.ingramcontent.com/pod-product-compliance
Lightning Source LLC
Chambersburg PA
CBHW052042300426
44117CB00012B/1941